Psychology in Prisons

Forensic Practice

Series Editors: Adrian Needs, University of Portsmouth, and Graham Towl, HM Prison Service

The books in this series take a research-based applied psychological approach to a wide range of topics in forensic psychology, and are aimed at a range of forensic practitioners working in a variety of settings. They will be of use to all those working within the criminal process, whether academics or practitioners.

Published

Psychology in Prisons
Edited by Graham Towl

Forthcoming

Applying Psychology to Forensic Practice
Adrian Needs and Graham Towl

Psychology in Prisons

Edited by

Graham Towl

BPS Blackwell

© 2003 by the British Psychological Society and Blackwell Publishing Ltd
except for editorial material and organization © 2003 by Graham Towl
A BPS Blackwell book

THE BRITISH PSYCHOLOGICAL SOCIETY
St Andrews House, 48 Princess Road East, Leicester LE1 7DR

BLACKWELL PUBLISHING
350 Main Street, Malden, MA 02148-5020, USA
108 Cowley Road, Oxford OX4 1JF, UK
550 Swanston Street, Carlton, Victoria 3053, Australia

First published 2003 by the British Psychological Society and Blackwell Publishing Ltd
Reprinted 2003, 2004 (twice)

Library of Congress Cataloging-in-Publication Data

Psychology in prisons / edited by Graham Towl.
    p. cm. — (Forensic practice ; 1)
  Includes bibliographical references and index.
  ISBN 1–4051–0028–1 (pbk : alk. paper)
    1. Psychology, Forensic—Great Britain. 2. Prison psychology—Great
Britain. I. Towl, Graham J. II. Series.
  RA1148 .P785   2003
  365′.66—dc21
                                                    2002011184

A catalogue record for this title is available from the British Library.

The views expressed are those of the authors and are not necessarily those of the
National Probation Directorate or Prison Service.

Contents

Foreword

I am delighted to welcome this book, and indeed this new series, as representing a very great advancement in knowledge about forensic psychology. As Graham Towl points out in his chapter, forensic psychology is booming, especially in the prison service. The potential and actual contributions that psychologists can and do make to research and practice in criminal and juvenile justice are enormous and are becoming more widely appreciated. Arguably, psychologists are the best trained and most competent researchers in the prison and probation services, and they should take the lead in organizing a nationally co-ordinated programme of research on criminological issues.

The particular strengths of this book lie in its descriptions of current practice in assessment and treatment. There have obviously been great advances in risk and needs assessment (e.g. OASys) and in interventions such as Enhanced Thinking Skills (ETS), Controlling Anger and Learning to Manage it (CALM) and Cognitive Self-Change (CSC). This book is a valuable source of information about the application of these methods with sex offenders, violent offenders, life-sentence prisoners, young offenders and female offenders; Lorraine Mosson points out that female offenders tend to be marginalized and that more interventions should be designed specifically for them.

The book is also extremely useful in describing interventions designed to prevent suicide and bullying to manage hostage incidents and disruptive prisoners; Sarah Selvey notes the difficult challenges facing staff in Close Supervision Centres and the need for individualized care plans. I would particularly recommend the thoughtful and innovative chapter on 'Applying the research on reducing recidivism to prison regimes' by Phil Willmot (chapter 5). After reviewing numerous risk factors for offending (employment, education, marital, criminal associates, substance abuse, etc.) he argues that effective regimes should address not only offending behaviour but also these other areas of life success or failure.

This book is the second published showcase of research and practice by psychologists in the prison service which helps to answer outsiders' curiosity about

'What do they do?' The first book (*Applying Psychology to Imprisonment*, edited by Barry McGurk, David Thornton and Mark Williams) was published 15 years ago in 1987. What has changed in the meantime? It is clear that psychologists have developed risk and needs assessments enormously. Also, interventions have become far more uniform, evidence-based, systematic and of course accredited. Psychologists are working more as consultants rather than solely as treatment implementers, and they are more integrated with operational needs and more involved in joint working with other agencies.

A critic may wonder (along with Karen Brady and David Crighton) whether there is a danger that accredited programmes too much represent a 'one-size-fits-all' approach, and how far this is compatible with the careful matching of types of treatments to types of offenders. For example, it is perhaps difficult to imagine some of the programmes described in the 1987 book (e.g. 'A stimulus satiation treatment programme with a young firesetter' by Chris Daniel) being implemented in present-day conditions, but then again there is at least some emphasis on individualized care plans.

No-one surely can doubt that methods of dealing with offenders should be based on the best possible evidence about 'what works', and psychologists in prison have been very much in the forefront of implementing this approach. However, there is still a great need for well-designed, high-quality evaluations of the effectiveness of intervention programmes. While experimental and quasi-experimental designs are usefully reviewed by Caroline Friendship and Louise Falshaw, it is clear that more and better evaluations are needed. Also, these evaluations should include cost-benefit analyses to demonstrate how much money is saved by money expended on treatment programmes, as recommended by Phil Willmot.

My conclusion after reading this book is that the future is bright for forensic psychologists, who are highly valued and are doing extremely useful work. Graham Towl should be commended for assembling this collection of chapters which give an excellent snapshot of what psychologists in prison do. I am happy to recommend the book to psychologists and others who are interested in the assessment and treatment of offenders in criminal-justice settings.

David P. Farrington
Professor of Psychological Criminology
Cambridge University

Contributors

Names are accompanied by Prison Service area.

Zoë Ashmore – Action against Crime and Disorder Unit, London

Martha Blom-Cooper – Kent, Surrey & Sussex

Karen Brady – Kent, Surrey & Sussex

David Crighton – Kent, Surrey & Sussex

Louise Falshaw – HQ, London

Danielle Forbes – Eastern

Caroline Friendship – HQ, London

Jane Ireland – Personality Disorder Unit, Ashworth Hospital and Psychology Department, University of Central Lancashire

Serena Jackson – Kent, Surrey & Sussex

Michael Jennings – Lancashire & Cumbria

Lorraine Mosson – West Midlands

Sarah Selvey – High Security, London

Wayne Stockton – Greater London

Debbie Tanner – HQ, London

Michelle Thomas – Kent, Surrey & Sussex

Graham Towl – HQ, London

Phil Willmot – East Midlands North

Series Editors' Preface

The demands faced by forensic psychologists arise from some of the most pressing issues in society. Yet whilst concern over issues such as public safety, the rights of individuals and the efficient and appropriate operation of society's services and institutions is widespread, it is not always matched by accurate knowledge. Even the settings in which forensic psychologists work are unfamiliar to many members of the public, and, for that matter, to a substantial proportion of psychologists in other fields.

Promoting awareness of the work-contexts of forensic psychologists is one of the aims of the series of which the present book is a part. This is balanced by an additional aim. This centres around illustrating continuities in approach between forensic and other branches of applied psychology. In particular how forensic psychologists often draw in the course of their work upon theories, methods and findings from other traditions (e.g. cognitive, social and developmental psychology). This aspect helps underpin the versatility which is evident in the work of many forensic psychologists, a feature which, as the series also seeks to demonstrate, has arisen largely in response to the complex and varied nature of work requirements in settings concerned with criminal and civil justice.

The employment of forensic psychologists has increased markedly in recent years. Nowhere is this truer than in prison services. This expansion in numbers (Towl, in chapter 1 of this volume) can be attributed to a constellation of factors. Political and societal pressure to reduce crime and make imprisonment a more constructive process combined in the 1990s with the availability of structured evidence-based approaches to the rehabilitation of offenders. Forensic psychologists in HM Prison Service have played a key role in the design and large-scale mobilization of work in this area. The achievement has been remarkable, not least in the unprecedented degree of effective multi-disciplinary working which has also helped redefine the role of many prison officers. The process was assisted by changes in the managerial structure of psychologists which promoted greater integration within establishments (McDougall, 1996) and set the scene for the development of a more co-ordinated service. Not that the contribution of forensic psychologists to the work of the prison services has been confined to work directly related to group-based interventions with offenders. Many psychologists have continued to work in areas such as staff training, organizational consultancy and research, hostage negotiations, and the design and implementation of staff selection procedures. Some still have occasion to undertake the kind of individually based work with prisoners represented in an earlier publication on the work of psychologists in HM Prison Service (McGurk, et al., 1987), although the field has now moved on considerably to reflect current developments in areas such as risk assessment. Perhaps the overriding reason why the employment of forensic psychologists in this setting has continued to expand is that their work is valued.

The chapters in the present volume reveal a pragmatic approach. It could be argued that this orientation towards practical aspects and a shared conceptual base has been vital to establishing the work described, particularly in relation to gaining the necessary co-operation of other professionals (and prisoners) in the institutional context. For related reasons many of the chapters are essentially descriptive. The result is a clear picture of what at present forensic psychologists in prisons actually do.

It might be tempting to suggest that, having established itself, forensic psychology in prisons should now scrutinize its roots in research and theory and review its practice in order to inform and enhance its continued evolution.

In George Kelly's (1955) terminology, 'circumspection' and 'pre-emption' should be alternating and complementary phases of a cycle of creative and adaptive engagement. Circumspection refers to a wide-ranging consideration of possible courses of thought and action. Pre-emption is a more single-minded following through of a decided course. Each has its own place in avoiding the potentially adverse consequences of dwelling too long on the other mode (paralysis of marginalization on the one hand and rigidity and imperviousness on the other). It is neither to denigrate recent achievements in the field nor the work of the present authors to raise the idea that now is the time for psychology in prisons to embark once more on a disciplined process of circumspection. There are indications in several of the chapters that this is already happening.

Adrian Needs and Graham Towl

Preface

This book includes a range of perspectives on forensic psychological work in prisons. The contributors would by no means all claim to being 'experts' in the fields they cover (although some undoubtedly are). What the contributors share is an enthusiasm and commitment to write about important areas of their psychological practice in prisons. It should be noted, however, that the views expressed are those of the authors and do not necessarily reflect the views of HM Prison Service, the editor or publishers.

Some of the chapters are primarily research-focused in their approach, for example in the chapter by Caroline Friendship and Louise Falshaw on the evaluation of groupwork in prisons. Other chapters give very much a practitioner perspective on particular areas of work. For example, Michael Jennings reflects on his experiences in undertaking anger management groupwork in prisons. This rich collection of perspectives, perhaps particularly those from some of the newer contributors to the field (e.g. Michelle Thomas and Karen Brady) bode well for the future. The forensic field is moving apace.

One pervasive theme is the recent rapidity of change surrounding the structure and delivery of psychological services. An important recent development has been the linking of psychological services between probation and prisons.

In my role as Head of Psychology for HM Prison and Probation Services I am keen to support and develop emerging talent within the field. This book is one manifestation of this.

I am grateful to the contributors for giving their time and efforts to this volume. I very much hope that it will be of interest to a range of readers.

Professor Graham J. Towl

Chapter One

Psychological Services in HM Prison Service

Graham Towl

Introduction

The forensic psychological field is booming. Nowhere is this more so than in HM Prison Service, which is now the largest single employer of applied psychologists in the UK. It is no surprise therefore, that it is also the largest single employer of forensic psychologists. HM Prison Service currently employs over 600 psychological staff. In the past three years over 100 psychology graduates have been recruited annually (Towl, 2001).

Much of the recent growth in numbers of, especially trainee forensic psychologists and psychological assistants has been, in large part, accounted for by the increases in structured groupwork interventions aimed at reducing the risk of reoffending. Most recently there has also been an increase in interest and activity in individual work with life-sentenced prisoners. Such work is focused upon assessing and reducing the level of risk of reoffending (Willmot, chapter 5 of this volume). Two other areas of activity have been in relation to the management of suicidal prisoners (Towl and Crighton; 1998, Towl and Forbes, 2000; Towl, 2000) and incident management, for example, hostage incidents (Ashmore, chapter 4 of this volume). Women (Horn and Warner, 2000) young offenders (Dalkin and Skett, 2000) and juvenile prisoners (Blom-Cooper, chapter 12 of this volume) are also groups with increasing demands for services. The areas mentioned above are illustrative rather than comprehensive in terms of the range of work undertaken by forensic psychologists in prisons (Towl, 1999). What is also changing is the way in which psychologists undertake work. This point is explored more fully later in this chapter.

This chapter is structured in three parts. The first part focuses on the organization of psychological services within prisons. The second part considers what may be termed the functions of psychological services. Thirdly there is a focus upon future developments and directions.

The Organization of Psychological Services in Prisons

The organization of psychological services is linked to arrangements for the management of prisons throughout England and Wales. HM Prison Service has 12 geographical areas with a range of different types of prisons in each. 'Area managers', who in turn manage the operational managers of the prisons, lead each of these areas. Each area manager has an area team, one of whom is an area forensic psychologist.

Area psychologists are responsible for ensuring the professional, economic, efficient and effective delivery of psychological services in prisons in their area. Nationally there is some variation in precisely how this is achieved in terms of their management arrangements with individual heads of psychology units; however the core functions outlined above are common to all. One recent and significant development has been the joint recruitment of psychologists for both prisons and probation services, for a fuller discussion of this see chapter 2. In addition to the 12 Prison Service areas based on geographical boundaries there are also two 'functional' areas – high-security prisons and women's prisons with their own area psychologists.

The area psychologists meet regularly with the head of psychology for prisons and probation. Such meetings and training events are used to inform professional, leadership and management issues with the support of a small administrative group at Prison Service HQ.

Forensic psychology units within prisons have tended to be there for historical reasons rather than being based upon current prisoner, staff and organizational needs. This is changing markedly with the recent introduction of the national network of area psychologists. Area psychologists are well placed to look constructively and critically at the psychological services provided in their area. Such reviews of services have led to the redeployment of resources in some areas to meet prisoner, staff and organizational needs more appropriately. Workforce planning is an important part of this with the need to focus on future needs and the levels of staffing required to meet such needs. Nationally, with the rapid growth in the forensic field there is a relatively short supply of experienced forensic psychologists. However, competition for trainee forensic psychologist positions within HM Prison Service is stiff. This means that the organization can attract some high calibre staff in the current graduate market-place. This bodes well for the future of psychological services.

Needs assessments undertaken or driven by area psychologists are important in informing broader management decisions about the appropriateness of the design of particular activities or regimes available in individual prisons. One core function of the area psychologists in relation to the maintenance and development of professional standards is in the supervision and Continuing Professional Development (CPD) arrangements that they put in place in their areas. This is critical work in terms of delivering professional services (Towl, 2002). Also, without such supervision and CPD the organization is exposed to significant corporate risk if it can be shown not to have provided appropriate support when services are being delivered directly to prisoners. Such supervision and professional support are also likely to be important in terms of impacting upon staff retention levels.

Individual forensic psychology units in prisons vary in terms of the focus of their work. As mentioned earlier highly structured groupwork interventions have in recent years tended to account, in large part, for the growth in trainee forensic psychologist posts and those for psychological assistants. Such interventions are routinely referred to as 'offending behaviour programmes' in prisons and increasingly in probation services too. For most forensic psychology units this is however only one aspect of their work. Some units have a major focus on individual interventions with life-sentenced prisoners. Others are involved in the range of areas of work touched upon within this volume.

Increasingly area psychologists are making effective links with universities to ensure that applied psychology in the Prison Service is kept at the forefront of broader developments within psychology. This is a two-way street. Area psychologists often contribute to psychology courses in universities, sharing their expertise. This is another important element of keeping forensic psychological services in prisons upon a firm academic and professional footing. With an eye to the future it is anticipated that there may be the development of joint posts with universities, particularly for more experienced forensic practitioners. Area psychologists clearly have a pivotal role to play in the shaping of the future of psychological services in prisons.

The Functions of Psychological Services in Prisons

Critical to the work of forensic psychologists is a need to address the question of why particular work is being undertaken. The two key drivers of the work of psychologist in prisons should be, and increasingly are; organizational needs and psychological expertise.

The organization at various levels has a series of aims and objectives. Such aims and objectives are represented in a variety of forms. For example, individual prison establishments have 'business plans' where the tasks or outputs that need to be delivered are outlined. Psychologists working within prisons seek to contribute to undertaking some of these tasks and outputs. Notwithstanding this there are, of course, some broader national and regional tasks and outcomes which psychologists contribute to achieving too. Indeed, contributing at a regional or area level is becoming more commonplace with the introduction of area psychologists in the organization of services. However, the key point here is that the work undertaken by psychological staff should meet an organizational need (at whatever level of the organization).

The second key driver of the work undertaken is the competencies that the forensic psychologist has to offer. Readers interested in the details of the areas of knowledge and skills required of forensic psychologists should refer to the literature produced under the auspices of the British Psychological Society's Division of Forensic Psychology (BPS, 1997, and 2001).

Forensic psychologists may have a range of their skills drawn upon in undertaking work for the Prison Service. At a basic level some of the skills they have as graduates may be used from time to time. This may be in relation to undertaking a variety of project-management work. However, more commonly, and ultimately more appropriately, their skills in working with prisoners and staff from a psychological perspective are drawn upon. Much of such work may be usefully conceptualized as involving risk assessment and management (Towl, 2001).

Psychologists draw from a range of risk-assessment methods and tools, in what may be referred to as a multi-modal approach. However, virtually irrespective of the particular field or favoured method the logic of risk-assessment work remains relatively fixed (Adams, 1995). One framework used in the forensic field is what is sometimes referred to as the Cambridge model of risk assessment (Crighton, 1999).

Three basic concepts underpin good quality risk assessments (Crighton, 1999). First, it is vital to identify appropriate and accurately defined predictor and criterion variables. Predictor variables are those which may be used to predict a particular outcome. For example, in a forensic context previous convictions may be used as a predictor of future convictions. In terms of the criterion variable this is what is being predicted. Thus the predictor variable may be age at first offence and the criterion variable may be future violent offending. The hypothesis here then may be that early involvement in crime and the criminal justice system may be a useful predictor of the likelihood of subsequent violent offending.

Second, it is important to have a thorough understanding of the base rates of a particular behaviour. Base rates are the frequency with which a particular event or behaviour occurs. For example, the base rate for shoplifting would be relatively high given that it happens frequently. However the base rate for homicide would be low because it is an infrequently occurring event. Low base rates result in particular and systematic problems of prediction (Needs and Towl; 1997, Crighton, 1999).

Third, there is the notion of the acceptability or tolerability of a particular level of risk. A level of risk of an event, or criterion variable, occurring amounts to a matter of opinion rather than an informed judgement based on a range of germane information. Psychologists have no distinctive expertise in this aspect of riskassessments; it is conceptually distinct from the process of making an assessment of the level of risk (Towl and Crighton, 1996). The contribution of psychologists in risk-assessment work lies in drawing together the data to make an informed judgement about the level of risk which is evident, not in indicating what is or is not acceptable. However, this is not to say that the psychologist will not have a view on such matters. Indeed it is generally important to give such a view either at relevant meetings or in report form.

Most commonly perhaps, the term 'risk assessment' in the context of psychological interventions in prisons is often viewed as relating to the risk of reoffending for an individual prisoner. Risk-assessment work with individual prisoners, particularly lifers, remains an important part of the work of forensic psychologists in prisons. Such interventions may take the form of highly structured groupwork interventions aimed at reducing the risk of reoffending. Alternatively, or sometimes in addition to the groupwork, individual work may be undertaken. The theoretical approach underpinning such interventions in prisons tend to draw from a broad cognitive-behavioural school. Multi-modal risk assessments of prisoners and structured interventions to reduce the risk of reoffending are clearly crucial areas of work to which psychologists have much to contribute. Such work is the subject of a number of chapters in this book.

Perhaps less well known are the interventions undertaken by psychologists with, for example, suicidal prisoners or prisoners who intentionally self-injure (ISI). Again, this subject matter is covered in chapter 14 of this book. However, what is important to note in terms of the contributions of psychologists is that the logic of the work is essentially the same as that used when attempting to reduce the risk of reoffending: namely, a multi-modal risk assessment is undertaken and a risk-management plan is outlined with the prisoner and other staff (Towl and Crighton, 2000). The purpose of subsequent interventions is to reduce the risk of suicide and self-injury.

These are just two examples of the applications of structured clinical models of risk assessment. There are numerous other areas of such applications e.g. prison disturbances, hostage incidents and bullying. Elsewhere in this book a more detailed coverage of the range of interventions undertaken by forensic psychologists in prisons is given.

Earlier in the chapter it was mentioned that psychologists are working in different ways from those of the past in ensuring the delivery of organizational goals. An example of this can be seen in relation to a set of highly structured groupwork-based interventions with offenders. These are commonly, in prisons, referred to collectively as 'accredited offending behaviour programmes'. As mentioned above these interventions draw directly from cognitive-behaviourally based approaches to working with offenders with a view to to reducing their risk of reoffending. During the earlier stages of the development and implementation of such interventions psychologists were, and are, very involved in the direct delivery of the groupwork and key members of the local management-support team in providing supervision to groupworkers. This has been helpful for the organization in the early stage of the development of such interventions. However, with such manualized approaches to working with offenders once the initial implementation phase of such interventions is in place, the question of the continued involvement of experienced psychologists in such roles needs to be raised.

Psychologists are, and will continue to be, a relatively small proportion of the workforce in prisons. Manualized approaches to working with offenders are also likely to be on the increase over the coming years. There are some clear benefits to such approaches and these are ably covered elsewhere in this book in a number of chapters.

One unfortunate product of this area of work has been in relation to the jargonistic language used. Terms such as 'criminogenic' and 'high dosage' spring to mind. Both are jargon and do not add anything to our understanding. This is regrettable because the use of such jargon is unhelpful in terms of conveying to a wider audience some of the very good work that has been achieved in recent years in this key area. As can be seen elsewhere in this book such work is, and will continue to be, the subject of rigorous evaluation. However, in terms of the roles of psychologists there is a need to think afresh about how psychologists may develop new approaches to working with offenders whilst also having a role in ensuring that manualized interventions are rigorously delivered. Area psychologists play a key role in contributing to ensuring that such groupwork is available to meet identified needs. Also given the widespread knowledge and skills base of psychologists in this area, work may be undertaken in training a range of grades of staff to deliver such groupwork. In general terms perhaps the most helpful functions for psychologists to fulfil are twofold. One is to have a key role in quality control, e.g. through staff training. The other is to address at a strategic level implementation issues working closely with operational managers.

Another area, which has been neglected in the past, is the contribution that psychologists can make nationally to research. Particularly given the national structure of area-based services, psychologists are very well placed to make a number of contributions. Area psychologists are experienced and well-qualified practitioners, of whom some hold visiting academic positions with universities, and a number have direct links with universities. Collectively they have a significant amount of research expertise.

Given that psychologists have expertise in this area, how may the organization benefit from this? One area of potential benefit is in undertaking research, which informs policy and practice within prisons. For example, research undertaken by psychologists has informed policy and practice in relation to the management and support of suicidal prisoners (Towl and Crighton, 2000). Area psychologists themselves may undertake such research, or more commonly they may help and support the research of a psychologist colleague. Nationally within the prison service there is considerable scope for the expansion of this role. One area of development is in proactively brokering links between universities and prisons in looking at the most cost-effective way of delivering research which is most likely to be linked into policy and practice. Psychologists can play an important gate-keeping role for operational managers in assessing the aims, methodology and ethical basis of research proposals submitted to be undertaken in prisons. Area psychologists will be aware of what research is needed locally; they will also have a national perspective. This is an important point about the relevance of research. Often what appears to have happened is that individuals have approached operational managers in prisons requesting research access to pursue *their* research interest for *their* postgraduate qualification. However, there may be more pressing research needs. It is helpful for both the organization and the prospective researcher if work that is undertaken is directly relevant to the organization. For the organization this has the significant benefit of providing an evidence base for informing policy and practice. For the prospective researcher the benefit lies in the research being used by the organization and the work being more likely to be linked into similar research nationally. So often research is done and the only output is a dissertation which meets university requirements for a particular postgraduate degree with no impact whatsoever on policy and practice. Trainee forensic psychologists frequently undertake research funded by the organization; area psychologists are responsible for ensuring that such research contributes to organizational needs.

In this discussion of research the focus has been on postgraduate research; however there is much other research undertaken within prisons either in terms of nationally commissioned research or indeed local research to address a particular local operational concern. The expertise of psychologists in prisons has perhaps not been tapped as much as it could have been: again an area for future development.

Psychologists working in prisons have not over the years tended to have a great deal published in terms of both research and psychological practice. This has been of concern in that such work, if undertaken but not externally published, will not have the benefit of peer review. This is changing. Over the coming years there is likely to be a proliferation of research activity and publications in this important area of forensic practice.

Future Developments and Directions

The field of forensic psychology in prisons is currently in a state of flux. The numbers of psychologists working in prisons continues to grow. There is a broad range of areas of work where forensic psychologists make key contributions. There is a continuing need to reassess the appropriateness of particular roles so that we may ensure that the organization concerned is getting the best possible value out of this comparatively small but expensive group of specialist staff. On the point of the costs of psychologists it is perhaps worth mentioning that nationally approximately £10 million pounds is spent on psychological services within prisons.

In terms of best practice in public-sector service delivery there is a need to focus on some key themes driven by government policy. Working practices and organizational structures need to ensure and facilitate effective service delivery from psychological staff. Additionally, a clear focus on the organization's needs in providing a service for the public, and indeed other key stakeholders, is necessary. Clearly, as a profession we need also to be setting high national standards.

One major theme on which there has already been considerable work is the development of an infrastructure for psychological services in probation services nationally. One good example of this has been the first joint recruitment exercise of psychologists for prisons and probation. Such partnership working is increasingly emerging as a core theme in the delivery of public services. The potential is enormous in terms of more effective working with offenders, the opportunity is being grasped but clearly there is still a long way to go. Area psychologists have been a vital link with probation services.

The partnership working between prisons and probation is set to grow. Psychologists are well positioned to respond to this need given the structure of services; a joint head of the profession, area psychologists with probation links and with joint recruitment procedures in place. The partnership work will continue to be a core theme in the professional contribution of forensic psychologists in both the prison and probation services. Such a partnership is good for the development of forensic psychology. One core challenge for the profession to contribute to, as public-sector employees, over the coming years, will be constantly striving to improve the quality and reduce the overall costs of service provision.

Chapter Two

Psychologists' Recruitment

Zoë Ashmore and Debbie Tanner

Background

Psychologists (both chartered and trainees) have been employed in HM Prison Service for nearly 55 years now. The number of trainee forensic psychologists recruited to work in the Prison Service in England and Wales has increased significantly in recent years. In the 12-month period from April 2000 to the end of March 2001, 84 trainee forensic psychologists were recruited. New trainees, in these numbers, have been recruited annually for about the past five years, bringing the number of trainees, chartered forensic psychologists and psychological assistants in the total group to over 600.

The first joint Head of Psychology for the Probation Service and the Prison Service was appointed in 2000. One key aim was to develop the psychology service in England and Wales for the new National Probation Service. A joint recruitment process to fill trainee forensic psychologist posts in both the National Probation Service and the Prison Service began the following year. This was an element of the partnership between the National Probation Service and HM Prison Service.

In recent years, the large number of new vacancies has been driven by the use of trainee forensic psychologists to work, under the supervision of chartered forensic psychologists, on the delivery of cognitive-behavioural groupwork programmes, based on 'What works?' principles. An external body of experts (a Joint Accreditation Panel) accredits these programmes, which are running in both the National Probation and Prison Services, as being likely to reduce offending because of they way they have been developed and are operating.

The recruitment of trainees needs to take account of their ability to apply previous skills and experience to the groupwork programmes, but it also needs to take account of the full range of tasks which can fall to the psychologist. The recruitment procedures need to be able to identify the competencies required and test for them. For example, psychologists are required to make assessments of risk for a range of different reasons. In many cases it is the risk of reoffending which is being assessed, perhaps in the case of a life-sentenced prisoner who is being considered for release or a sex offender who has completed a groupwork programme. It may be that it is the risk of suicide or intentional self-injury by the offender which requires a risk assessment. Equally, psychologists are called to make other types of assessment such as an offender's suitability for a particular intervention. One example of this would be an assessment of a prisoner's appropriateness for a therapeutic community. A number of psychologists will work on therapeutic communities within prisons where they will co-lead groups and support other prison staff working with prisoners (Cullen et al., 1997). Some psychology posts require research skills, for example to evaluate the effectiveness of a regime for juvenile offenders. Others will require psychologists to be able to pass on their psychological skills and knowledge to staff through training and support. Some psychologists advise at incidents, mainly hostage-taking incidents, and the recruitment process will need to select those candidates who have the potential to take on a range of different roles and tasks throughout their career as a psychologist (Towl and McDougall, 1999).

Current Policy and Practice

The external recruitment of psychologists is managed centrally. Devolving the process was found to be expensive and difficult to manage effectively. Maintaining high standards and consistency in the recruitment process was more readily achieved through a central process.

Targeting desirable candidate groups

The location of appropriate publications in which to place advertisements is critical in reaching the desired target group. Advertisements are placed in the ethnic minority press, a professional journal, the 'Appointments Memorandum' of the British Psychological Society and a national daily newspaper, usually the *Guardian*. The Prison Service website (www.hmprisons.gov.uk) hosts information about the recruitment of psychologists and is linked to the website of the company contracted to manage the administrative support for the recruitment process such as issuing application forms to candidates. Additionally, it links to the website of the British Psychological Society so that candidates can gain general information on professional issues and qualifications related to a career in applied psychology.

The provision of accurate information about the organization and the job to potential candidates is vital. When candidates are recruited with realistic information including values and aims of the organization, that is given a Realistic Job Preview (RJP), the satisfaction and retention of those employed is increased (Wanous, 1992). The information package sent to applicants includes a summary of the role of a psychologist working in the National Probation and Prison Service settings. It is evident from table 2.1 that there remains a great deal of interest amongst Psychology graduates in training in the challenging area of forensic psychology practice. There is a great deal of competition for places.

Minimum requirements

Candidates must possess a degree, (at least a 2.2 classification), have the basis for graduate registration (GBR) with the British Psychological Society and submit a completed application form.

Sift Criteria

Candidates are sifted using a scoring system where points are allocated according to relevant experience and qualifications. Applications are then placed in rank order and the highest-scoring candidates are invited to attend an assessment centre. Stronger candidates successful at this stage would have relevant experience and postgraduate qualifications.

This method of selection does not tap into the candidates' ability to perform as it is based on what they have done educationally and experientially rather than on competencies. There are plans to sift using responses to competence-based questions in addition to experience and qualifications.

Table 2.1 The number of applicants successful at each stage

Recruitment Campaign	A/F to candidates*	A/F returned*	Success at sift	Success at assessment
June 200	Unavailable	322	108	41
November 2000	831	367	108	43
June 2001	1053	272	168	59
November 2001	1199	411	196	46
May 2002	1274	511	216	Unavailable

A/F = Application Form

The assessment-centre approach

The qualities of the people in an organization largely define organizational design ... the qualities of the people hired are critical for the short and long-term effectiveness of organizations. (Schneider, 1987)

The use of unstructured interviews for recruitment has been shown to be ineffective in differentiating between suitable and unsuitable candidates possibly as a result of interviewers' biases. Interviewers frequently make their decision regarding the suitability of candidates well before the completion of the interview, often very early in the process (Tullor et al., 1979). The assessment-centre approach has high face validity and is positively endorsed by candidates.

Competencies

A job competency is an underlying characteristic of a person in that it may be a trait, a skill, an aspect of one's self image or social role, or a body of knowledge which he or she uses. (Boytzis 1982)

Competencies are the descriptions of job outputs or work tasks or the descriptions of behaviours. They have been increasingly used in assessment and training over the past 15 years. Their use has allowed organizations to develop a common language to identify effectiveness and to consistently assess performance levels across the organization (Whiddett and Hollyforde 1999).

The accurate identification of the competencies required for effective job delivery is key to identifying the most capable candidates for the job. The Prison Service has developed the Core Competency Framework (CCF) as the basis for recruitment, appraisal and staff development. The competencies identified are considered to include those required to be successful in any role within the organization.

The recruitment of psychologists for the Probation and Prison Service is based on these competencies. In addition, discussions with Probation Training and Recruitment Consortium has identified further competencies. The following competencies were measured in the last recruitment (November 2001).

Care and concern for the individual
Verbal communication
Judgement
Team skills

Written communication
Motivation and commitment
Systematic approach
Planning and reviewing
Analytical skills
Rehabilitation orientation
Problem solving

Each competency is broken down into behavioural indicators, which demonstrate that particular competency. More detailed examples of positive and negative behaviour relating to each competency are currently being developed.

The exercises

Five different exercises are used currently.

The exercises are developed to allow the assessment of competencies in various situations, for example 'Care and concern for the individual' in both a group and one-on-one scenario. The candidate is told what competencies are measured prior to each exercise and is given full instruction together with ample opportunity to ask questions. As a result, candidates should be clear exactly what is expected of them and what is being assessed before each exercise begins.

Exercises are videotaped and assessed by two assessors who mark independently. In the case of there being more than one mark difference between each assessor's score, the exercise is marked again by another assessor. Generally, there is a high level of agreement between assessors. Each exercise is marked by different assessors. This means that each candidate is assessed by ten different assessors.

The assessors

Assessors are practising probation officers and psychologists drawn from their posts across the National Probation and Prison Services. Assessors are trained in the exercise they will mark and assess the same exercise throughout the assessment centre. The detail and content of training is currently being further developed with a view to training and accrediting a small group of practising psychologists drawn from the field to act as assessors.

In the first joint recruitment process with the National Probation Service, it was agreed to add a further and final stage to the process. This consisted of a structured board interview with the area psychologist and either the Governor (or his or her representative) of the prison establishment or the Chief Officer (or his or her representative) in the relevant National Probation Service area, as well as the proposed line manager of the candidate. The final structured interview was usual practice for the National Probation Service in the recruitment of trainee probation officers and was seen to add value as it ensured the involvement of the managers in the area where the new recruit would work.

Feedback

Feedback is an important component of any assessment process, not only feedback to the candidate but also feedback to the organization from the candidate about the process in which they have been involved. It is important that candidates feel that the process is fair and transparent and that they have been given the chance to demonstrate what they can do. Feedback from assessors about the process or the content is also valuable. The organization must be responsive and consider feedback, incorporating it into assessment centre development to contribute to improvement over successive recruitment campaigns.

The provision of useful feedback to candidates can be time-consuming. It is more efficient when the mechanism for feedback is built-in as part of the assessment process. A system for the delivery of useful feedback to the candidates is currently being piloted. Once a candidate has been scored on a particular exercise, both assessors discuss their performance and agree feedback, which highlights areas of good performance and suggests areas for the candidate to improve, and it is recorded on feedback sheets. Each candidate receives feedback when the recruitment process is complete unless they request otherwise.

Equal opportunities

Ensuring that the recruitment process is fair among different applicant groups is the central issue in employee selection and each group is faced with unique challenges. The law prohibits discrimination in employment opportunities on the basis of disability, gender or race but care also needs to be taken over a range of possible stereotypes, issues or other irrelevant factors which can unfairly affect the performance of some candidates or how they are viewed by the assessors.

Our approach has included the monitoring of each stage of the recruitment process to show the success rates by race, gender and disability. Additionally, by listening to the psychologists who have been successfully recruited from minority ethnic groups, awareness among assessors and managers has been raised and changes made to the recruitment process.

SUMMARY

There has been considerable growth in the number of trainee forensic psychologists in the probation and prison services in recent years. Central recruitment, drawing on identifying competencies through an assessment centre approach, has been found to be the most effective model. The role of the forensic psychologist is described and the recruitment process needs to select candidates who are able to fulfil a number of roles in their career in the National Probation and Prison Service.

The current policy and practice is to target desirable candidate groups through advertising in the national newspapers and the professional press. The website, as well as information sent to candidates, is used to increase the match between suitable candidates and the organization in which they will work. Objective criteria are used to sift application forms to identify those candidates who meet the basic criteria. An assessment centre is used to identify the candidates with the required fit to the competencies needed. Each competency is broken down into behavioural indicators from which the exercises are developed. The competencies can then be assessed in different situations. The process takes approximately four hours and includes a debriefing.

The assessors are drawn from the field of practising psychologists and probation staff. The first joint recruitment process with the National Probation Service added a third stage, a structured board interview. All candidates are offered feedback on their performance. Ensuring that the recruitment process is fair among different applicant groups is now the central issue in employee selection and each group is faced with unique challenges.

Chapter Three

Staff Training

Danielle Forbes

This chapter considers psychologists' contributions to the area of staff training in the Prison Service.

The chapter begins by looking at the purpose of staff training in large organizations. Psychologists' involvement in training is then raised generally, with specific consideration being given to the role of forensic psychologists working in prisons.

Those training courses currently on offer in HM Prison Service which were designed and/or delivered by forensic psychologists are outlined. These courses tend to focus on topics in which psychologists have expertise, for example, groupwork interventions focused on offending behaviour. Next, forensic psychologists' role in training other HM Prison Service psychologists is explored, both in relation to formal training courses and in relation to on-the-job training and supervision as part of the British Psychological Society's chartership requirements. Finally, the chapter concludes that the future looks very positive for increased psychological involvement in staff training in HM Prison Service. In particular this is felt to be the case because of the inclusion of 'Staff Training' as one of the 'key roles', or areas of work, on which trainee psychologists can be examined to achieve chartership.

Introduction

Training aims to promote learning by developing attitudes, knowledge, ability and skills in order to improve performance in a given task (Holding, 1965; Goldstein, 1980, 1986; Patrick, 1992). In a work situation (rather than, for example, in a psychotherapeutic situation), the aim is to produce an improvement in an 'on-the-job' task or set of tasks (Goldstein, 1980).

Training of all grades of staff within an organization is necessary in order to improve the efficiency and effectiveness of the organization (Eyre and Pettinger, 1999). The aim is to maximize the performance of individuals both for themselves (e.g. by making them more marketable and by increasing their job satisfaction) and for the organization (to ensure effectiveness and efficiency). Training and re-training are necessary to ensure that employees behave and continue to behave, at least at a predetermined level (Analoui, 1993).

Staff training is usually considered under three headings:

professional training – required as the result of being in a particular occupation;

organizational staff training – required as the result of being in a particular organization; and

personal training – chosen by individual preference (Eyre and Pettinger, 1999).

In HM Prison Service, all three types of training are available to staff. Certain pieces of training are 'mandatory' for all staff working in HM Prison Service establishments, for example, basic training in security. Other pieces of training are 'mandatory' only for certain professional groups, for example, basic level 'control and restraint' training is mandatory for all prison officers. Some staff in HM Prison Service are funded to undertake further educational or professional training, for example, whole or partial funding to complete part-time higher education.

Psychologists and Training

At present, the majority of psychologists employed by HM Prison Service are chartered forensic psychologists or forensic trainees – graduate psychologists working towards chartership as forensic psychologists. Forensic psychologists in prisons are the largest single group of applied psychologists working for an individual employer, namely HM Prison Service (Towl, 2001).

Applied psychology can be defined in a number of ways (Patrick, 1992); however, essentially, it is concerned with the application of psychological theory to practical, 'real world' situations. Examples in the forensic field include prisoner risk assessment, prisoner groupwork-facilitation or project management. This chapter will consider the contribution made by forensic psychologists in prisons to the area of staff training.

A large body of psychological research exists which is of enormous relevance to the field of staff training. For example, research has focused on theories of learning and skill acquisition, on the behaviour of individuals in group situations, on the links between attitudes and behaviour, and on methods for evaluating the performance of individuals on key tasks (see Patrick, 1992, for a review of the contribution of these theoretical concepts to the field of staff training). Psychologists have therefore contributed to the development of many now well-accepted conceptual formulations underpinning practice in the field of staff training. Some organizations routinely employ applied psychologists (usually chartered occupational psychologists) in a more direct training role, to work with a team of staff devising, delivering and evaluating staff training. Sometimes, forensic psychologists working in prisons are asked to take on a role similar to that of occupational psychologists in other settings, and apply their laboratory-based psychological knowledge when assisting in the design, delivery and evaluation of staff training.

In general however, staff working for HM Prison Service's training services are not psychologists. Personnel staff, administrative staff and 'operational' staff all work together to assess, design, deliver and evaluate training to fit the needs of the organization. So whilst training services staff may work within accepted guidelines to develop training which aims to ensure transfer of learning, a psychologist is not always on hand to advise on how this should take place. Instead, forensic psychologists' involvement in staff training tends to take one of two forms: firstly, involvement in developing courses on topics within their area of expertise; and secondly involvement in the provision of training for forensic trainees.

As well as their occasional use by training specialists to advise on design, delivery and evaluation of specific courses, forensic psychologists in prisons have made and continue to make a significant contribution to the content of some courses. This tends to be the case when the topic of the training course is felt to be a topic in which forensic psychologists can make a distinctive and helpful contribution. For example, courses exist which aim to improve participants' communication skills or increase staff's awareness of specific groupwork interventions available for prisoners. These courses are discussed in more detail below. There are also some situations in which forensic psychologists are involved in delivering training courses in the role of tutors. Once again, these courses tend to be those on topics which forensic psychologists have expertise. Examples of these kinds of courses are discussed in the second part of this chapter.

As well as their involvement in the training of HM Prison Service staff from other disciplines, forensic psychologists have a very important part to play in training each other. This chapter considers their role in providing training and supervision of forensic trainees and in training other psychologists too.

Forensic Psychologists' Involvement in the Design and Delivery of Training Courses

Offending Behaviour Groupwork – tutor training and staff awareness training

Offending Behaviour groupwork (sometimes referred to as 'Accredited Programmes') refers to highly structured groupwork interventions designed to reduce prisoners' risk of reoffending post-release (see chapters 6–9).

The interventions include three types of staff training, each of which usually involves forensic psychologists: tutor training, tripartite manager training and staff awareness training.

'Tutor' training   Staff from a range of professional groups act as 'tutors' or facilitators for such programmes.[1] All staff involved in tutoring must pass a series of training courses specifically designed to develop their knowledge and their skills. The courses and their content are partially dependent upon the particular structured groupwork involved. Broadly speaking, one course is concerned with the development of generic groupwork skills, and another course is concerned with the development of knowledge and skills specific to the groupwork intervention in question. When new tutors have passed both of these courses they can start co-tutoring with an experienced tutor in their establishment. After a specified time spent tutoring the 'Programme', staff are required to complete further skills refresher and development courses as they move from novice to 'expert tutor' status. For example, to tutor on the most commonly run accredited programme (Enhanced Thinking Skills), tutors must firstly pass a three-day course on groupwork skills. Then they must pass a two-week course which familiarizes the tutors with the material of the programme and develops their skills and knowledge in techniques for putting the material across. At this point they are able to tutor the programme in conjunction with other more experienced tutors. After they have tutored the 'programme' on two occasions, they are then required to complete a further 'booster' training course which looks to 'refresh' their knowledge whilst developing an advanced level of skill in the delivery of such interventions.

Psychologists were heavily involved in the design of the tutor training courses and continue to work to develop the course content and methods in response to evaluative information. Psychologists continue to be involved in the delivery of tutor training courses. In general, one or two psychological staff experienced in a particular groupwork intervention work on each tutor training course alongside experienced staff from other professional groups.

Tripartite manager training   Accredited programmes are managed at establishment level by three members of staff. This 'management team' is known as the Tripartite Management Team and is usually made up of a senior manager in the prison (the Programme Manager), a member of staff from the Probation Service (the Throughcare Manager) and a member of staff who can be from a range of grades of staff (the Treatment Manager). Each of the tripartite managers is required to attend training to develop their knowledge of the specific groupwork intervention they plan to run. The treatment manager is also required to complete training aimed at developing skills in aspects of his or her role, for example, supervising tutors.

Forensic psychologists are heavily involved with the design, delivery and evaluation of these courses, although it is likely that the roles of psychologists, particularly chartered psychologists will change in emphasis over coming years (Towl, 2001).

Staff awareness training   One of the requirements of an establishment running an accredited programme is that it ensures that staff in the establishment at all grades and from all disciplines are given training to make them aware of the nature and demands of the programme. This training is known as 'Staff Awareness Training' and the requirement is that a proportion of staff in establishments delivering accredited programmes are trained each year. For some programmes, the requirement is for an increasing proportion of staff to be trained on a year-on-year basis. For example, for the Enhanced-Thinking Skills Programme, in the first year that the programme is run in an establishment, 25 per cent of staff must receive staff-awareness training. By the end of the second year of programme delivery, 50 per cent of the staff must have been trained, by the end of the third year, 75 per cent must have been trained, and by the end of the fourth year, 100 per cent of staff must have received training. For other programmes, for example the Sex-Offender Treatment Programme, the requirements are that a proportion of the total number of staff must be trained each year.

Psychologists are often involved in the management and delivery of accredited programmes.[2] Psychological assistants often take on the role of tutor and sometimes of 'Treatment Manager'. Psychologists (forensic trainees) sometimes take on the role of treatment manager, as in a few cases do chartered forensic psychologists. Whilst all establishments running the programmes are expected to deliver staff awareness training, there is not, as yet, a standard format for the training. Hence, treatment managers and tutors are often involved with the design of the course which will run in their establishment. There is also a requirement that one of the tripartite managers of the programme is involved in the delivery of the training. This task often falls to the treatment manager.

Hostage-negotiation training

HM Prison Service has a well-defined set of policies and procedures which come into operation during the comparatively rare incidents in which individuals are taken hostage. One policy is to use only trained hostage negotiators to communicate with hostages and hostage takers during incidents.

A group of forensic psychologists and operational managers from HM Prison Service (Evans and Henson, 1999) drew up the training pack which was adopted as HM Prison Service's mandatory training for hostage negotiators. The same pack is used nationally in order to ensure that trained staff from any establishment are able to work within the same set of procedural and operational guidelines when negotiating.

The rationale for the involvement of psychologists is that whilst operational managers are well placed to tutor on aspects of the negotiator's role which is grounded in HM Prison Service procedures for incident management, psychologists are well placed to provide constructive, evidence-based skills feedback.

The lifer course

Probably more than with any other group of prisoners, life-sentence prisoners' release is dependent upon their risk of reoffending. Forensic psychologists are acknowledged to have a high level of expertise in the area of risk assessment, be it of suicide, homicide, grave or minor reoffending (Towl and Crighton, 1996). As such psychological staff worked alongside operational staff to design the five-day training course used to train HM Prison Service staff who work with life-sentence prisoners.

Suicide prevention

HM Prison Service recently produced a revised Suicide Awareness Training pack for use in establishments across England and Wales. Psychological staff worked alongside operational staff to devise the programme which is made up of a quiz and a series of case studies as well as more traditional information giving sessions.

Training services' accredited courses – Counselling Skills and Groupwork Skills

Forensic psychologists are sometimes involved with the design of training courses in response to an identified need. An example of this is two courses which were accredited to run across the prison estate, and were designed by forensic psychologists. The first of these courses is entitled 'An Introduction to Basic Counselling Skills' and is a four-day course aiming to equip staff from any professional discipline with a knowledge of basic non-directive listening and verbal communication skills for use in interpersonal interactions (Bailey and Hudson, 1997). The second of these courses is entitled 'An Introduction to Groupwork Facilitation' and is a four-day course aiming to equip staff to run prisoner or staff groups using a largely non-directive approach (Towl and Hudson, 1997). Both of these courses comprise a mixture of information-giving and role-play sessions.

'One-off' training

One-off training involves training, for example, for governors and senior management teams in prisons. As well as their involvement in the standard set of courses delivered across the prison estate, forensic psychologists are often asked to provide training in a range of topics on an *ad hoc* basis in their own or neighbouring establishments. For example, an establishment starting a new area of work may wish to train its senior managers in some of the key concepts associated with that work prior to its commencement. If that area of work is one in which psychological staff have expertise, then they may be asked to contribute to the training. Similarly, training managers often ask for help, advice and support from forensic psychologists in developing, designing and delivering pieces of training to meet identified needs in their establishments. Psychologists' knowledge and experience in the area of training can make them a useful resource at establishment level.

Forensic Psychologists' Role in Training Other Psychologists

In addition to providing training for staff from other professional groups, forensic psychologists in prisons also design and deliver training for each other. This training generally takes one of the following forms.

New entrant psychologist training

'New entrant psychologists' (psychologists who have recently commenced work for HM Prison Service and HM Probation Service) are provided with a week-long training course which aims to develop a basic level of knowledge in a range of job-related areas. Topics which tend to be covered include: risk assessment, groupwork, interviewing skills and suicide and self-injury. More experienced psychologists are involved in the organization, design, delivery and evaluation of these training events.

Area training

In general, HM Prison Service establishments are divided into operational groups by geographical area[3] and managed in those groups. In many 'Areas', the area forensic psychologist (the lead psychologist for a group of prisons) runs a training programme for psychologists working in the area. This is worked out on an area by area basis, but often includes training delivered by forensic psychologists working in HM Prison Service. For example, a member of staff with a high level of knowledge and experience in a particular topic might provide a training session on that topic for other psychological staff in their area. This form of training has the advantage of being cost-effective and of providing useful developmental opportunities for both the staff delivering and the staff receiving the training. Topics which might form the basis of an area training session include: working with the suicidal, risk assessment, working with sexual offenders and psychometric testing. However, the range of topics is likely to depend upon the areas of expertise of the staff within the geographical area and the needs of staff working in that area.

Supervised practice

The assurance of quality of psychological services and maintenance of professional standards is partially achieved via the British Psychological Society's award of the title of Chartered Psychologist. For psychologists practising in forensic settings, chartership is examined and awarded by the British Psychological Society's Division of Forensic Psychology. Chartership requirements are based around competence in three domains: research methods appropriate to forensic settings, academic knowledge in forensic psychology and supervised practice in a forensic setting. The element of chartership regulations which involves professional practice (i.e. the 'supervised practice' element involves supervision and on-the-job training for a period of between two and five years (BPS, 2001).

A forensic trainee working towards chartership through the Division of Forensic Psychology is supervised by a chartered forensic psychologist who takes on the role of 'co-ordinating supervisor'. Their role is to design a programme which will provide the trainee with a range of experience and ensure that they are guided to achieve an appropriate standard and breadth of practice to meet the guidelines set down by the Division (BPS, 2001).

A range of different forms of 'supervision' can be included, for example, attendance at formal training courses, reading and discussing relevant research literature, attending prisoner interviews as an observer and completing written reports. Some of these 'supervisory' elements could clearly be described as closely related to training within a broad definition. Other elements of supervision are less likely to be seen as 'training'. In practice, many of the 'training' elements (and most of the 'supervision' elements) will be provided by chartered forensic psychologists already practising within prisons. Whilst it is not compulsory that all training is delivered by a chartered psychologist (or even a psychologist), in practice this is often the case.

Conclusion

This chapter has summarized the current level of involvement of forensic psychologists working in prisons in the area of staff training. Their current level of involvement in training is generally limited to the design and delivery of those courses on topics in which psychologists have expertise, for example, training as part of accredited programmes delivery or hostage-negotiation training. Forensic psychologists often provide a consultancy service to their establishment or their area for delivery of one-off pieces of training. In addition, forensic psychologists deliver a considerable amount of training to other psychologists working for HM Prison Service.

The future for forensic psychologists' involvement in staff training is positive. The new guidelines for supervised practice (BPS, 2001) issued by the British Psychological Society's Division of Forensic Psychology, include four key roles in which psychologists must demonstrate experience and competence in order to be awarded Chartered Forensic Psychologist status. Key role 4 is 'training other professionals in psychological skills and knowledge'. The role is broken down into five sub-sections, which encourage the application of a systematic approach to the assessment of need, design, delivery and evaluation of staff training.

Psychological service provision in HM Prison Service is, quite rightly, largely dictated by organizational need and performance. This often precludes involvement in areas of work not seen to be central to the role of particular professional groups. At present this tends to limit the amount of time psychological staff spend on staff training. The inclusion of staff training within supervised practice guidelines is, however, likely to reintroduce into forensic psychologists' core role the area of staff training, and hence increase the amount of time which they feel able to devote to the area. In addition, the Head of Psychology in the Prison and Probation Service is committed to ensuring high quality skills in forensic psychology. Managers are generally keen to assist psychologists in achieving chartered status as it increases the range of work they are able to conduct. Hence, time spent on training will be seen by both trainees and managers as central to forensic psychologists' roles and as beneficial to the individual, the profession and the organization.

NOTES

1 It is unusual that the term 'tutor' has been adopted to describe this role in a groupwork intervention programme. The term 'facilitator' might be more appropriate.
2 Whilst none of these roles are exclusively delivered by psychological staff, such staff make a valuable contribution. In the future this may change as the organization develops and the role of psychologists broadens (Towl, 2001).
3 Two other 'areas' also exist: one comprises women's prisons, the other comprises high security prisons.

Incident Management

Zoë Ashmore

Background

Psychologists in HM Prison Service have been advising at hostage-taking incidents in prison establishments for more than twenty years. The role has expanded to encompass advice on a range of other incidents such as riots, barricades or rooftop protests. However it is on the psychologist's contribution to the successful management of hostage incidents that this chapter will concentrate, as it forms the major contribution to this area of work. The aim in managing incidents is to resolve the incident as effectively as possible without incurring injury to anyone.

Hostage-taking and hijacking became more frequent internationally in the late 1960s. Between January 1968 and June 1975, there were 77 international hostage incidents, excluding airline hijacking and kidnapping of business people (Jenkins 1976). Hostage-taking in British prisons became more common from the 1970s (Cooke et al. 1990). Hostage-taking in prisons in the United States of America in the 1970s, 'became an increasingly common adjunct to, and latterly a control feature of, rioting' (Adams and Campling 1994).

Approaches to the Management of Hostage-Taking Incidents

Cooke et al. (1990) describe three approaches to the management of hostage-taking incidents which were used in the 1960s:

    the 'hard' approach
    the 'soft' approach
    the 'softly softly' approach.

The 'hard' approach, sometimes known as 'go in', is where a team of highly trained intervention staff enter the siege area and attempt to overcome the perpetrators and release the hostages as quickly as possible. This method has the benefit of surprise but is high risk. Whilst the approach has had dramatic successes in international hostage incidents, it has also produced a number of deaths. For example, in 1972 in Attica Prison in the USA, 15 hostages were killed during shooting when the National Guard stormed the prison. Afterwards, it was found that the rescuers, not the perpetrators, had fired all the bullets. Garston (1972) reviewed 25 prison riots in the 1950s which involved hostages, and he looked at the effects of different approaches in the management of these incidents. He found that no hostages were killed regardless of whether the riot was ended by force or in a more restrained way. In contrast, in 12 riots, also in the 1950s, force was used and deaths occurred.

The 'soft' approach, the 'give in' option, has advantages in that the situation is resolved quickly. The limits of this are evident. Rewarding inappropriate behaviour means that it is now more likely to be repeated, if not by the perpetrators, then by others who have learned how productive hostage-taking can be.

Cooke et al. (1990) reviewed a number of international hostage-taking incidents where this approach was used. They conclude that the approach led to an increase in demands and the more frequent occurrence of hostage-taking. Psychologists involved in training prison staff as hostage-negotiation advisers will see the 'balance of power' shifting in favour of the perpetrators if, in role-playing exercises, their behaviour is rewarded in any way, even by seemingly small responses such as the gaining of a cigarette or a cup of tea. Any perceived progress by the perpetrators will quickly be followed by more frequent and higher-level demands. Within a prison setting, a hostage situation resolved by 'giving in' will undoubtedly lead to other potential perpetrators attempting this course of action.

The third method, known as the 'softly softly' approach, is the approach adopted by the Prison Service since the early 1980s. Negotiators work initially to calm the situation, build rapport with the perpetrators and use this, together with the information they have gathered, to persuade the perpetrators to come out without harming the hostages or themselves. Miron and Goldstein (1978) spell out the benefits of this approach (p. 7):

> If there is one generalisation that has come from experiences in these sorts of situations, it is that time is our best ally. If we can move past the early minutes of a crisis and bring some sort of stability to the situation, the longer it remains stable, the higher the probability that it will end favourably.

Adams and Campling (1994, p. 175) cite hostage situations that shaped the policy in Britain, including the 'Spaghetti House siege' where 'police used talk rather than force.' The siege occurred in 1975 when three escaping offenders kept six staff of a London restaurant hostage in the restaurant basement and released them after six days of negotiation by the police. The 'softly softly' approach is likely to be the most successful strategy although as Cooke et al. (1990, p. 115) admit: 'It is not an easy approach.' It certainly is not easy for the victims who may have to spend days in the situation before being released and may suffer severe psychological problems after the incident. It is, however, as Cooke et al. conclude, 'the best approach we have'.

Current Policy and Practice

The Stockholm syndrome

'Playing for time' and adopting the 'softly softly' approach may also allow for the Stockholm syndrome to develop (Lanceley, 1981). This effect was named after events occurring in Sweden in 1973, when a hostage victim fell in love with and married her abductor. The syndrome has been described by Mackenzie (1978, p. 98) as: 'A normal process of bonding accelerated by severe conditions, coupled with attitude changes resulting from an inability to refute arguments' and Strentz (1979, p. 4) as: 'an automatic, probably unconscious, emotional response to the trauma of becoming a victim'. Holding the perpetrator and the victim in similar extreme conditions, seems to unite them against the 'outsiders'. In the prison setting it is the prison staff negotiating and managing the incident. 'The primary experience that victims of the syndrome share is positive contact with the subject. The positive contact is generated by the lack of negative experiences, i.e. beatings, rapes or physical abuse, rather than by an actual positive act on part of the abductors' (Strentz, 1980, p. 145).

During the incident the psychologist will carefully monitor the Stockholm syndrome. Achieving a positive relationship between the perpetrator and the victim is significant in helping the victim survive. Certainly, the syndrome is not present in all incidents and it takes time to develop fully (Strentz, 1980), but if it takes hold, it can mean that the victim begins to work with the perpetrator and in some cases joins in the pleas for demands to be met. Prison staff negotiating are often distressed when the victim, who may be a member of staff known to them, appeals directly to them for a relatively minor item if they have been instructed to refuse all demands, however small. The psychologist will support the negotiator through this process. They will also need to be alert to opportunities for the perpetrator and the victim to interact positively and to foster this relationship. By drawing out similarities, for example between the perpetrator and the hostage, or by praising the perpetrator for his 'reasonable' treatment of the hostages, the negotiators arc working to protect the hostages and make it increasingly less likely that the perpetrator will harm them.

Defining the incident

Often the first task of the forensic psychologist is to help define exactly what sort of incident is being managed. Is it a hostage incident? If so, how many people are involved? How many of them are being held as hostages? Sometimes an incident begins as a protest by a few prisoners. An example is when a prisoner barricades him/herself in a cell with cellmates. After a few hours a cellmate wants to leave and the prisoner is reluctant to let anyone go. The barricade protest turns into a hostage incident. The reverse situation can also occur when an incident which began (or was considered to be) a hostage-taking becomes a barricade. On other occasions, the incident begins on a rooftop with a number of prisoners. Sometimes there are no hostages involved but there would clearly be significant risks if staff were to go on to the rooftop to remove the prisoners. Negotiation, which leads to the prisoners coming down safely of their own ac-cord, is the preferred option.

The most difficult situations are those where a number of prisoners are riot-ing and may also have taken hostages. Adams and Campling (1994) found that hostage-taking was not a noteworthy feature of prison riots until the twentieth century. The siege area in a riot may be larger and negotiators are faced with the task of negotiating with a number of different prisoners who may move away from the point where the negotiators are standing in order to negotiate. The larger the area, the more difficult it is to control. In the Strangeways riots in Manchester in April 1990, some prisoners were in control of parts of the prison for 24 days. During the next few months there were five further serious riots and numerous smaller disturbances. It was during these riots that psycholo-gists became increasingly involved in incident management as well as post-incident care and support (Vagg 1994).

The roles of the psychologist

The more traditional and well-known role of the psychologist is that of the hos-tage-negotiation adviser supporting the negotiation process. This was the ini-tial role adopted by psychologists advising at hostage incidents in the early 1980s. Psychologists in the Prison Service were well placed to be able to apply their skills to incident management.

One spin-off from the ascendancy of the rehabilitative ideal was the presence in and around penal systems in Western 'developed' countries after the Second World War of sociologists and psychologists with an interest in exploring a range of responses to violence, in individual and group situations. There was a growing interest in manipulating the interaction between the authorities and rioters so that, with the minimum of risk or injury, the authorities came out on top.

(Adams and Campling 1994, p. 174)

Acting as the hostage-negotiation adviser (HNA) the psychologist will be based either at the actual incident or within the command suite. Initially, the psychologist will be trying to help the negotiators to calm the situation and gain control of the hostage area. Evans and Henson (1999) summarize the role as 'supporting the incident commander in designing negotiation strategy and tactics, and then helping the negotiators with the implementation of these tactics by advising on suitable techniques'. The role will include debriefing negotiators to ensure that as much relevant information as possible is gathered. Psychologists can help enrich this process because often information known by the negotiators at the scene may not have been conveyed back. A systematic approach, clarifying exactly what is and what is not known can be fed back into the negotiating process and help shape the strategy decided on.

Communication is critical to the negotiations and the psychologist will work with the team to identify and remove any barriers to communication. It is crucial that the negotiation team and the command team work out a basic, clear communications strategy so that the negotiating team is following the commander's strategy. It is equally important that the commander is receiving timely, accurate and salient information from the scene. The psychologist will advise on implementation but the decision regarding the choice of strategy to follow clearly sits with the commander, although the psychologist will very probably have helped the commander to think through which strategy is more likely to be effective at each stage.

This role, primarily based on the negotiation process, is the one initially developed by forensic psychologists in the Prison Service but as Evans and Henson (1999) outline, this is not the only role adopted by psychologists in support of incident command teams. They describe the roles performed as

in the areas of 'command' or 'support'. In the former, the psychologists are trained to advice on negotiation strategy and the appropriate tactics, which will lead to a safe resolution of the incident. In the latter, there are a range of tasks supporting the negotiation team, interpreting perpetrator profiles, and debriefing and briefing negotiation teams.

(pp. 67–8)

A significant role has been the monitoring of other members of both the negotiation and command teams. It is the psychologist at the scene, trained as an HNA, who will often carry out both roles. Sometimes tasks such as 'profiling' can be delegated to other psychologists who are based at the establishment where the incident has occurred. This experience of a hostage incident is invaluable for training forensic psychologists who will need a variety of incident-related experiences as well as specialized training in order to take on the role of HNA. After the incident there is another role for the psychologist who will be required 'to offer emotional support to the negotiator and make suggestions on how to deal with stress' (Wardlaw, 1983, p. 186). The victims too may well need post-incident support and a psychologist who has not been involved in advising at the incident is best placed to take on this role.

Since the early 1990s, a psychologist with significant experience of acting as HNA, as well as the skill and experience to work well within senior teams, has been routinely deployed at incidents. This role has included advice on the negotiation strategy and tactics for the command team.

There are numerous ways of monitoring the progress of any individual incident towards its successful resolution and the HNA will be critically assessing the negotiating strategy. In the initial stages, negotiators should be calming the perpetrator and building rapport. In incidents of multiple perpetrators this process can take longer as it needs to be repeated and multiple perpetrators can act to keep each other focused and in high state of agitation.

The involvement of the media can affect the progress of the incident. In some British prisons, if prisoners have attained access to a roof top, they may be able to communicate directly with others. Sometimes it is visitors to other prisoners who relate what they have heard and the media may become involved. Perpetrators with access to radio can be encouraged by press interest. The aim of the command team is to work with the media to minimize the risk to the hostages and to resolve the situation as quickly as possible.

The negotiator will be gathering information from the perpetrator, the victim, though usually not through direct contact, and from the sounds heard from within the siege area. The state of the victim is critical information for the command team. In persuading the perpetrator, the negotiator will be trying 'to build a climate of successful negotiation by dealing with smaller, easy-to-settle items first' (Miron and Goldstein, 1978, p. 127).

The prime advantage of incident management in the Prison Service, in comparison with incidents occurring elsewhere, is that staff often not only know who the perpetrators are but also know a great deal about their previous behaviour and current functioning. This intelligence allows for more accurate assessment of the risks involved.

People who perpetrate incidents

The majority of perpetrators are adult male prisoners who take available staff, usually prison officers, or other prisoners, as hostages. When the perpetrators are young offenders the incidents are normally shorter than those perpetrated by adults. Planning of incidents is unusual and they are often characterized by the type of impulsive behaviour familiar to staff working with young offenders in secure settings. Negotiators with experience of working with young offenders have an advantage in working with these perpetrators.

Hostage-taking by women is a very rare event although barricading of a cell or other room is a more common feature and there is always a danger that when a number of prisoners are involved in a barricading incident that hostage-taking may develop. On some occasions when the situation is treated as a hostage-taking it is not until the incident is over that it is clear that collusion was a feature, and the incident would have been more appropriately handled as a protest. Best practice is to err on the side of caution and treat the incident as a hostage-taking if there is doubt.

A small number of perpetrators go on to repeat their hostage-taking behaviour. It might be thought that this is because their previous hostage-taking led to the meeting of some of their demands but there is no evidence that repeat hostage-takers are able to use hostage-taking to gain their demands.

SUMMARY

The 'softly softly' approach is the strategy adopted by HM Prison Service since the early 1980s. Negotiators 'play for time' by talking to the perpetrators. They aim to calm the situation, build rapport with the perpetrators and persuade them to give themselves up without harming anybody. The strategy has significant advantages over other methods employed in the 1950s and 1960s when 'the hard approach' and 'the soft approach' were both found wanting.

The advising psychologist will carefully monitor the Stockholm syndrome during the incident. Its effect can create difficulties for the negotiator who is working to reduce high-level demands. However it can also act to help reduce the risk of the perpetrator harming the hostage.

Acting as the HNA at the scene of the incident the psychologist works with the team to formulate the negotiation strategy and then helps the negotiators follow the commander's brief. Although supporting the negotiating process is the primary role, the psychologist will also carry out a number of other roles including monitoring the members of the teams and perpetrator profiling.

After the incident another psychologist, who was not involved, will offer post-incident support. Many factors affect the progress of an incident such as peer pressure and media interest but there are clear indicators that the negotiating process is effective. When progress is made the higher-level demands will fall away gradually. The ending of a hostage-taking incident requires patience, careful planning and control.

The majority of perpetrators are adult male prisoners who take available staff or other prisoners as hostages. The skills of the psychologist can help to ensure that incidents are managed to a successful conclusion without incurring injury to anyone.

Chapter Five

Applying the Research on Reducing Recidivism to Prison Regimes

Phil Willmot

Why Do Offenders Offend?

There is a large amount of research about the reasons why people offend which shows a number of factors, sometimes known as 'criminogenic factors', which are common to a lot of offenders. For example Andrews and Bonta (1994) identified a number of these factors:

Employment   Some offenders lack the skills to get or hold down a job. This makes them more likely to resort to crime to support themselves. As well as specific technical skills there is a range of general 'employability' skills which offenders lack. These include communication skills, planning and problem-solving skills, being able to work with and manage other people, as well as attributes such as self-confidence, honesty, initiative and motivation which employers look for.

Education   Some offenders have a poor educational attainment, either because they dropped out of school, or because they have learning disabilities, or specific learning difficulties, such as dyslexia. This limits the sort of work that is available to them. They may also have missed out on the social skills that children learn in schools, for example learning to work together, resolve conflict without violence and see other people's points of view.

Partner and family   Stable family support, and in particular a supportive partner, tend to protect offenders from committing further crime.

Criminal social networks   Offenders tend to mix with other offenders outside as well as in prison. They may live in the same high-crime areas. They may have other family members who are also offenders, and they may socialize with other offenders. Perhaps not surprisingly, prisoners who have these sort of social networks are more likely to reoffend.

Substance abuse   Alcohol and drug abuse are related to crime in a number of ways. For example, people are more likely to offend when their judgement or inhibitions have been impaired by alcohol or drugs; substance abuse can interfere with other factors such as employment or relationships which protect people from offending; or offenders may commit crime in order to buy drink or drugs.

Poor community functioning   This heading covers a number of areas, such as financial problems, poor accommodation and a lack of social support, which can lead to offending.

Personal and emotional factors   There are a number of patterns of thinking and behaviour which are known to be more common among offenders. For example, offenders are often impulsive, aggressive, or find it difficult to see other people's points of view or solve problems effectively.

Anti-social attitudes   Some offenders have particular attitudes or sets of beliefs, which encourage crime, for example they may have anti-authority, racist, sexist or other anti-social beliefs which encourage offending.

The link between these factors and crime is complicated. Offenders will not necessarily have all or any of these factors in their background and, on the other hand, having any of these factors will not make a person into an offender. All we can say is that these factors are more common among offenders than among the rest of the population, and on the whole, the more of these factors are present, the likelier it will be that a person will offend.

What Does This Mean for Prisons?

In recent years, there has been a rapid expansion in offending-behaviour programmes in prisons. These programmes, such as the Enhanced Thinking Skills (ETS), Reasoning and Rehabilitation (R&R) and Sex Offender Treatment Programme (SOTP) are thought to have a significant effect on reducing reoffending among prisoners who successfully complete them. However, these programmes tend only to address the personal and emotional factors and anti-social attitudes from the above list. They do little to address the other problem areas listed.

Motiuk (1998) followed up 3,380 prisoners to investigate which of these eight areas were the strongest predictors of recidivism after release. He found that, for adult male offenders, the strongest predictors of recidivism after release were, in order, unemployment, substance abuse, criminal associates, marital/family breakdown and personal/emotional problems. While it would be dangerous to draw too strong conclusions about the relative importance of these different factors, Motiuk's results suggest that other factors may be of comparable importance in reducing reoffending. This chapter describes some of the research into other factors, and what can be done to address them through prison regimes.

Employment factors

Lipsey (1992) identified the fact that finding employment on release was the best single predictor of not reoffending for young offenders on release from custody. However, this result is ambiguous; it could mean that employment protects young offenders from reoffending. On the other hand, since criminality is known to be associated with factors such as poor educational attainment, poor employment skills and poor cognitive skills, it is also possible that this finding reflects the fact that better educated, more socially skilled, less criminally minded offenders are less likely to reoffend and are also better equipped to find stable employment. More recent North American studies have investigated the link between work and training in prison and subsequent reoffending. Simple comparison of those with good and bad work records in prisons have the same problems as Lipsey's results; those with good work records in prison are arguably more socially skilled and less delinquent than those with poor records, and so may reoffend less anyway. Saylor and Gaes (1996) followed up after release US prisoners who had worked in prison industries or received vocational training, and compared them with other prisoners who were carefully matched in terms of their background and level of risk. They found that prisoners who worked in federal prison industries adjusted better to prison, were less likely to return to prison within their first year of release, were more likely to find a job on release and were likely to find slightly better paid jobs on release. In the long term, although reoffending rates for the two groups were not significantly different, the industries subgroup survived 20 per cent longer and the training subgroup 28 per cent longer in the community before reoffending than the control groups. This suggests a slight, but hardly overwhelming effect of employment in prison on recidivism.

More recently the Correctional Service of Canada has moved its attention away from simply putting prisoners to work and has conducted a number of studies in an attempt to analyse the concept of employability, in other words the generic skills, attitudes and abilities that employers consider when looking for potential employees. Fabiano et al. (1996) summarize a number of these studies. First of all, looking at work attitudes, they found that the best workers in prison industries found the work motivating, felt more involved in their job, felt responsible for their work and confident in their abilities. Also, the more prisoners expressed feelings of involvement, responsibility and competence, the less they expressed criminal attitudes. Their supervisors also rated these prisoners as more dependable, co-operative, safety-conscious and productive.

A second study used workshop supervisors to identify the general work skills that contribute to work performance. These were developed into a set of performance measures which could be used to give constructive and specific feedback to prisoners about their work performance in 12 areas which covered attitudinal, behavioural and interpersonal factors, as well as job performance.

A third study examined the characteristics of effective work supervisors and demonstrated the positive effects of leadership training for these staff in terms of developing more positive attitudes to work for themselves and the prisoners they supervised, and improving workshop productivity.

Fabiano et al. argue that workshop supervisors have a key role to play in providing prisoners with a sense of purpose, promoting positive values and problem-solving. They have developed the Performance Evaluation Scale so that workplace supervisors can give feedback to case managers on employability skills. They also argue that there is considerable overlap between employability skills and the cognitive skills taught in programmes such as the Reasoning and Rehabilitation programme which also teach problem-solving, pro-social skills and positive values. Thus, with appropriate training, workplace supervisors can reinforce the learning in these programmes and give valuable feedback on progress to case managers.

The idea put forward by Fabiano et al., of using workshop supervisors to reinforce the learning from cognitive-skills programmes in a practical setting appears to be a simple and effective means of enhancing the learning from such programmes. It may also have other positive effects, for example in improving the job satisfaction of workshop supervisors and improving workshop productivity.

Education factors

An unpublished report commissioned by HM Prison Service (Palmer and Hollin, 1995) concluded that there were 'remarkably few relevant outcome studies' looking at the link between education in prison and recidivism. There appears to be an untested assumption that education is effective in reducing recidivism.

Palmer and Hollin quote a number of arguments that have been put forward for the benefits of education, such as:

> It improves employment skills
> It promotes attitude change and motivates offenders to change their behaviour
> It improves self-esteem
> It relieves boredom and improves institutional behaviour
> It mirrors work patterns outside, so helping their reintegration into society.

Palmer and Hollin noted that a number of different approaches had been tried which have attempted to meet one or more of these goals. However, they found very little effective evaluation of the impact on recidivism.

An earlier study by Hill (1985) reviewed 12 studies and found only three that showed any positive effect of prison education on recidivism. Palmer and Hollin did find one more recent study (Porporino and Robinson, 1991) with more positive results. Porporino and Robinson (1991) followed up 1,736 prisoners in Canada who had started basic education in literacy and numeracy. They found that, of those who completed the programme, 30 per cent reoffended in the follow-up period, compared with 36 per cent of those who were released before the end of the programme and 42 per cent of those who dropped out of the programme. This result seems open to the criticism that those who complete the programme are less delinquent and so less likely to reoffend, but the study also found that, amongst high risk offenders, those who had completed basic education were the least likely to reoffend. Indeed, basic education seemed to have the greatest effect on recidivism amongst high risk offenders.

Clark (2000), looking at education in British prisons, found that education in basic literacy and numeracy skills, when properly targeted, does have an effect in reducing recidivism.

The correlation between dyslexia and delinquency has long been recognized (e.g. Critchley, 1968), though it is still unclear why dyslexia is relatively common among offenders or why it should lead to offending.

Marital and family factors

Paolucci et al. (1998) reviewed the literature on links between family background and crime and found evidence that poor parenting, such as inappropriate discipline and lack of parental supervision, as well as conflict, abuse and a lack of affection are all predictive of later criminal behaviour. There was also evidence that early paternal influences are stronger than maternal influences in fostering violent criminality. These historical factors cannot be changed; however, it does suggest that interventions which improve family contacts, prevent abuse and teach parenting skills may have a long-term benefit for the children of offenders. Paolucci et al. also found that maintaining an active family interest while incarcerated and establishing a mutually satisfying relationship after release were associated with reduced recidivism.

Sampson and Laub (1993) described an 18-year follow up study of 500 adolescents described as 'delinquent', together with 500 'non-delinquent' cases. They found that adult social bonds, such as employment or a strong marriage, had a strong protective effect in reducing offending in later life.

Social-network factors

A number of studies have found that this area was one of the strongest predictors of recidivism. Goggin et al. (1998) divided this area into three components, of which association with criminal companions was the strongest predictor of recidivism, followed by crime rate in home area and criminal family. They commented however that, although surveys had often identified associating with criminals as one of the most prevalent problems among adult offenders, this is one of the least-researched areas of 'criminogenic need'. It is also, arguably, one of the hardest to influence directly within prisons.

Substance-abuse factors

Several studies have identified a link between substance abuse and recidivism. A literature review for the Prison Service (Home Office, 2000b) summarizes the results of evaluations of the commonest treatment methods used in prisons: therapeutic communities (TC), cognitive-behavioural programmes, methadone and 12-step models. That report concludes that a number of studies of TCs for substance abuse have produced very positive results. While these have some methodological flaws, the overall results are encouraging. The report concludes that the other techniques, while showing promise, have not yet been properly evaluated to determine their effect on recidivism. The report notes three characteristics of effective drug treatment programmes from its literature review:

1   matching the treatment to the needs of each offender;
2   effective throughcare and aftercare to manage the transition into the community when the offender will be most at risk of relapsing; and

3   the more time offenders spend in treatment, the more effective the outcome.

The report concludes that the most effective treatment programmes will probably include elements of all these techniques and quotes in conclusion the comment of the (US) Executive Office of the President, Office of National Drug Policy (1996):

> . . . a successful course of treatment will combine therapies, services and methods that produce favourable outcomes. Since drug users, especially hardcore drug users, face many related problems (e.g. high risk environment, unemployment, lack of education and physical and sexual abuse), effective treatment requires several critical elements, including the following:
>
> > complete and ongoing assessment of the client
> > a comprehensive range of services, including pharmacological treatment, if necessary; counselling, either individual or group; in either structured or unstructured settings; and HIV-risk reduction education;
> > a continuum of treatment interventions;
> > case management and monitoring to engage clients in an appropriate intensity of services; and
> > provision and integration of continuing social support.
>
> These elements, rather than the specific treatment models, determine whether a program will be successful in treating the individual clients and affecting the broader social or community problems that exist because of drug abuse

Community-functioning factors

This heading includes factors such as poor accommodation, debts, poor health, literacy problems, absence of support and lack of hobbies. A detailed study of these areas by Gates et al. (1998) found the most significant of these factors in relation to recidivism to be use of leisure, followed by finance problems, accommodation and support. Self-presentation, hygiene and physical health were found to be unrelated to recidivism.

Personal and emotional factors

There are a number of factors included under this heading, including poor problem-solving skills, rigid thinking, impulsivity and risk-taking, as well as other personal characteristics such as low self-esteem, neuroticism and mental disorder.

Robinson et al. (1998) identified that, while many interventions target self-esteem, its effect on recidivism was weak. Many other interventions teach offenders assertiveness. While the authors found no correlation between assertiveness and recidivism, they found that, in combination with other skills deficits, a lack of assertiveness may be relevant. For example assertiveness does appear to be effective in reducing recidivism among substance abusers. They also conclude that there is no evidence for low intelligence or mental disorder being relevant to the prediction of recidivism. They conclude that the personal and emotional-needs domain consists of four principal components that are relevant to offending:

1   cognitive problem-solving skills and thinking skills;
2   self-control, impulsivity and life-planning deficits;
3   interpersonal problem-solving and empathy;
4   aggression and anger.

Lösel (1995) reviewed a number of studies to look at the overall effectiveness of offending-behaviour programmes and found that they reduced the proportion of offenders who reoffended by between 5 and 20 per cent. These effects are relatively small when compared to psychological treatments for non-offenders and Lösel suggests three reasons for this:

1   Offenders are a particularly difficult group to treat.
2   The environment in prisons is not particularly conducive to treatment.
3   These studies probably underestimate the effect because 'untreated' offenders in the control groups will still have got some benefit from the prison regime.

A common finding is that prison-based programmes are less effective than community-based programmes. Lösel suggests that this may be because prisons tend to treat more persistently anti-social and dangerous offenders. Also, programme effectiveness is affected by other factors such as the physical environment and design of prisons, the degree of repression, isolation from the outside community and the characteristics of staff, such as motivation, attitude, role definition and training. Lösel found that prison programmes were sometimes as effective as community programmes, and argues that, where environmental and staff factors are positive, this can counteract the negative aspects of prison.

Anti-social attitudes

Anti-social attitudes include negative attitudes towards the criminal justice system, towards employment, the family and relationships and minority groups, attitudes that value substance abuse, violence and crime, and values which disrespect societal values and other people. Law (1998) found that anti-social attitudes towards the criminal justice system, violence and lifestyle were the most strongly related to recidivism.

While many cognitive-behavioural programmes include elements designed to address such anti-social attitudes in prison, outcome measures looking specifically at attitude change are rare, so it is hard to say how effective such programmes are in addressing these attitudes.

Pro-social modelling is a concept that is more widely recognized in the National Probation Service. Trotter (1993) describes pro-social modelling as involving 'the practice of offering praise and reward for pro-social expressions and actions . . . [Also] the probation officer becomes a positive role model acting to reinforce pro-social or non-criminal behaviour'. While it is more difficult to evaluate the effectiveness of a process such as this than it is to evaluate a discreet and specific programme, this has been done by Trotter (1996), who trained a group of Australian probation officers in pro-social modelling techniques and then compared the breach and recidivism rates of probationers supervised by these officers with probationers supervised by other officers. The study found significantly fewer breaches and lower rates of imprisonment after four years' follow-up among the group exposed to pro-social modelling than among the control group. Although there is no literature on pro-social modelling in prisons at present, pro-social modelling does form a central part of the regime in the successful Buckley Hall bid, and staff training was due to start there towards the end of 2001.

Legitimacy is related to pro-social modelling, and is another concept that is more widely recognized in the Probation Service, though it, or the lack of it, was referred to in the Woolf report (1991). Bottoms and Rex (1998) argue that people will comply with authority more readily if they perceive that authority to be legitimate. As with pro-social modelling, it is harder to evaluate a process or a set of values like legitimacy, and, while this may appear a somewhat idealistic notion to apply to prisoners, there is some limited evidence that people in authority who act legitimately can have an impact not only on the current behaviour of those they deal with, but also on their future behaviour. The best known example of this comes from the Milwaukee Domestic Violence Experiment (Paternoster et al., 1997), which found that when police dealt in a procedurally fair manner when arresting assault suspects, the rate of subsequent domestic violence was significantly lower than when they did not. Moreover, suspects who were arrested and perceived that they were treated in a procedurally fair manner had subsequent assault rates that were as low as those suspects given a more favourable outcome (warned and released without arrest).

Paternoster et al. identify a number of elements that make systems appear legitimate:

Representation   The subject has the opportunity to play a part in the making of important decisions.
Consistency   The authority treats all subjects alike.
Impartiality   The person in authority suppresses his or her personal biases when acting professionally.
Competency   The person in authority seems competent to make high quality decisions.
Correctability   Low-level decisions can be appealed against where necessary.
Ethicality   The person in authority treats subjects with respect and dignity.

Though there do not appear to have been any formal evaluations, the different cultures in private-sector prisons and in women's prisons appear to match these ideals more closely.

One of the theories underlying cognitive-skills programmes such as the Enhanced Thinking Skills course is that of moral development. Kohlberg (1969) proposed that people pass through a number of stages of moral development. In the 'pre-conventional' stage, moral reasoning is determined by selfish considerations and obedience to rules in order to avoid punishment and seek reward. In the next stage, the 'conventional' stage, individuals become aware of the reciprocal nature of rules and decisions are made to maintain social contact. Finally, in the 'post-conventional' stage, individuals are able to understand the underlying moral principles of society's rules. There is some evidence (e.g. Thornton 1987) that offenders tend to function at lower levels of moral development.

Thornton (1987) proposed that moral climate in prisons can have an effect on prisoner behaviour, which to some extent overrides the moral stage of the individual. For example, prisons, with their clear emphasis on reward and punishment and their coercive and authoritarian approach to rules, tend to reinforce a preconventional way of moral reasoning, which could undermine the teaching of cognitive-skills programmes. Thornton proposed that moral development progresses through exposure to conflicting or more advanced arguments. A culture of reciprocity and equality, such as those outlined above, may therefore foster moral development. Studies into the dynamics of cognitive-behavioural programmes such as the STEP evaluation of SOTP (Beech et al., 1999) has shown that pro-social modelling and legitimacy are key elements of successful tutoring.

What Doesn't Work?

Before drawing conclusions about what works, the evaluation literature also contains much information on the interventions that are not effective, or which are counter-productive in reducing offending.

Punishment

Evaluations of punitive programmes show that punishment by itself leads to worse rates of recidivism. The general literature on psychology indicates that, under certain circumstances, punishment can be an effective means of reducing unwanted behaviour, though on balance, behaviour change that is based on positive reinforcement works better. For punishment to be most effective the following conditions need to be met:

Inevitability   When the undesired behaviour appears, it will definitely be punished.

Immediacy   To be most effective, punishment should occur more or less instantaneously following the behaviour to be reduced.

Severity   The most effective punishments are those that occur at the maximum possible severity.

Availability of alternative behaviours   Punishment works best when, instead of the unwanted behaviour, other responses can be made and are reinforced.

Comprehensibility   With people, as opposed to laboratory animals, punishment needs to be understood in relation to the behaviour that has brought it about.

None of these conditions are met in the criminal justice system in general, and it is difficult to imagine how they could be. This is not to say that punishment does not serve other purposes such as retribution or deterrence. However, the research is unequivocal; as a means of controlling criminal behaviour punishment on its own is ineffective, indeed it may even be counter-productive. An evaluation of American 'boot camps' by Mackenzie and Souryal (1994) concluded that the impact of these programmes in reducing recidivism was 'at best negligible'. Moreover they found that camps with the strongest emphasis on punishment produced an increase in recidivism compared with control groups, whereas the camps that seemed to be least damaging were those that had some element of treatment-related work such as education, counselling or substance-abuse treatment.

Gendreau et al. (1993) found a similar result with their evaluation of Intensive Probation Supervision (IPS) in the US. IPS involved more intensive contact with probation officers as well as other, more punitive measures such as home confinement, curfews and random drug-testing. The researchers found that, overall, IPS had little impact on recidivism (indeed, perhaps unsurprisingly, the closer supervision resulted in more offenders being breached). However, they found that, in those programmes that did reduce recidivism, the effective element was more 'treatment' rather than more intensive punishment or surveillance. Andrews (1990) found that, overall, the effect of increasing the severity of a penalty was a slight increase in recidivism, together with a slight tendency to dilute the positive effects of any treatment. Since a recurring theme in this body of research has been the need to address the deficits of offenders, these results should not be surprising. Punishment on its own will do nothing to tackle these deficits, and may indeed further limit the skills and support networks of offenders.

Incentives-based regimes

Regimes run on strictly behaviourist lines, such as token economies, in which participants are awarded tokens for specified good behaviours, may have some effect in improving institutional behaviour, though there is no evidence that these changes translate into reduced recidivism (Rice et al., 1990). The limited effectiveness of token economies in reducing recidivism is further diluted in a programme such as the Prison Service's Incentives and Earned Privileges System which does not comply with the strict behaviourist criteria of token economies. Thus, while the IEP system appears to be effective in changing institutional behaviour, its effect on recidivism is likely to be negligible.

Assessment of 'Criminogenic Needs'

There is no simple explanation for criminal behaviour and, while there are common patterns, each offender will be different in terms of the factors that lead to offending. Effective assessment of the needs of offenders must therefore be at the heart of any regime that is designed to reduce recidivism. Some measures have been designed specifically for this purpose, for example the Level of Service Inventory – Revised (LSI-R) (Andrews and Bonta, 1995) and the Assessment Case Management and Evaluation System (Probation Studies Unit, 1998). Both of these instruments are extremely time consuming to administer and are not really feasible for mass screening of prisoners. The Offender Assessment System (OASys) is designed to fulfil a similar function to the LSI-R, though its implementation date is still uncertain. In the shorter term, officers at HMP Garth have designed a needs-assessment process which is both effective and resource efficient (Horn, 2000). This involves a two-stage process; first a general induction process over the prisoner's first three months, followed by a more detailed assessment of his or her particular needs. The system also incorporates a behavioural monitoring process used by wing officers and workplace supervisors to monitor aspects of behaviour that relate to the needs-assessment process, such as aggression, impulsivity and vocational skills.

Cost Effectiveness

One of the strongest arguments holding back the expansion of effective programmes in recent years has been that such programmes are extremely costly to run. Apart from the social and ethical counter-arguments, there is now a growing body of evidence from North America that effective programmes provide large savings over time for both taxpayers (in terms of reduced costs of police, courts and prisons) and victims (for example medical costs, stolen property or reduced earnings).

Aos et al. (1999) calculated that each dollar spent on effective programmes saves on average $5 for the taxpayer and $7 for potential future victims. In contrast, punishment-based programmes such as boot camps yielded substantially lower economic returns of around 75¢ for each dollar spent.

Conclusions

To be effective in reducing recidivism, an activity must specifically target factors empirically linked to reducing reoffending. This is not only true of offending-behaviour programmes, it also holds for other activities such as employment and education in prisons.

Accurate assessment of such needs is crucial to any effective regime that aims to reduce recidivism.

Though few of the evaluations of prison-based programmes have included evaluation of the follow-up, those which have done so in the areas of offending-behaviour programmes and substance abuse, show that effective aftercare to manage the transition from prison to the community has a significant effect on reducing recidivism.

It seems that simply putting a prisoner in a workshop or on education will have little effect on his likelihood of reoffending, unless this targets specific 'criminogenic' needs. The Canadian model of targeting specific employability skills through workshop supervisors appears to be a promising approach.

The effects of pro-social modelling are hard to quantify. However there is research to indicate that it also has a positive effect in reinforcing the positive effects of specific programmes, while conversely, anti-social behaviour by staff is likely to undermine effectiveness. It appears possible to teach pro-social modelling skills, and all staff could benefit from this training.

Targeting offending-behaviour needs should not be seen as a role for specialist groups in prisons such as offending-behaviour programmes, psychologists, teachers or probation officers. There are a wide range of regime activities which can contribute to targeting relevant prisoner needs *providing they are properly and specifically targeted.*

Elements of effective regimes

Assessment   Any effective regime that addresses factors linked to the risk of reoffending must be based on accurate assessment of such prisoner needs. In the medium to long term the OASys should meet this need. However in the shorter term a system like that at HMP Garth may be effective and should be investigated further.

Education   The current policy of prioritizing basic literacy and numeracy skills in education appears to be sound and should be strengthened. There is currently little evidence that other forms of academic education are as effective in reducing reoffending. Education resources should be focused on addressing other offending-behaviour needs which are not widely addressed, such as teaching of parenting skills, constructive use of leisure time, budgeting skills and education on health. Education screening should routinely include a screening for dyslexia. Education provision should also include remedial work for people with dyslexia.

Employment   If employment in prisons is to have any significant effect on recidivism there needs to be a fundamental change in the culture of Inmate

Activities groups. At present, work for prisoners appears to serve a number of diverse functions; it provides essential services such as cleaning and catering; it keeps prisoners active and 'out of mischief'; it often functions as an informal 'Incentives and Earned Privileges' (IEP) system, rewarding good behaviour with well paid, easy or interesting jobs. Relatively rarely does work seem to be allocated on the basis of offending-behaviour needs. In order to match employment opportunities with appropriate needs, there would need to be a job analysis of each area of work in the prison to identify the interpersonal, problem-solving, attitudinal and job-specific skills required for that job. These could then be matched to the deficits and needs identified for each prisoner. Work supervisors would need to be trained to assess and develop these employability skills and to play a more active role in contributing to and developing the sentence-management system. Education could also enhance employability skills by teaching such generic skills as presenting CVs, interview skills and self-employment skills. Building links with potential employers in the local community would help to overcome the reservations that employers have about employing ex-prisoners, as well as giving them the skills to work with ex-prisoners. It could have other benefits such as improving employment prospects for offenders and sharing skills and training between prisons and business.

Marital and family   Some aspects of relationships are addressed in other areas, such as teaching problem-solving, interpersonal and perspective-taking skills on cognitive-skills programmes. Greater emphasis should be placed on teaching specific relationship and parenting skills through education departments.

Social Networks   Though the literature suggests that this is one of the most important factors linked to the risk of reoffending, it is one of the least researched. More research is required into how this can be effectively addressed. At a very simple level there may be lessons to learn from the Sex Offender Treatment Programme. It seems ironic that, although most sex offender offend alone, the SOTP gives a very clear message that they should avoid mixing with other sex offenders on their release, and this seems to be a message which is readily reinforced by personal officers and probation officers. However, this message does not appear to be given to other groups of offenders with anything like the same force, even though they are arguably more likely to be influenced by offending friends. Simply raising this issue regularly may have some effect in prompting prisoners to consider it, rather than automatically returning to the same home environment and social network on release.

Again with sex offenders, personal officers and probation officers expend a great deal of energy in setting up safe release plans for prisoners, such as finding suitable accommodation away from schools or vulnerable people, checking on the whereabouts of victims and developing support networks. While this is undoubtedly costly, it can be justified by the need to protect the public. While this approach will not be necessary for every prisoner, there are skills and procedures which are used by staff working with sex offenders that should be used more widely in planning the resettlement of prisoners.

Substance abuse   There is evidence for the effectiveness of certain types of substance-abuse intervention. The recent Prison Service study highlighted the characteristics of effective programmes. Existing programmes should be evaluated against these characteristics. The same literature review highlighted that some interventions, such as assertiveness training, were effective with substance abusers, although they do not appear to be effective in reducing recidivism for other groups. This should be borne in mind when assessing the need for 'non-accredited' programmes.

Community functioning   Specific basic 'life skills' such as budgeting, cooking and nutrition, health and hygiene should be assessed by education departments and taught where necessary. Links with external agencies should be fostered, particularly those which can provide support in the community. While this is already done, it often seems to be done on an *ad hoc* basis which can be overly reliant on personal contacts and the enthusiasm of individual members of staff. These contacts should be made more systematic and thorough.

Personal and emotional   Much greater emphasis needs to be given to ensuring that the pro-social messages taught on offending-behaviour programmes are reflected and reinforced by the rest of the regime. Pro-social modelling training for all staff would help achieve this, but the staff awareness training which is already run alongside such programmes should also help. This training should be targeted at different groups of staff and focused on the specifics of how each group can reinforce these treatment goals.

Attitudinal   Pro-social modelling training has been shown to be effective in the community with community-service supervisors. The Buckley Hall pilot project should show whether these techniques could be applied to other prisons. The pro-social modelling literature makes it clear that pro-social modelling should not only be done by the 'front line' staff, who have the most contact with offenders. Pro-social modelling works on staff just as much as it does on offenders, and it therefore needs to be practised by all levels of management and different departments within the organization.

Sentence planning targets currently often seem to focus on activities which the prison is obliged to provide for prisoners, such as particular courses or employment options. Greater emphasis should be placed on targets which prisoners can achieve themselves or where they can take the initiative in seeking help from others, for example maintaining and building links with family, probation or other agencies outside, identifying a suitable support network in the community, taking greater responsibility for their own hygiene, work and behaviour and taking responsibility for others as a wing representative or in the workplace.

General   There seems to be a widespread assumption that addressing offending behaviour and recidivism are the sole responsibility of accredited offending-behaviour programmes or specialist staff such as psychologists or probation officers. A clear message from this literature review is that not only do other areas such as education and industries have a role to play in reducing recidivism, but all Prison Service staff have a role to play in modelling and reinforcing pro-social behaviour and values. This is a message which needs to be broadcast and given much greater attention in all the Service's business.

Culture change is always a difficult process to manage. However, different sectors of the Prison Service such as the private sector and women's prisons appear to have a culture which involves more pro-social modelling and legitimacy.

Much of the past research and evaluation in this field has been of poor quality. If any of these changes are to be implemented then they should be properly evaluated from the outset in order to provide reliable recidivism data.

Research from North America into the cost-effectiveness of various interventions indicates that many effective criminal justice programmes are extremely cost effective, when the full costs of repeat offending to victims and the criminal justice system are taken into account. Given the current emphasis on government agencies providing value for money, it would be useful to develop a similar system of costing programmes and other regime elements in order to produce a stronger case for funding.

Chapter Six

Evaluating Groupwork in Prisons

Caroline Friendship and Louise Falshaw

Introduction

The evaluation of offending-behaviour programmes for prisoners has been identified as an important principle of effective practice in the 'What Works' literature (McGuire and Priestley, 1995). On-going evaluation is one of the
accreditation criteria for programmes run in HM Prison Service and the National Probation Service as governed by the Joint Prison and Probation Service
Accreditation Panel.

The primary aim of offending-behaviour programmes is to reduce reoffending,
and so assessing the impact of treatment on reconviction rates is the ultimate
goal of evaluation. This is often referred to as the long-term evaluation of programmes, owing to the length of time that is needed between finishing a treatment programme and completing at least two years in the community after
discharge from prison. Gendreau and Andrews (1991) differentiate between
factors that sustain criminal behaviour and those that do not. Offending-
behaviour programmes, therefore, need to reduce reoffending by targeting the
factors that are linked to offending behaviour. These factors or intermediary
treatment targets are monitored before, after, and at six weeks following treatment using clinical assessment measures. These measures assess attitudes, behaviour and skills, and monitor change attributable to treatment. Evaluating
clinical change is indicative of the short-term impact of treatment programmes.
This chapter describes the process of both long-term evaluation and short-term
impact assessment of offending-behaviour programmes.

Evaluation practices in HM Prison Service are informed by 'best practice' in
other organizations and these have included both governmental and academic

bodies such as the Home Office and relevant university departments. A Home Office Committee, which meets quarterly and considers both Prison Service and National Probation Directorate initiatives, oversees the programme evaluation studies in the Prison Service. The Evaluation of Offender Programmes Committee is tasked to act as an advisory committee for the Crime Reduction Programme (offender programmes) and similar evaluations. Its primary role is to advise on appropriate standards for evaluation methodology and to act as a forum for sharing knowledge gained from the evaluation of probation and prison programmes. This committee has had a profound influence on the evaluation practices adopted by the Prison Service and these are also described in this chapter.

Long-Term Evaluation

The aim of long-term evaluation is to assess the impact of offending-behaviour programmes in terms of reducing reoffending. Most programme-impact studies in the UK have used reconviction as an outcome measure but in the United States recidivism is the typical outcome measure. It is important for researchers and evaluators alike to clearly understand these terms. The criminological literature can be criticized for using the terms reconviction, reoffending and recidivism interchangeably. They are distinct terms and a definition for each is proposed, together with a recommendation that researchers adopt these to ensure clarity and consistency in the outcome measure they are reporting.

Table 6.1 Definition of reconviction, reoffending and recidivism

Reconviction	Conviction for any offence during a specified time period
Reoffending	Perpetrated an illegal act during a specified time period whether caught or not
Recidivism	Commited an offence-related behaviour, legal or illegal, during a specified time period

Recidivism covers the broadest range of criminal behaviour or activity. It includes both reoffending and reconviction but also may include patterns of behaviour that are linked to offending e.g. arrest or breach of probation order. Reoffending relates to behaviours which are defined in statute for a particular jurisdiction and this includes not only offending behaviour that is detected, recorded and convicted within the criminal justice system but also offending behaviour which is not reported or detected by the authorities. Reconviction has the narrowest focus and refers to officially recorded crime only, and it is this definition that most publications in the UK have adhered to.

For most jurisdictions the government routinely records criminal conviction histories – often referred to as 'official records'. In England and Wales there are two sources of official data (Friendship et al., 2001). Firstly, the Home Office holds a computerized database, which is accessible to independent researchers, called the Offenders Index. Secondly, the police centrally collate data from police force areas (microfiche data for offences prior to 1994 and the Police National Computer) but access to this source is for restricted personnel only. The Offenders Index is the most commonly used source of data for reconviction studies.

Reconviction rates tend to express the proportion of the sample who were reconvicted, therefore, reconvicted/not reconvicted as an outcome is a dichotomous variable. This type of dependent variable influences the statistical analysis of the data (e.g. *chi*-square statistic and logistic regression). In the UK, reconviction is typically expressed within a specified time period commonly referred to as a standardized reconviction rate. Reconviction within two years has been the convention and is common in government statistics. Two factors influence this. Firstly, there is a long time delay in the criminal justice system between charge and conviction of an offender. Secondly, national data suggests that most of those who are going to be convicted will be within two years of release. For example, 55 per cent of prisoners discharged from prison in England and Wales were reconvicted within two years while the four-year rate was 64 per cent, only a 9 per cent increase (Kershaw et al., 1999).

Reconviction rates that offer in excess of two years are more reliable. For some specific groups of offenders, such as sexual offenders, however, the low base rate of sexual conviction means far longer follow-up periods are required for reliability (Friendship and Thornton, 2001). The advantages of the standardized follow-up period are that it aids direct comparison from study to study. Recently, variable time periods have been used. These studies make more efficient use of the data, especially in samples where the actual period of observation varies widely, and survival analysis, a statistical technique, aids such studies (Lee, 1992).

The criminological literature predominately focuses on the limitations of reconviction as an outcome measure, most commonly the fact that official conviction records are a gross underestimate of reoffending (Maguire, 1997). The values of reconviction have recently been appraised in Cooke and Michie (1998), who described its use in the development of actuarial risk instruments and in the assessment of the impact of sentencing and offender management strategies, including programmes for offenders. Reconviction data are accessible for researchers and are computerized. Their use has been described as an essential tool of the trade for criminologists (Lloyd et al., 1994) and has now become an important key performance indicator within the criminal justice system (Carter et al., 1992).

Design of the evaluation study

Ideal paradigm   The ideal experimental design for the reconviction study is a randomized control study. The methodological advantages of randomization in criminal justice research are outlined by Farrington (1983). He describes a randomized experiment as '. . . one in which people (or units) are assigned to conditions according to a table of random numbers, with every person having the same probability of being assigned to each condition' (p. 257). Farrington also highlighted the fact that within the criminal justice system there are both practical and ethical problems with randomization. Denial of treatment has specific ethical issues for imprisoned offenders as it can affect sentencing, recategorization of security level in prison and parole decisions, all of which may impact on the chances of a prisoner's early release. Evidence from the 'What Works' literature also states that selection of offenders for treatment should be based on need, not on whether an offender is randomly selected for treatment. In reality, few reconviction studies in the UK have adopted a random design over the past twenty years. If such a design were implemented currently in a prison setting, offenders who were allocated to the 'no treatment' cell could apply to the European Court of Human Rights or through the Judicial Review process for the right to participate in interventions.

In practice   In the absence of random allocation, the majority of reconviction studies in England and Wales have controlled for extraneous variables by the retrospective matching of a comparison group (a quasi-experimental design). In this method a comparison group is matched to the treatment group on relevant variables after the intervention. In the criminological literature, it has been demonstrated that a number of variables have a statistically significant relationship with reconviction; that is, they predict reconviction. It is important that these theoretically relevant variables are matched between the treatment and comparison group. For example, Ward (1987) identified 16 variables predictive of reconviction and these included type of index offence, age at first reconviction and previous criminal history; and Lloyd et al. (1994) found that age, number of previous sentencing appearances, previous appearance rate, current offence type, average number of previous appearances, convictions per appearance, number of youth custodial sentences and gender all had a significant impact on reconviction. The major disadvantage of retrospective matching is that it is only possible to match on a small subset of extraneous variables and this is further limited by a lack of recorded variables for the comparison group. Typically, the intervention or treatment group is subject to rigorous pre- and post-treatment assessment.

The evaluation design of Prison Service programmes has built on the retrospective quasi-experimental design described above incorporating recommendations from Home Office guidelines for evaluators of offending behaviour programmes (Colledge et al., 1999). These guidelines do emphasize the importance of a control group or a well-matched comparison group. Further recommendations, however, were also made. Firstly, it is important to know what would happen to offenders anyway in order to assess the additional benefits of an intervention or treatment. This can be achieved through the analysis of national criminal history data to model predicted outcomes. The Home Office has generated such a model called the Offender Group Reconviction Scale (OGRS) which was based on the criminal careers of some 30,000 offenders. OGRS predicts from a limited number of demographic and criminal history factors whether an offender will be reconvicted within two years of release from prison or the start of a community penalty for a standard list offence (Taylor, 1999). Secondly, it is essential to compare known risk factors between the treatment and comparison group in the analysis (e.g. previous conviction history, age or OGRS likelihood of reconviction score) to counteract selection effects. Apparently good outcome results for a treatment programme may simply reflect the fact that less risky offenders completed treatment, rather than that it had a real impact. Finally, the outcomes for treatment drop-outs must be included within the treatment group.

An evaluation of the Prison Service Cognitive Skills Programmes is a sound working example of this research design in practice (Friendship, et al., in press). In this study the comparison group was retrospectively matched to the treatment group on the following variables: current offence, sentence length, year of discharge, number of previous sentencing occasions and the probability of reconviction score as calculated using OGRS. Treatment drop-outs were kept within the treatment group. There was a significant difference between reconviction rates for the treatment and comparison group. Further analysis using logistic regression was also undertaken to measure the unique effect of treatment when all the other factors significantly related to reconviction had been controlled for. Treatment produced a robust reduction in the probability of reconviction.

Improving practice　　An improvement of current practice would be to move from the retrospective matching of the comparison group to a prospective approach. In essence, this would mean identifying comparison group cases when treatment counterparts are being identified for treatment. Prospective matching has advantages over a retrospective design. Firstly, researchers can potentially be more aware of the variables that may be important for comparison group matching. Secondly, researchers can also have more opportunity to record a wider subset of extraneous variables. Finally, a prospective design also allows researchers to collect the same data for the treatment and comparison group e.g. full pre-treatment assessment. This approach has not been used routinely in the Prison Service because of the resources required to assess large cohorts of untreated offenders.

One main difference between the treatment and comparison group is the effect of selection for treatment. Offenders who participate in programmes have volunteered and there may be fundamental motivational differences between offenders who agreed to participate and offenders who did not. What is more, these differences are rarely assessed or controlled for when the comparison group is matched to the treatment group. One way to overcome this difficulty is that in addition to the conventional reconviction study, researchers could also assess the impact of treatment for participating offenders only. Within the treatment group motivational characteristics are more likely to be similar. A within-subjects research design is discussed in the short-term impact section of this chapter. This methodology could be used to assess how offenders have 'changed' during treatment as measured by the clinical assessment measures. The relationship between short-term change and long-term reconviction could also be assessed.

Policy decisions for evaluation

The main policy decision for the evaluation of offending-behaviour programmes has been which research group should conduct the evaluation. In HM Prison Service the long-term evaluation role was conducted by internal researchers closely affiliated to the programme developers and implementers. The benefits of an internal function were speed, flexibility and low cost. Whilst a series of controls was in place to ensure the reliability of these results (e.g. the steering committee, Home Office review of data sets for completed studies and peer review publication) it was considered that the credibility of the research was compromised by this arrangement.

A policy decision was made to give the evaluation research more independence, and therefore credibility, by shifting the emphasis from internal to external evaluation. Internal evaluation continues to play an important role giving timely feedback to programme developers, senior Prison Service management, Ministers, the Treasury and the National Audit Office. The programme of external evaluation of offending-behaviour programmes aims to ensure a judicious mix of both internal and external research. External research projects in broad terms are aimed to replicate the internal projects but also go beyond the scope of internal studies. External research should be designed to overcome any limitations in the methodological design of internal projects and could also adopt methods that are not possible within the resources of the small-sized internal evaluation unit. A new body, the External Evaluation Steering Committee has been established to identify research priorities for programme evaluation and oversee the external research programme. Contracting-out research typically involves the identification of the research need, drawing up the research specification and design of invitations to tender, and selecting from a shortlist the research organization to be awarded the project. This new committee will be chaired by the Home Office Research, Development and Statistics Directorate and will also includes membership from the National Probation Directorate, an appropriate independent university-based academic, the Head of Psychology for Prison and Probation Services, the heads of prison programmes and the head of internal evaluation. The internal evaluation function is involved with day-to-day management of contractors and is responsible for ensuring quality outputs, delivered in a cost-effective way and within the project timetable. This arrangement ensures independent verification of results.

Short-term Impact

Long-term evaluation has proved to be an effective method for assessing the influence of offending-behaviour treatment programmes on rates of reconviction. However, the length of the process means evidence for the short-term impact of programmes is absent when using this approach. Without an indication of the short-term impact of treatment, programme content cannot be modified where necessary. A partial, but potential solution to this problem comes from psychotherapy outcome research.

Historically, different indicators of treatment efficacy have been used in psychotherapy research making the comparison of results nearly impossible. In addition, there has been an over-reliance on using group means and statistical significance to measure treatment effect. These criticisms have also been levelled at the evaluation of other non-psychotherapeutic interventions. Group means mask individual variability in response to treatment and reflect only the majority or largest influence in the group. Statistical significance merely indicates whether the differences found between, say, pre- and post-treatment scores are real and unlikely to be due to chance. It does not indicate whether, for instance, the extent of change is sufficient to be of clinical significance. Group statistical significance is therefore not the same as individual *clinical significance* and applies to all intervention research. These factors mean outcome research was having little bearing on the practical aspects of therapy. As a result, questions such as 'What proportion of clients have benefited from treatment?' and 'To what extent has each participant benefited?' remained unanswered.

In an effort to address some of the problems inherent in psychotherapy outcome research, Jacobson et al. (1984) proposed a convention which, when systematically applied, would detect the presence of clinically significant treatment effects in programme participants. This criterion is not exclusive to psychotherapy research, but in fact has already been used to good effect in the forensic field via the evaluation of the Prison Service's Sex Offender Treatment Programme (Beech et al., 1999). Whilst there have been criticisms of this methodology (e.g. Lunnen and Ogles, 1998) and suggestions for change (Christensen and Mendoza, 1986; Tingey et al., 1996) the formulae presented by Jacobson and Revenstorf (1988) have remained the standard for evaluating the clinical impact of treatment.

Jacobson et al. (1984, 1986, 1988, 1999), and Jacobson and Truax (1991) define clinical significance in the following way. Clinical significance is dependent on the position of the score following treatment and whether this score would be observed in an individual considered to be functioning 'normally' in relation to that particular problem. For example, when an offender enters a treatment programme their level of functioning on the targeted factor is considered to be in the 'dysfunctional' range, hence their need for intervention. Following therapy, their new level of functioning has to fall within the 'functional' or 'normative' range for their improvement to be considered clinically significant, that is equivalent to that found within the normal population. The magnitude of change, in and of itself, required for the shift from one population to the other would vary depending on the offender in question and his or her score prior to treatment and so would be a less definitive indicator of treatment efficacy than the position of the post-treatment score. Furthermore, Jacobson et al. suggested that researchers should not consider the outcome variable as a dichotomy, in the form 'cured'/ 'not cured' (as this is rarely achievable with problem behaviours), but should recognize the continuum of scores which represent normal functioning. In the words of Jacobson et al. (1984) therefore, '. . .a change in therapy is clinically significant when the client moves from the dysfunctional to the functional range during the course of therapy on whatever variable is being used to measure the clinical problem' (p. 340).

The method required to identify this shift is two-fold. The first part determines whether the difference between the offender's pre- and post-treatment functioning is statistically significant (i.e. that the difference is not just due to measurement error). This formula (taken from Jacobson & Truax, 1991, p. 14) is known as the Reliable Change Index (RC) and is calculated by:

$$RC = \frac{(x_2) - (x_1)}{S_{diff}}$$

Where: x_1 = the offender's pre-treatment score
x_2 = the same offender's post-treatment score
S_{diff} = the standard error of difference between the two test scores which can be calculated using the standard error of measurement SE:

$$S_{diff} = \sqrt{2(S_E)^2}$$

Jacobson and Truax (1991) suggest that if the RC value obtained is greater than 1.96 then the level of change is unlikely ($p < 0.05$) to be due to chance.

The second part of the methodology establishes whether the offender's post-programme level of functioning falls within the normal, preferably non-offending, population for that particular function. However, as with most behaviour problems, anti-social behaviour included, there will not be distinct functional and dysfunctional populations. This is particularly the case when working with incarcerated offenders. Prisoners are offenders who have been caught and convicted of a crime. There are likely to be a small number of offenders in the functional population whose crimes have not yet been detected by the authorities and whose behaviour and attitudes mirror those of the incarcerated offenders. This will result in an overlap between the two populations of the factors sustaining offending. Within the confines of this overlap the in-

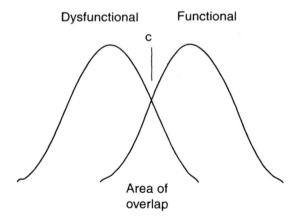

Figure 6.1   Distribution of scores for both the functional and dysfunctional populations

dividual's level of functioning could be categorized as belonging to either the functional (normative) or dysfunctional (offender) group (shown in figure 6.1). If such an overlap exists, and the distributions of both the functional and dysfunctional populations are normal and the variances equal, then the cut-off point for belonging to one range or another is the midpoint between the means of these two populations (shown by c in figure 6.1). This cut-off point is based on the assumption that a programme participant is equally likely to be a member of either distribution. A score beyond this cut-off represents a change in level of functioning which is considered clinically significant: where an offender has moved from the dysfunctional to the normal range of functioning and the change in the level of functioning has proved statistically significant. However, if the variances of the two ranges are not equal then the formula (taken from Jacobson and Revenstorf, 1988, p. 135) required to calculate the cut-off point is:

$$C = \frac{s_0 M_1 + s_1 M_0}{s_0 + s_1}$$

Where: s_0 = the standard deviation of the normative sample
s_1 = the standard deviation of the dysfunctional offender population
M_1 = the mean of the normative sample
M_0 = the mean of the dysfunctional offender population.

It must be noted that this formula requires norms for the functional population. Jacobson and Revenstorf (1988) do, however, suggest an alternative method if normative data is unavailable. In such circumstances the cut-off is defined as two standard deviations, in the desired direction, from the mean of the dysfunctional offender population. In addition, the cited authors suggest that normative data be collected for the dysfunctional offender population in general rather than using the prisoner sample under study. This would then improve comparison between offender studies.

The cut-off point yielded from this formula must be treated with caution. A discrete cut-off is likely to misclassify some offenders as treated when they are not and vice versa, due to measurement error. As a solution, Jacobson et al. (1988) and Jacobson and Truax (1991) propose the calculation of confidence intervals around the cut-off. Whilst this would then classify offenders into three groups – functional, still dysfunctional and unclassifiable – it would provide a more accurate estimate of the proportion of prisoners who have improved as a result of treatment.

The criterion for detecting clinically significant change, as described here, assumes that only one psychometric test is used to measure treatment effect. In offending-behaviour treatment work, both for living-skills and sex offender treatment programmes, a battery of psychometric assessments are administered to offenders, both prior to and following participation in a treatment programme. Gudjonsson (2000) explains this practice (p. 118):

> There are advantages in administering a battery of tests rather than one single test. First employing tests that measure different aspects of psychological functioning gives a broader base from which inferences can be drawn. . . . Secondly, using tests that measure similar aspects of psychological functioning may support the findings from the two tests.

However, this poses us a problem, since the proportion of offenders identified as having improved is likely to be dependent, to a significant extent, on the measure used. However, Jacobson et al. (1988) discuss the issue of multiple measures. In such a case as this they suggest several methods of deriving one statistic to represent all measures, but only if they are tapping into the same construct. If measures are aimed at different constructs then their conclusions cannot be amalgamated into one. In these circumstances it is assured that no one measure will reflect change in all areas of the dysfunction targeted. Whatever the method employed, it should be kept in mind that the convention for evaluating clinically significant change discussed here can only ever be as good as the measures used.

The methodology put forward by Jacobson and colleagues provides information previously unavailable to us through long-term evaluation procedures. It allows us to detect improvement in individual offenders enabling us to identify those who are most likely to benefit from treatment for inclusion on future programmes. In addition, the proportion of participants who have changed can be calculated, thus providing more accurate group findings. In relation to long-term evaluation, this latter factor proves most beneficial. To date, rates of reconviction have been compared for those who have participated in a particular offending-behaviour treatment programme ('treatment' group)[1] with matched offenders who have not ('non-treatment' group)[2]. This additional methodology would allow us to identify those who have benefited from treatment ('treated' group)[3] and compare them to those who haven't ('untreated' group)[4], as well as those who have not participated in a treatment programme ('non-treatment' group). This would provide us with much more accurate definitions of group membership and thus improve the conclusions we can draw on the differences in reconviction rates between the groups.

SUMMARY

The long-term evaluation of prison-based programmes involves assessing the impact of these interventions on reconviction rates. The evaluation methodology adopted by the Prison Service aims to follow best-practice in evaluation research. Recent policy decisions regarding a substantial programme of external research ensure that evaluators are not closely involved with designing or running programmes and this removes any conflict of interest. The short-term impact evaluation of programmes for offenders assesses changes in attitudes, behaviour and skills attributable to treatment. Monitoring clinical change has adopted methods originally applied to psychotherapy outcome research and these have only recently started being used in offender settings. The importance of robust evaluation is not in dispute and is one of the accreditation criteria set by the Joint Prison and Probation Service Accreditation Panel. Hollin (1999), in an address on offender treatment, has inspiringly articulated the importance of evaluating treatment programmes for offenders (p. 6):

> [T]he rise of What Works is directly attributable to the meta-analytical research, providing strong empirical evidence that treatment can be effective in reducing offending. If enthusiasm for treatment is to be maintained, particularly in the current climate of evidence-based practice, then it is incumbent upon those administrators and managers responsible for developing new programmes that they make provision to provide robust evidence of treatment effectiveness. Failure to provide strong evidence will, almost inevitably precipitate another demise in funding and resources. I fear it will be a long way back if we fail to deliver on the promise of What Works.

NOTES

1 Defined as all offenders who attended a treatment programme irrespective of improvement in functioning.
2 Defined as offenders who have not been involved in treatment but are matched to the treated offenders on factors predictive of reoffending for comparison.
3 Defined as offenders who have participated in a treatment programme whose improvement in functioning has proved clinically significant.
4 Defined as offenders who have participated in a treatment programme but have remained the same or have not improved to a clinically significant degree.

Chapter Seven

Sex-Offender Groupwork

Wayne Stockton and David Crighton

Background

Sexual assaults constitute a serious social problem. Such assaults also lead to long-term and severe effects on those who are assaulted. The occurrence of such offences has been recognized for many years but in recent decades the true extent and nature of sexual assaults has been increasingly recognized and researched (Marshall et al., 1990).

In line with this there has been a growth in efforts to intervene effectively and reduce such offending (Abel et al., 1978; Amir, 1971; Brecher, 1978). Efforts have also been made to develop interventions with those who have been sexually assaulted (Mezey and King, 2000) and to develop crime prevention strategies (Adams and Fay, 1981).

The role of prison services in relation to sexually assaultive offenders has traditionally been one of preventing further offending by containment of those offenders felt by the courts to require removal from society. In recent years however the limitations of this approach have become evident and resources have increasingly been directed towards the use of evidence-based interventions with offenders. Such interventions are undertaken with the aim of reducing the level of risk posed by sexually assaultive offenders on release from custody and, indeed, whilst in custody.

A broad range of interventions has been attempted with such offenders. These have included a range of individual and group-based psychotherapeutic interventions, based on a range of theoretical models (Marshall and Barbaree, 1990). Early attempts tended to be based on psychoanalytic or behavioural approaches. Early behavioural approaches in particular were often based on simplistic models of sexual offending and produced disappointing results. Psychoanalytic approaches tended to be more difficult to evaluate but produced similar poor results in terms of subsequent reoffending.

More recently cognitive-behavioural approaches have appeared more promising. Drawing on approaches developed to intervene with other psychological difficulties such as anxiety and depression (Beck, 1976; Meichenbaum, 1977) this approach has increasingly been developed and used with sexual offenders.

Within the Prison Service interventions using this approach have developed on the basis of one-to-one assessment and treatment work, and also group-based intervention work. Individual intervention work has been predominantly with those who have received indeterminate sentences.

In early 2001 there were over 50,000 men and women in prison in England and Wales and of these just over 5,000 had been convicted of sexual offences. This in turn underestimates the actual numbers of sexual offenders in prison, since it excludes those who have prior but not current convictions for sex offences. It also excludes those who are sentenced for offences such as murder and manslaughter, where there may have been evidence of sexual motivation.

The proportion of those convicted of sexual offences and sentenced to prison has also been increasing (Home Office, 2000). There are a number of reasons for this including a greater public awareness of sexual offending and a greater willingness to prosecute such offences.

In line with its duty to protect the public this has led to the expansion of efforts in prison to reduce the risk posed by sexual offenders on release. The focus of this chapter is on group-based interventions with these offenders. Over 800 prisoners complete 'accredited' sex-offender group interventions in prison annually.

Current Policy and Practice

Sex-offender groupwork

The Prison Service has developed and implemented a 'family' of group-based programmes designed to address sexual offending. These are all based on cognitive-behavioural approaches and, as such, are all fundamentally similar but are tailored to specific areas of need. Such groups are designed to complement and support individual work with offenders. Priority is also given to offenders facing indeterminate sentences.

All group-based sex-offender interventions are structured and intensive. They are also delivered using a 'treatment manual', although there is some degree of flexibility open to group facilitators. There is also flexibility in relation to the time taken to complete particular parts of the group programme, depending on the intervention goal in question and the performance of the group participants.

Below are outlined the family of group interventions currently in place.

The 'core' sex-offender treatment programme   In this group programme the intervention begins with prisoners who have been assessed as suitable to attend the group and who have also consented to participate. The membership of the group then remains the same, except for those who drop out during the programme. Suitability is assessed using a combination of clinical and psychometric assessments. It is also important that participants accept some responsibility for their offending, although those who deny the offence or offences that they were convicted for are not, necessarily, excluded.

The intervention is focused on a number of cognitive and behavioural aspects commonly seen in sex offenders. These include beliefs and cognitions that appear to support sexual offending (Murphy, 1990). Deficits in victim empathy are also addressed. The programme also stresses the avoidance of high-risk situations and the development of an individual 'relapse prevention' strategy (Pithers 1990).

This programme runs for around 86 sessions each lasting about three hours. In 2000 the programme was revised and retitled 'Core 2000'. Group facilitators were also retrained in the delivery of the revised programme from April 2001.

The 'rolling' sex-offender treatment programme   This programme is similar to the 'core' programme except that individuals enter and leave the programme on a flexible or 'rolling' basis. It is designed as an intervention for three groups of sex offenders. Firstly it is designed for offenders assessed as being at low-to-medium risk of sexual reoffending. Secondly it is designed for prisoners who have completed the 'core' programme but who still have unmet intervention needs. Thirdly the programme may be used for prisoners who are assessed as needing intervention work to reduce risk but who would not be in custody long enough to complete the 'core' programme.

Because of the flexible nature of this programme there is no set number of sessions that need to be completed. Group members will therefore attend sessions designed to address their individual needs. The group runs continuously addressing different intervention needs. Group facilitators and group members therefore change on a regular but structured basis.

The 'adapted' sex-offender treatment programme   This is essentially the same as the 'core' programme but, as the name suggests, is adapted to a set of specific needs. It is aimed at sexual offenders with literacy difficulties and/or those with IQ scores of less than 80. The presentational style and materials for the programme draw less heavily on written materials and complex ideas are presented using simpler language.

The 'extended' sex-offender treatment programme This intervention lasts for around 70 sessions, with provision for further individual work to be undertaken in smaller groups or on a one-to-one basis, where particular needs are identified. Prisoners may be referred to this programme once they have successfully completed the 'core' or 'rolling' programmes.

Here additional input is given in relation to cognitive aspects of sexual offending, the role of sexual fantasies in offending, relationship skills and relapse-prevention strategies. The programme also includes the use of psychophysiological measures (the Penile Plethysmograph or PPG) of sexual arousal and the use of behavioural approaches to controlling sexual arousal.

The 'booster' sex-offender treatment programme This is not an intervention in its own right since it is aimed exclusively at prisoners who have completed one of the groups above. The 'booster' programme primarily involves the revision and practice of skills previously acquired. This intervention is intended for prisoners who are within 18 months of release back into the community.

Theoretical basis

The family of sex-offender group programmes used within HM Prison Service is based on cognitive-behavioural approaches. Early attempts to implement this approach with respect to sexual offenders tended to be guided by practical considerations, rather than a theoretically cohesive model of such behaviours. In this respect the approach has been ostensibly similar to that used for other forms of criminal behaviour such as non-sexual violence (see chapter 8 for a fuller discussion of this).

More recently attempts have been made to develop integrated theories of sexual offending (Marshall and Barbaree, 1990). There have also been significant developments in relation to specific aspects of sexual offending such as the role of cognitive processes (Murphy, 1990), the role of social and cultural factors (Finkelhor, 1979) and the role of interpersonal skills (McFall, 1990). Overall the approach currently adopted draws from the broad range of cognitive behavioural approaches to assessment and intervention (Towl and Crighton, 1996).

However, attempts to provide a unitary model of sexual offending have generally been seen as unsuccessful. Perhaps the most obvious reason for this is the broad range of behaviours subsumed within this category of criminal behaviour. It is also worth noting that much of the research and practice to date has been predicated on groups of offenders convicted of particular offences.

There is in fact often very considerable variation within even a single offence category. Factors such as these have confounded a number of studies of sexual offenders. Indeed it can be argued that studying sexual offending as if it described a unitary group is as inappropriate as attempts to study 'dangerous' offenders as a single group (Prins, 2002).

Selection criteria

Offenders are identified as potentially needing to attend sex-offender groups on the basis of 'throughcare'. Throughcare refers to the process of planning a prisoner's time in custody and under supervision in the community. As such the process is multi-disciplinary. It also draws heavily on joint working between the Prison Service and the National Probation Service. One of the primary aims of this process is to seek to ensure that the public are protected by reducing the risk presented by sexual offenders in custody and on release back into the community.

To be eligible to participate in the 'core' or 'rolling' groups prisoners must meet a number of specific criteria. They must have a previous or current conviction for a sexual offence, or alternatively they may have a previous or current conviction for a violent offence with evidence of a sexual 'element' to the offence(s); for example they may have committed a homicide in which the victim was sexually assaulted. Prisoners may also be advised to participate in sex-offender groups on this basis where a sexual 'element' is suspected rather than proven.

A standardized actuarial risk assessment is completed prior to attending the group. For adults (over 21) this is used to inform decisions about whether the 'core' or 'rolling' group is more appropriate. Assessment of the level of risk is based on existing data relating to adult sex offenders released in recent years. Prisoners assessed as being 'low' to 'medium' risk may be allocated to the 'rolling' group. Those assessed as being higher risk should be allocated to the 'core' group. This assessment is not however undertaken with young offenders. It may also be worth noting that the basis of this selective allocation is questionable given the current state of knowledge about the levels of risk posed by sexual offenders.

In order to attend the 'adapted' group the prisoner should have an assessed IQ of less than 80, or have learning deficits evident from the pre-group assessment that would make it difficult for them to cope with the written and verbal content of the 'core' or 'rolling' groups. Again allocation to this group is not dependent on the level of assessed risk.

Prisoners attending the 'extended' sex-offender group must have completed the 'core', 'adapted' or 'rolling' programme. They must also be motivated to undertake further intervention work and consent to this. Those participating in the 'extended' group should show signs of particular problems in relation to at least two of the following areas: distorted patterns of thinking relating to their offending and lifestyle, difficulties in managing emotions, difficulties in managing intimate relationships, problems with offence-related fantasies, inappropriate physical sexual arousal and poor relapse-prevention skills.

The 'booster' group is designed primarily as a revision course for those who have completed other sex-offender group programmes. As such it is designed for prisoners in their last 18 months in custody. For indeterminate-sentence prisoners it is a requirement that they complete this programme in open prison before progressing towards release into the community.

As noted above, prior to attending sex-offender groups prisoners must accept some degree of responsibility for some of their sexually assaultive behaviours. Where this is not the case then it is generally more appropriate to seek to address this through individual work with prisoners. However, it is not necessary that they accept responsibility for all their offending, or their current conviction. Prisoners are also initially assessed by group staff and the nature and content of the group is outlined in order that prisoners can give their consent to attend the programme on an informed basis.

There are several exclusion criteria common to the whole family of sex-offender groups. All those participating in the groups must be able to speak English. Prisoners are excluded from the groups if they were found to be suffering from a 'mental illness' at the time of their offence. They are also excluded from the groups if they are showing evidence of 'mental illness' that has not been stabilized with medication. Group management teams are also advised to exclude those with significant hearing impairments and those with 'severe personality disorders'. Those who totally deny their sexually offending are excluded along with those who are appealing against sentence and/or conviction.

Where consent is given by prisoners who meet the criteria to attend group-based work a pre-group assessment is undertaken. This serves to provide a baseline against which to assess progress and also intervention needs. Elements of this assessment are repeated following completion of the group.

The process

As noted above, the 'rolling' group differs organizationally from other sex-offender groups in that prisoners may flexibly join and leave the group in order to address specific intervention needs. This type of group also progresses at a pace that depends on the progress of group participants.

The other sex-offender groups do not have this degree of flexibility, and progress in a fixed manner. Again the speed of progress is dependent on the progress of group participants.

In common with other cognitive-behavioural interventions the groups are governed by a number of 'rules' that apply to participants and group tutors. These are agreed at the outset of the group and are intended to ensure that the group can progress effectively. Participation in sex-offender groups is voluntary but group members must agree to abide by rules such as having respect for others, completing 'homework' assignments, attending all sessions, being punctual and participating constructively.

Group participants may choose to leave the group. They may also be removed from the group when they are failing to abide by the group rules. Such conduct would not necessarily prevent future attendance in other sex-offender groups but group members cannot generally leave and rejoin the group.

Sex-offender groups are modular in format and address the following areas:

1   cognitive and behavioural deficits in sex offenders;
2   'cognitive distortions' used to justify offending;
3   individual accounts of offending;
4   deficits in victim empathy;
5   relapse-prevention;

The 'extended' group adds to this the development of skills in relation to controlling intrusive sexual fantasies and the control of emotions. In addition further input is given in relation to developing strategies to prevent relapse into sexual offending (Laws, 1989).

Staffing

Group interventions with sex offenders are multi-disciplinary, involving a broad range of practitioners. As with other types of group programmes, management and quality control are the responsibility of a tripartite team of programme, treatment and throughcare managers. The aim of this is to integrate the provision of intervention groups with the more general activities of the prison such as education and work.

The role of the throughcare manager is to facilitate the continuity of supervision and support between prison and the community, primarily through liaison with the National Probation Service areas. The programme manager is responsible for the issues such as logistics and staffing for groups and for the management of physical resources. The treatment manager is responsible for supervising the quality of delivery in group sessions and also for leading supervision sessions with group facilitators. They are also responsible for overseeing the quality of pre and post group assessments.

Prospective treatment managers are required to have a broad range of competencies in relation to groupwork with sexual offenders. Many will therefore have experience of individual and groupwork with sexual offenders, the provision of supervision and current research and practice in the area of sexual offending. The majority of treatment managers are probation officers or forensic psychologists.

Research undertaken in the early stages of setting up group interventions with sex offenders suggested the likelihood of negative impacts on group facilitators, which could be minimized by the provision of regular counselling support. In line with this, group facilitators are required to attend a minimum number of regular counselling sessions, to identify any developing difficulties. Such counselling support may also be increased where this is felt to be appropriate or is requested.

All staff involved in sex-offender groups are required to undertake training delivered by a multi-disciplinary team. Training includes coverage of research and practice issues in relation to sexually assaultive behaviours. Group facilitators also receive practical training in basic groupwork skills and the intervention targets that are addressed within the standardized treatment manuals. The performance of potential group facilitators is assessed and only those who meet minimum standards of performance on the course go on to become group facilitators.

Group facilitators are drawn from a range of different disciplines and, after successfully completing initial training, are regularly assessed by means of monitoring videotapes of group sessions. They also attend regular supervision sessions led by the treatment manager. Here issues relating to treatment quality can be reviewed on the basis of the video monitoring and issues arising within the groupwork team.

SUMMARY

In this chapter we have examined the main group-based approaches to working with sexual offenders in prison custody. In doing so we have briefly outlined some of the main considerations involved in the assessment of sexual offenders, and also in undertaking intervention work with this group of prisoners.

Following on from this we have looked in greater depth at the family of group programmes that have been developed to address a range of individual and organizational needs. These include the 'core', 'rolling' and 'adapted' groups which are aimed at reducing the level of risk of further sexual offending in a broad range of sexual offenders. We have also looked at the 'extended' group intervention, which is designed to further address specific areas of concern remaining after completion of 'core', 'rolling' or 'adapted' groups. The 'extended' group is generally used to address the intervention needs of sex offenders assessed as presenting a particularly 'high risk' of further sexual offending. Finally we discussed the 'booster' group. This is in essence a revision group for those who have completed previous intervention work on a group basis prior to release back into the community.

HM Prison Service and National Probation Service are currently in the process of developing integrated and evidence-based approaches to sexual offenders. As with other interventions designed to reduce criminal offending, the current research base is generally limited both in terms of theory and methodological limitations of existing studies. Research to date does however suggest that cognitive-behavioural interventions, both group and individually focused, are the most promising approach to reducing sexual reoffending (Marshall et al., 1990; Towl and Crighton, 1996).

Individual and group-based interventions with sex offenders in both the Prison and National Probation Services are multi-disciplinary in nature. Both are also subject to systematic monitoring of quality and the provision of ongoing supervision and support to practitioners. Group-based interventions have become increasingly manual-based, with the exception of the 'rolling' group, which runs against this trend by allowing slightly greater flexibility in facilitating the group. All groups however remain highly structured and as such allow a wider range of practitioners to become involved in delivering group interventions.

As with other forms of offence-related groups this does also raise a number of difficulties. These would include the concern that whilst a standardized approach to this group of offenders may be managerially convenient, it may be less clinically effective than a more flexible approach. The standardization of approach also runs counter to many of the fundamentals of the cognitive-behavioural approach, with its stress on individual analysis and intervention (Beck, 1976; Meichenbaum, 1977). Standard cognitive-behavioural interventions run the risk of becoming less relevant to individuals needs and therefore potentially having less impact in reducing sexual reoffending. The approach can also be criticized as exercising too much control over practitioners and, in the process, not fully drawing upon their skills.

Recent changes to sex-offender groups have generally involved minor revisions to established groups, along with an expansion to address the needs of prisoners with learning difficulties. It seems likely that there will be a need to develop groups which allow interventions to be more closely targeted to reduce an individual's future risk of sexual reoffending. It also seems likely that to maximize the effectiveness of sex-offender groups in prisons these will need to link effectively with a broad range of other individual and group interventions both in prison and in the community.

Chapter Eight

Violent Offender Groupwork

Karen Brady and David Crighton

Background

Violent criminal behaviour clearly imposes substantial social, economic and human costs on society. Official crime statistics give some idea of the extent of violent criminal behaviour. The British Crime Survey (Home Office, 1998a) reported 3,381,000 violent incidents. It is not surprising then that 21 per cent (10,928) of the current prison population are serving sentences for an offence of violence (Home Office, 1999).

It is estimated to cost an average of £18,000 per person, per annum to keep an individual in prison (Home Office, 1999). In crude financial terms, then, the economic costs are clearly high. In terms of the suffering of victims and the wider effects of violent crime on society, the 'cost' is difficult to calculate but such costs are almost universally seen as unacceptable.

Research into prisoners released in 1994 demonstrated a reconviction rate for violent offending of approximately 6 per cent within two years of release. Within the 1994 sample it is notable that those individuals reconvicted within two years for an offence of violence were twice as likely as those reconvicted for other types of offence to have a previous conviction of violence (Home Office, 1999). It is also perhaps worth noting that the studies focus on reconviction and as such are likely to have produced a marked under-estimate of the true rates of violent reoffending.

Such evidence does, though, highlight the potential value of undertaking effective interventions and throughcare both in prison and in the community. Effective interventions will allow offenders to address their choice to use violence, with the aim of reducing rates of violent offending.

In terms of the work undertaken with violent offenders in HM Prison Service this can be divided into two main types. Firstly a large amount of individual work is undertaken with violent offenders by a range of practitioners. Secondly, a range of group-based interventions have been used.

The nature of the individual intervention work undertaken is diverse and has involved a variety of approaches, in line with assessed need. Much of this work is focused on indeterminately sentenced prisoners since release and supervision arrangements in the community are dependent on assessment and intervention work in custody. In line with current broader trends in applied psychology, and the developing research base, a majority of such work is grounded in cognitive and behavioural psychology. The main approaches included under this broad heading are interventions using personal-construct approaches, Cognitive Behavioural Therapy (CBT) and Dialectical Behaviour Therapy (DBT).

In addition to specific individual intervention work, several aspects of effective 'throughcare' of prisoners are explicitly and implicitly designed to reduce levels of violent offending. These include efforts to improve the social integration of such offenders by, for example, improving family ties, enabling offenders to avoid anti-social and violent peer groups and providing effective 'pro-social' models. In addition specific forms of violence may be subject to intervention work, for example domestic violence. Such work takes place in prisons and in the community (Willmot, chapter 5 of this volume).

In support of effective throughcare planning and individual work with offenders HM Prison Service has developed and implemented a number of cognitive-behavioural groupwork interventions. Some of these may indirectly address violent offending. Such indirect group interventions would include 'Enhanced Thinking Skills' (ETS) and 'Reasoning and Rehabilitation' (R&R), as discussed in chapter 9. Such groups address a broad range of cognitive and behavioural aspects that are believed to impact on a range of offending behaviour.

In addition there are specific group interventions used by HM Prison and National Probation Services which are aimed to address violent offending. These are explicitly based on cognitive-behavioural approaches. In addition, such interventions are assessed by an independent panel and 'accredited'. Such accreditation applies where the group intervention adheres to aspects of the cognitive-behavioural approach that are thought to be related to reductions in criminal reconviction. Such programmes tend to be fundamentally similar. Therefore, for the purposes of this chapter, we have focused primarily on one group programme as an illustrative example – the Cognitive Self Change Programme (CSCP). Like much of the individual intervention work described above, the CSCP is aimed at those offenders thought to pose the highest risk of subsequent violent reoffending.

When examining the experimental underpinnings of the cognitive-behavioural approach, it is clear that in its initial stages such work focused on the relationship between the environment and subsequent reaction of the subject following the process of learning (Pavlov, 1927; Watson and Rayner, 1920; Skinner, 1971). Early behavioural research adopted an approach which, with a few exceptions, did not accept that cognitions and emotions were appropriate areas to study. This has significantly changed as exclusively behavioural models, which work well in explaining simple behaviours, have increasingly being found to be inadequate models for explaining and modifying more complex behaviours (Dolland and Miller, 1950; Kelly, 1955; Piaget, 1932; Neisser, 1976; Meichenbaum, 1977).

In recent years there has been a convergence of 'Cognitive' and 'Behavioural' models in psychology to yield 'cognitive-behavioural' models (Beck, 1976). Such models have increasingly explored the role of individual's thoughts and attitudes in influencing behaviour. This model has become much more dominant within psychology and particularly within applied psychology, where it has been shown to have good utility in terms of positive clinical outcomes from both individual and group-based interventions (Beck, 1976; Marshall et al., 1999).

In applying cognitive-behavioural models, the integration of elements of behaviour and cognition is central. The approach makes explicit the notion that changing thought processes can change behaviour (Bandura, 1977). Such approaches assume an important and usually dominant role for cognitive processes such as thoughts and feelings (Towl and Crighton, 1996).

In terms of violent behaviour, the role of cognitive appraisal of a situation in relation to the individual's emotional experience of that situation has been the focus of a significant body of work (Schacter and Singer, 1962). A pioneering example of such work, of relevance to both individual and group-based approaches, explored the functions of anger. Novaco (1975) suggested that anger performs six main 'functions':

1 energizing;
2 disrupting (effect of the emotion on the ability to process information);
3 expressing (the role of the emotion in the communication by the individual about what is making them angry);
4 defending (role of the emotion in the protection of the ego);
5 instigating (the role of the emotion in the use of aggression);
6 discriminating (role of the emotion in the value judgement about 'what is threatening').

Novaco's work, therefore, highlights the potential role that cognitive processes may play in aggressive and violent behaviours. However, it is important to make a distinction between the experience and expression of anger (Towl and Dexter,

1994; Spielberger et al., 1995). Anger and violent behaviour are clearly not mutually exclusive. Equally, feelings of anger are not inevitably, or even generally, associated with the outward expression of aggression or violence.

Work such as that of Novaco has played a seminal role in informing the practice of interventions designed to aid the appropriate expression of anger. Generally, interventions aiming to develop effective anger management have focused on three main areas:

1   increasing awareness and regulation of the physiological arousal associated with anger;
2   increasing awareness and control over cognitive aspects of anger;
3   the development and practice of behavioural strategies to improve effective anger management (Towl and Crighton 1996).

It is clear when examining current groupwork interventions aimed at reducing violent reoffending that they fit into this model of practice. In recent years, HM Prison Service has focused significant efforts on two significant groupwork initiatives. These are the Cognitive Self Change Programme (CSCP) and the Controlling Anger and Learning to Manage It (CALM) programme. The former is considered in more detail below.

Current Policy and Practice: The Cognitive Self Change Programme

Theoretical basis

The Cognitive Self Change Programme (CSCP) is a groupwork intervention for 'high risk' violent offenders. The CSCP is based on cognitive-behavioural principles, and aims to change violent behaviour by modifying the thoughts, feelings, attitudes and beliefs that appear to support the behaviour. The intervention is skills-based and aims to equip individuals with the practical skills which may help them to avoid violent offending.

Bush (1995) states that there are three premises upon which the intervention is based: the first is that violent behaviour is not a distinct or isolated criminal behaviour; in other words, that offenders are criminally diverse as illustrated by Beck's (1987) finding that individuals originally convicted of offences against property were just as likely to offend against the person as an individual with violent previous convictions.

The second premise is based on work by Bandura (1973) and Goldstein (1988) which suggests that violence is behaviour learnt in a social context, often as a means of 'coping'. Bush (1995) argues that for violent offenders, violence is an '. . . effective, reliable and often used response which reinforces their feelings of power and self-efficacy'.

The final premise is that patterns of violence and criminal behaviour are embedded in patterns of thinking or cognitive schemata. It is therefore hypothesized that criminal violent behaviour may be actively promoted and supported by patterns of thinking and beliefs held by violent offenders (Andrews, 1990). The CSCP seeks to address a number of these areas.

Selection criteria

Potential CSCP participants are assessed to ensure that they fall within the 'high risk' of further violent criminal offending group. This is assessed using a combination of 'static' and 'dynamic' risk factors. Static risk factors include such things as current conviction for violence, previous convictions for violence, and are historical. Such factors have been identified as related to violent offenders' likelihood of reoffending violently (Webster et al., 1997).

Such static risk factors are assessed using the Violence Risk Scale (Wong and Gordon, 1999) and include current age, age at first violent conviction, number of convictions prior to the age of 17 and the occurrence of violence throughout lifespan. Offenders are scored for each item (0–3, with scores of 2 or 3 on each item equating to high risk) and are assigned a final score out of 18. To be included on the group intervention, candidates must score 2 or 3 for violence throughout lifespan and should have an overall score of 7 or more.

Offenders are also assessed in terms of transient or changeable indicators of risk such as their levels of violent fantasy, ability to manage feelings of anger, moral and critical reasoning, social perspective-taking and self-control.

Such transient risk factors are identified as part of an initial assessment, whereby prisoners are interviewed and assessed using a number of psychometric assessments. The offender's motivation to undertake treatment is also assessed via a semi-structured interview. This aims to ensure that a potential group member's expectations reflect the purpose and function of the intervention and that such expectations are linked to appropriate treatment goals.

The CSCP group intervention is aimed primarily at individuals within the 24 to 45 years age range. This is based on research that suggests that risk of reconviction declines with age; combined with concerns regarding less mature offenders having difficulty with the length and nature of the intervention.

Candidates for the CSCP have their IQ assessed; generally individuals are excluded when their score is less than 80. They are also required to be literate and numerate in order to follow the course materials. For those individuals for whom there is evidence that their violence was significantly increased by their substance use, it is generally recommended that intervention work to address their substance abuse is undertaken, prior to commencing the CSCP.

A number of offenders are excluded from the CSCP, including offenders with a current conviction for sexual violence. These individuals are initially referred to the Sex Offender Treatment Programme (SOTP) as discussed in chapter 7; with the option to undertake the CSCP following completion of SOTP, should this be deemed appropriate. Offenders whose violence is perpetrated against an intimate other (e.g. their spouse) or those who utilize violence as a means of attaining something (e.g. as part of a robbery) would also be excluded. The somewhat controversial rationale for the exclusions of perpetrators of 'domestic violence' is that such intrafamilial violence is distinct from extrafamilial violence and therefore requires a somewhat different approach to intervention work.

The process

Group participants progress at their own pace via four distinct stages of the intervention. Progression is based upon their ability to understand each stage, the methods used and their ability to apply these to their own violent behaviour. Participation and progress is linked strongly to the extent that the group member takes responsibility for their participation, progress and choices in order to apply the intervention to their own behaviour.

Group members who volunteer to undertake the CSCP are asked to show that they have the potential to change their behaviour. The intervention aims to facilitate understanding of the role of cognitive processes in behaviour. The choice as to whether to implement change is the responsibility of the group member.

In common with many other cognitive-behavioural approaches, participation on the intervention is governed by a number of conditions, which enable the group to operate successfully. Participation is voluntary, but individuals agree to abide by the intervention conditions, which include respect for others, completion of assignments, attendance at all sessions, punctuality and constructive participation.

Continued participation is the responsibility of individual group members. They may choose to leave and are able to rejoin the group. However, group members are not permitted to continue to attend the group and at the same time breach the group rules.

The CSCP is divided into five parts, which address different aspects of the cognitive behavioural approach. These are:

1   the development of skills in the self-monitoring of thoughts, feelings, attitudes and beliefs;
2   identification of links between cognitions and behaviour;
3   development of new skills and attitudes;
4   development of a relapse-prevention plan;
5   practice of new skills in custody;
6   use of new skills and relapse-prevention plan in the community.

As can be seen, the CSCP follows a characteristic pattern seen in cognitive-behavioural approaches to anger management (Towl, 1995a; Towl and Dexter, 1994; Towl and Crighton, 1996).

The process of CSCP groups is tailored to the individual in terms of their motivation, understanding, ability to utilize the techniques taught in the intervention and to choose to do so. Individual group members therefore have the potential to move through the process at a slower or faster rate than outlined.

At the beginning of each group session, group members verbally recount situations where they felt they were 'at risk' or committed 'hurtful behaviour'. They move on to recount the thoughts, feelings, attitudes and beliefs that they had at the time with the aim of being able to describe the link between their cognitions and behaviour.

During the early stages of the intervention, members concentrate on developing the ability to monitor themselves. Therefore early accounts may take the form of a description of the situation followed by a list of their thoughts, feelings, attitudes and beliefs. However, as members become more proficient at utilizing the process and skill, accounts may contain explicit statements about the meaning of key thoughts and attitudes, and the way in which these may have led on to violence. They may also include the identification of thoughts and attitudes which helped them to avoid behaving violently.

As part of the development of self-monitoring skills, participants are required to monitor their thoughts and behaviour between group sessions. The aim of this self-monitoring varies according to the stage that the individual has reached. They may take a number of different forms ranging from simple lists of feelings associated with violence, through to an appraisal of the usefulness of the offender's thoughts when applied to real-life situations.

Staffing

Delivery of the CSCP is multi-disciplinary. At establishment level this involves a team approach including programme, treatment and throughcare managers. Each member of this team has distinct responsibilities in terms of delivery of the intervention including the quality of organization, delivery and support and care for offenders on release into the community.

Group facilitators are also drawn from multi-disciplinary backgrounds and are assessed in terms of a number of criteria including their openness to learning, ability to communicate with others and attitudes towards offenders. Facilitators are regularly assessed by means of monitoring of video tapes recorded during group sessions. Based on this monitoring, areas for development and support may be addressed during regular supervision sessions.

SUMMARY

In this chapter we have examined approaches to working with violent offenders in the Prison Service. In doing this we briefly outlined the role of individual assessment and intervention work with offenders. In addition we looked in depth at one group-based intervention developed for use in prisons – the Cognitive Self Change Programme. Both forms of intervention tend to be aimed at 'high risk' offenders. Clearly intervention work also takes place with offenders in prisons who present lower levels of risk. However, the principles involved tend to be fundamentally similar.

Both individual and group intervention approaches in HM Prison Service tend to be predicated on the basis of a multi-disciplinary working. Both are also subject to regular quality monitoring and supervision. Group-based interventions have also become increasingly 'manualized', with increasing levels of specification for the delivery of materials. This has had the advantage of enabling a range of practitioners to become involved in delivering group-based interventions.

However, such developments can also be criticized on a number of grounds. These include the fact that they have led to an increasing sense of 'one size fits all', with all offenders receiving the same intervention. This clearly runs counter to many of the key notions of cognitive-behavioural approaches that stress the individual nature of cognitive and behavioural processes. It seems likely that such increased standardization may lead to decreased clinical impact on individuals, as the intervention may become less relevant to their needs. The approach can also be criticized as being unduly centralized and as such potentially de-skilling, particularly for practitioners with high levels of prior training.

Future developments in relation to work with violent offenders in prisons might usefully focus increasingly on developing more flexible and individualized intervention work with offenders. In addition, it seems likely that the increasing collaboration between probation and prison services will lead to significant changes in both individual and group-based interventions to address violent behaviour. Most notably such joint working provides an opportunity to increase the emphasis on the planning of assessment and intervention work, with a view to integrating offenders into the community. As part of this HM Prison and the National Probation Services are developing integrated approaches to assessing risk and planning the throughcare into the community of offenders. This in turn has the potential to feed into a much broader range of evidence-based interventions with violent offenders, as part of the overall aim of reducing the risks such offenders pose to themselves and the community (Willmot, chapter 5 of this volume).

The common approach of HM Prison Service and the National Probation Service is to develop and implement evidence-based interventions with violent offenders. Founded on the (albeit limited) existing empirical research base, cognitive-behavioural interventions appear to be the most promising approach currently available to reducing violent offending.

Chapter Nine

Cognitive-Skills Groupwork

Michelle Thomas and Serena Jackson

Background

In the 1970s research in both the USA and UK suggested that interventions undertaken in prison to reduce criminal reconviction did not work. Lipton et al. (1975) reported the results of a review of studies of 'treatment' programmes that had attempted to reduce rates of recidivism. They reported that, despite wide variations in methodology, the most consistent finding from these studies was that nothing could be relied on to work effectively in reducing recidivism. This finding was supported by Brody (1976) in the UK.

This view became a virtual dogma during the 1970s and early 1980s. As a result little effort was put into developing interventions with offenders. However, this view was never universally accepted and both research and practice in this area continued (Towl and Crighton 1996). Ross and Gendreau (1980) compiled a number of research studies that showed positive results from intervention work with offenders. They went on to review which aspects of these interventions were associated with positive outcomes. They concluded that, amongst other attributes, interventions that acknowledged the role of cognitive processes, and particularly styles and patterns of thinking and problem-solving, appeared to be effective in reducing criminal reconvictions.

The development of the statistical technique of meta-analysis also provided researchers in this area with a method of evaluating the 'nothing works' view. This technique allows for the analysis of large numbers of different studies with a view to finding effects that may not be detectable at the level of individual studies. In its application to studies of intervention work with offenders such studies have measured the 'effect' size between groups that have completed interventions and those that have not.

Re-examination of the data used by Lipton et al. (1975) cast doubt on the veracity of their conclusions, suggesting that intervention effects were in fact evident. Two large-scale meta-analytic studies found a consistent reduction in the rates of reoffending for those offenders undertaking intervention work (Andrews et al., 1990; Lipsey, 1992). These findings have subsequently been replicated by Lipsey and Wilson (1998) and Redondo (1999). Overall, they report that the net effect of intervention work was a 10 per cent reduction in rates of reoffending. However, for some intervention approaches this increased to around 30 per cent.

Research has also focused on the most effective aspects of intervention work. D'Zurilla and Goldfried (1971) looked at which 'cognitive skills' were involved in effective problem-solving. They suggested that awareness and recognition of the problem, distinguishing fact from opinion, generating alternative solutions, the ability to make links between objectives and the means of reaching these, the ability to reason about consequences of actions and the ability to take on other perspectives were key skills in effective problem-solving.

Drawing on this evidence a number of intervention approaches have been developed for use in prisons and in the community with offenders (Ross and Fabiano, 1985). Ross and Fabiano went on to argue that persistent offenders were deficient in a range of 'problem-solving' skills and that these could be addressed by appropriate intervention work either in prison, or whilst in the community via probation services. They went on to adapt the training programme developed by Platt et al. (1980) and produced a 'training manual' for those undertaking such intervention work. This combined the skills thought to be needed for effective problem-solving with a range of other areas for intervention. These were reported as including:

> social skills
> negotiation skills
> management of feelings
> enhancement of values
> critical reasoning – the ability to evaluate one's own thinking.

Such interventions drew heavily on cognitive-behavioural approaches developed in other areas of psychology. The authors described their intervention programme as 'Reasoning and Rehabilitation' and this was piloted in prison and probation services in Canada in 1992 with promising results claimed by the authors.

Cognitive-behavioural intervention approaches have a lengthy history in both prisons and probation services in England and Wales, with the development of both individual and group-based intervention work. Group interventions such as 'Reasoning and Rehabilitation' were introduced in the 1990s as part of a growth in such work, and particularly as part of the use of this approach with a wide range of offenders. Alongside group training approaches imported from Canada, existing group work developed in the UK using cognitive-behavioural approaches was formalized and standardized in HM Prison Service, on a national basis, in the form of a group-based intervention entitled 'Thinking Skills'. This was developed alongside a number of offence-specific groupwork approaches developed in the UK (Towl and McDougall, 1999).

Current Policy and Practice

The 'cognitive skills' groups

As part of its commitment to reduce reoffending HM Prison Service has invested in the development of cognitive-behavioural group interventions to address offending in general. These were titled 'cognitive skills' groups and complemented existing individual intervention work, and also groups designed to address specific types of offending (e.g. violent offending).

In relation to cognitive-behavioural groups designed to address 'generic' offending most resources have gone into two types of group programme. Enhanced Thinking Skills (ETS) which at the time of writing was running in 85 prisons in England and Wales and Reasoning and Rehabilitation (R&R) running in 29 prisons. A small number of prisons run different generic cognitive-behavioural groups although the number of these has progressively reduced with the growth of ETS and R&R.

Reasoning & rehabilitation (R&R)   This is designed to run over 38 two-hour group sessions in which a range of cognitive and behavioural skills are discussed and practised. The group involves input in the following areas:

1 **Self-control**   Here the links between thoughts and behaviour are highlighted and skills are taught that aim to reduce impulsivity by the use of different ways of thinking about situations.
2 **Social perspective-taking**   Group exercises are used which attempt to develop the ability of group members to see things from a variety of perspectives.
3 **Interpersonal problem-solving**   Group and individual exercises are used to modify the approaches used by offenders to interpersonal problems.
4 **Critical reasoning**   The aim is to improve the ability of group members to reflect on the outcomes of their past thinking and behaviour, in order to improve future outcomes.

5 **Cognitive style**   The aim is to reduce the use of rigid, stereotypical and irrational thinking and behaviour and use this to improve future outcomes. Exercises are intended to improve the ability of offenders to think flexibly, consider likely consequences and plan and set effective, realistic goals.
6 **Moral reasoning**   Group members are encouraged to look at the reasons behind their expressed values through a series of debates on 'moral' issues.

Enhanced Thinking Skills (ETS)   This group is designed to be run over 20 two-hour sessions. It is essentially similar in terms of the areas covered to the R&R group as outlined above.

ETS Booster   This group is currently being piloted at a number of prisons in England and Wales. It is designed for prisoners who have already completed the main ETS and R&R group and are approaching release back into the community. It also seems likely that this group may be used for prisoners who have completed the ETS or R&R groups and are under the supervision of the National Probation Service in the community.

Theoretical basis

The theory behind these group programmes is that many offenders show deficits in certain areas of thinking and that these 'cognitive deficits' are related to anti-social and criminal behaviour (Ross and Fabiano, 1985). The aim of these groups is to target these areas of 'deficit' through structured exercises that first identify the links between thinking and behaviour. By being aware of this link it is suggested that behaviour can be better controlled. Consequently the group stresses that offenders can take effective control of their lives. In addition these 'cognitive skills' groups also teach a number of 'social skills' such as assertiveness and seek to provide motivation to practice and develop these skills outside the group environment.

In line with other cognitive-behavioural intervention approaches it has been suggested that effective interventions to reduce reoffending should incorporate a number of key features. Cognitive-skills groups in HM Prison Service are audited annually against the 11 criteria listed below (HM Prison Service, 2000a):

1   The groups are to be research-based and research-led. Interventions should be based on a solid theoretical background, and current research should be used as part of an ongoing process of modification.

2 The target group (i.e. who is the intervention intended for) and the selection process should be specified.

3 The groupwork should be designed to change factors that relate to offending behaviour.

4 The group should address a range of these factors in an integrated manner.

5 Methods should be used that are consistently effective with offenders, and specify the standards necessary for those methods.

6 Groupwork should teach 'pro-social' skills.

7 The frequency, sequence and spacing of sessions should be related to the seriousness of the offending and related factors. The intervention has to be carefully constructed to effectively challenge the target behaviour.

8 The methods used should be ones to which the target group are responsive.

9 Participants' progress should be followed up through internal and external monitoring and support.

10 The intervention should incorporate evaluation procedures within its design, and be adapted when necessary, based on the feedback received.

11 There should be ongoing evaluation of the effectiveness of the intervention.

Selection criteria

Offenders are identified as potentially needing to attend 'cognitive-skills' groups on the basis of 'throughcare' assessments. Throughcare refers to planning a prisoner's time in custody and in the community under National Probation Service supervision. A broad range of offenders are eligible to attend such groups and allocation is not simply dependent on the level of assessed risk. Sexual offenders are not generally excluded and it would usually be recommended that they attend the appropriate sex-offender treatment programme after completing a 'cognitive skills' group.

Prisoners may be excluded from groups where they have evident learning deficits that would make it difficult for them to cope with the written and verbal content of group sessions. Similarly prisoners may be excluded where there is evidence of inadequately controlled psychotic disorders.

It is not necessary that prisoners accept responsibility for all their offending, or their current conviction. However, prisoners are informed by group facilitators about the nature and content of the group, in order that prisoners can give their consent to attend the programme on an informed basis. Where such consent is given by prisoners who meet the criteria to attend group-based work, a pre-group assessment is undertaken. This serves to provide a baseline against which to assess progress and also intervention needs. Prisoners are expected to abide by the agreed rules of the group and may be deselected where they choose to breach these (e.g. repeatedly missing sessions without good reason).

The process

One of the 11 criteria for effective intervention work with offenders is that the methods used should be those, as far as they are known, that are most likely to promote effective participation. In seeking to achieve this cognitive-skills groups use three main techniques – pace, non-verbal communication and the Socratic style of teaching.

Pace refers to the speed of progress of each session and also the group as a whole. The rate of delivery may be modified to encourage motivation and participation of group members. If the pace of sessions is too slow for the majority of group members then boredom may ensue. If the pace is too quick then important opportunities for learning may be lost.

The facilitator's non-verbal communication is also felt to play a fundamental role in the efficacy of cognitive-skills groups. Facilitators are expected to model 'pro-social' behaviour for group members. Potential facilitators need to demonstrate the ability to support and encourage group members, through praise and reinforcement, in order to increase their self-esteem and motivation to change. A supportive environment also aids facilitators in effectively challenging and modifying anti-social ideas in a non-threatening way.

During group sessions facilitators aim to encourage positive change in each group member's behaviour, in order to increase group members' perceived control over their own lives. Behaviours and non-verbal communication which is felt to promote such change would include warmth, genuineness, empathy, respect, sensitivity and also 'open' and interested body language.

The Socratic style is a method of teaching that uses open questions to elicit information and reflect back this information in order to encourage group members to think about their own thoughts and behaviours. The ultimate aim of the method is to help group members to reach conclusions for themselves that are logical and consistent. This style of presentation incorporates active listening, in which the facilitator will at intervals reflect back and/or paraphrase responses before continuing with a line of questioning. It is important that questions are open-ended since this requires group members to think more carefully about their responses. The method is also used as a means of challenging particular styles of thinking and encouraging group discussion.

Staffing

All staff involved in this area of groupwork are required to undertake an initial three-day training course to assess their suitability for further training. Those who pass this stage of training may progress to a two-week training course delivered by a multi-disciplinary team. Training includes coverage of research and practice issues. Group facilitators also receive practical training in basic groupwork skills and the intervention targets that are addressed within the standardized treatment manuals. The performance of potential group facilitators is assessed and only those who meet minimum standards of performance on the course go on to become group tutors.

At establishments cognitive-skills groups are led by a tripartite management team. The management and delivery of these groups is multi-disciplinary and draws on a wide range of practitioners including prison officers, probation service officers (PSOs), teachers and psychologists. Groups are managed by a tripartite team comprised of a programme manager, a treatment manager and a throughcare manager. The programme managers are responsible for organizational and delivery issues. Treatment managers are responsible for the quality aspects of the group and the supervision of group tutors. Throughcare managers are responsible for ensuring effective links between establishments and those providing community supervision and support.

Prospective treatment managers are required to have a broad range of competencies in relation to groupwork with offenders. Many will therefore have experience of individual and group work and also the provision of supervision.

Group facilitators are drawn from a wide range of different disciplines and, after successfully completing training, are regularly assessed by means of monitoring videotapes of group sessions. Group facilitators also attend regular supervision sessions led by the treatment manager. Here issues relating to treatment quality can be reviewed on the basis of the video monitoring and issues arising within the groupwork team.

Evaluation

Group members undertake an in-depth assessment immediately before, immediately after, and two months after completion of the group programme. These are evaluated primarily to measure whether the group is achieving its aims in relation to modifying the 'cognitive deficits' described above. The results of these assessments are analysed at establishment level, to estimate the level of change seen amongst group members. Assessments are also analysed at a national level in terms of groups of offenders (women prisoners, young offenders, adult men and life-sentence prisoners). The results of this research can be used as a basis for developing such groups on an ongoing basis.

Robinson (1995) reported the results of a study of 4,072 offenders released from prison. Recidivism data was based on 2,125 of these offenders who had been released on licence for at least one year. Robinson defined recidivism as either the commission of, or conviction for, a further offence, or breach of licence conditions resulting in the individual being returned to prison. In total 1,444 (68 per cent) had completed a 'cognitive skills' group. A group of 379 were used as controls whilst a further 302 who had started but failed to complete a group were also studied.

The overall findings of this study were that cognitive-skills groups had no significant impact on those who had breached their licence conditions but were not returned to prison. There was an 11 per cent reduction in prisoners recalled to prison due to breach of licence conditions but the greatest impact was a 20 per cent reduction in reconviction for those who had completed a group.

Cognitive-skills groups were also found to have differing degrees of impact when looking at different types of offences and level of risk of recidivism. Those offenders classified as being at high risk[2] of recidivism did not appear to have benefited. Those offenders classified as being at lower risk of recidivism displayed a 20 per cent reduction in recidivism.

When looking at the impact of cognitive-skills groups on different offence types Robinson (1995) reported that those convicted of sexual offences showed a greater reduction in reconvictions (58 per cent), followed by those convicted of violent and drugs offences (35 per cent). Non-violent property, and robbery offenders showed very little change in reconvictions. This group was also classified as being at the highest risk of reoffending. This may be because such offending has little to do with 'cognitive deficits'.

In discussing the lack of impact on high-risk offenders Robinson (1995) suggests that such individuals may require a 'higher dosage' or, alternatively, may respond to different approaches to those classified as lower risk. The results for different offence types are more challenging to explain. Robinson (1995) suggests that sexual and violent offenders may have been more motivated to change their behaviour, although this seems at best highly speculative. A large number of such *post hoc* hypotheses could be generated and there would appear to be a clear case for more research into this finding.

It should also be noted that there are a number of methodological flaws in the Robinson study. For example, there is an assumption that the control group and treated group are similar, with the only difference being participation in a 'cognitive skills' group. In the absence of detailed data on the backgrounds of both groups the possibility that the control group differed in significant ways cannot be eliminated. Thus, for example, members of the control group may have been excluded from groups on the basis of poor literacy, learning difficulties etc. Equally the study could be criticized on the grounds that the researchers were not independent of the group programme and were not genuinely 'blind' to who had attended groups and who had not.

To date the efficacy of such groups in reducing recidivism and reconviction rates remains largely an open question. However, given the large-scale investment in such groups in both prison and probation services forensic psychologists should be well placed to address this issue in coming years.

SUMMARY

Overall forensic psychologists have been closely involved in the development of multi-disciplinary group programmes designed to address a broad range of criminal offending. Psychologists continue to have a central role in the development and evaluation of such groups. They also have an ongoing and indeed growing role in training staff to manage and deliver these and other cognitive-behavioural groups.

However, there are some caveats to current practice in this area of work with offenders. At present cognitive-skills groups are inflexible and, as a result, are often poor at addressing the individual needs of group members. Equally, group-based approaches are clearly not appropriate for all offenders.

In line with this there is a need for psychologists to be involved in developing and enhancing approaches to reduce levels of reoffending. At present such efforts include the development of 'booster' groups for use in prison and the community with those who have already completed cognitive-skills groups, often in the early stages of prison custody.

It also seems evident that in order to be optimally effective group interventions will need increasingly to become part of a much more broad-based approach to addressing the factors implicated in criminal and anti-social behaviour. Such an approach needs, as a first step, to recognize the role of areas such as family relationships, peer groups, employment, work skills, education and substance abuse. It has also been argued that there is a clear need for an increase in individual intervention work, and in particular one-to-one work with 'high-risk' offenders (Needs, 1995; Towl and Crighton, 1997; Willmot, Chapter 5 in this volume).

Forensic psychologists in the prison and probation services have been closely involved in cognitive-skills groups and in particular in the development, piloting and ongoing evaluation of this area of work. Psychologists are likely to have an increasing role in relation to evaluating the efficacy and further development of such groups in addressing various aspects of offending. They also have an important contribution to make in training a broad range of practitioners as group tutors. These areas of work by psychologists seem likely to grow in line with the projected rapid growth of such groups, particularly in community settings.

NOTES

1   'Cognitive skills' groups are part of a family of groups collectively refered to as 'living skills'. These include ETS, R&R, Think First, and Controlling Anger and Learning to Manage It (CALM).
2   For the purposes of the research risk was defined as the overall likelihood of 'recidivism' (not offence-specific) based on a 'static criminal history'.

Chapter Ten

Anger-Management Groupwork

Michael Jennings

Background

A book by Raymond Novaco, entitled *Anger Control: The Development and Evaluation of an Experimental Treatment* (1975), brought together a body of research in the field of self-management and transformed it into an anger-management programme, which the author then ran and evaluated. This book was used by many psychologists who wrote and then ran anger-management courses (Towl and Jennings, 1990). Anger-management programmes have been running in the prison system in England and Wales since the 1980s (Law, 1997). Pressure to run such groupwork interventions, often in the form of referrals, comes from a variety of sources.

These requests for anger-management interventions are common in HM Prison Service. They come from managers, professional staff working with prisoners, and from prisoners themselves. The motivation behind these referrals is interlinked. Managers are concerned to have an orderly prison, with a low number of assaults on both staff and other prisoners and with a minimum of other types of disturbances. Indeed, data such as the number of proven assaults forms part of the package of measures currently used to judge the performance of prison managers in England and Wales. Professional staff are given the task of dealing with offenders on a daily basis and have a personal interest in reducing the incidence of assaultative behaviour. A common expectation of prison staff is that they should reduce the risk of prisoners reoffending. For example, the current system of sentence planning in England and Wales aims to do this by addressing risk factors that lead to the original offence. For this reason, multi-disciplinary sentence-planning boards often highlight a need for anger-management work. Prisoners themselves may be aware that an anger-management problem is having a significant negative impact on their lives. Many offenders are imprisoned for violent offences; acting violently in prison will, if detected, bring negative consequences, such as having release delayed, and they are often under pressure from their own relatives to deal with this aspect of their behaviour. Other agencies, for example the National Probation Service, for the reasons outlined above, often try to motivate prisoners to seek such interventions.

In response to the very real demand and need for anger-management work it is a common intervention in HM Prison Service. This work is carried out both with individuals and with groups. This chapter focuses on group-based interventions. Often individual work is done using similar principles but without the advantages, and without some of the difficulties, offered by a group-based approach. This chapter, then, aims to look at the practice of anger-management groupwork and its effectiveness. It will also look at the development of 'accredited' programmes. These are programmes that are judged by a panel to meet the standards necessary for an intervention to be likely to reduce reoffending. These standards are drawn from the body of work, commonly referred to as the 'What Works' literature. The Prison and Probation Services use a joint accreditation panel to 'accredit' interventions as having all the features necessary to make it likely that they will reduce recidivism. Most anger-management groupwork programmes do not reach the standards necessary for this accreditation. Newer programmes, developed for accreditation, do so. These include programmes specifically developed to reduce violent reoffending and more general 'cognitive skills' programmes which include, in a broad syllabus, the management of emotions. In the light of these recent developments, the future of anger-management programmes will be discussed.

Policy and Practice

In the 1980s and the early 1990s many psychology staff in prisons were devising and running anger-management programmes, for example Towl and Jennings (1990) and Clarke (1988). Common features of many of these programmes can be identified. In doing this I am drawing on a number of programmes and I have emphasized the similarities between them to give what I hope is a representative and useful picture of such programmes. Similarly, when comparing some of the results of research in this area, I am not comparing like with like. However, many anger-management programmes, probably due to the influence of Raymond Novaco, are similar in methods, length, aims and goals and thus there is value in looking at them collectively. These programmes:

involve some form of selection process; they use a cognitive-behavioural model; they are typically structured around approximately ten two-hour sessions; and they use a range of exercises. I will look at these features in turn.

Selection

The selection method typically ensures that individuals referred to the course have an anger-management problem at the present time, in their present environment. This can be contrasted with the view of many prison staff that, because someone has a conviction for a violent offence, they must have an anger-management problem. Much violence is instrumental and does not involve a loss of control and, in any case, on most anger-management courses participants need to be experiencing ongoing anger problems in order to be able to use the exercises immediately and thus enable them to become a permanent part of their behavioural repertoire. Selection will also look at an individual's motivation to attend the course and any practical issues around their attendance.

Cognitive-behavioural models

The cognitive-behavioural approach aims to teach participants to see how their thinking is linked to their behaviour and to teach them to change both. Cognition here refers to a range of features of an individual, for example: personal beliefs, expectations, the inner dialogue they have, and the values they hold (Hunter, 1993).

Length of programmes

The duration of programmes varies greatly but is typically up to ten sessions. Often the final session is in the form of a follow-up session, some weeks after the main body of the course.

Exercises

The content of anger-management groupwork typically includes a series of exercises, which I will now describe. One key exercise is to look at the positive and the negative consequences of temper loss in a variety of situations. The aim is to show that the negative consequences frequently outnumber the positive consequences, and that the positive consequences are often short term compared to the negative consequences. For example, a common positive consequence is a feeling of relief, while a common negative consequence for this group is a prison sentence with all its ramifications. Participants are taught relaxation techniques to lower their level of arousal generally which they can use in situations where they feel themselves getting angry. Many people with an anger problem readily accept that there is a threshold of arousal beyond which they lose control and see that they need to stop themselves crossing this line. Teaching them the bodily signs to warn them that they are approaching this threshold is important, so that they can then employ relaxation or other techniques. To aid early warning and therefore self-management, participants are requested to keep 'anger diaries' both before, during and after attendance at the course. This will enable them to identify the patterns found in their anger loss and the key 'trigger points' for them personally.

Recognizing the vital role of cognition, a typical programme focuses on 'self talk', the things people say to themselves. This group of people usually have 'self talk' that serves to increase their level of anger in the face of perceived provocation and thus motivates them to act violently. This 'self talk' often reflects core, deeply held beliefs about the need to 'stand up for yourself'. Role plays of real-life difficult situations are often used to allow the practice of the skills taught. Video-taping role plays and playing them back to the group can be a particularly useful way of raising participants' awareness of their own non-verbal behaviour and using this to help them to broaden the range of skills they have available to de-escalate situations. Ways of classifying anger can be taught with either written or taped vignettes to help participants to understand their own anger better.

Throughout these exercises, attitudes embedded in the prison sub-culture are often expressed and form part of the core beliefs discussed above. There is also a commonly held belief by participants, familiar to any anger-management facilitator, that they become angry so quickly that there is nothing they can do to stop themselves. Having run courses for male and female offenders, I realized that these attitudes are not gender specific. Tackling these beliefs, and a general hostility to the groupwork programme, involves all of the techniques discussed above with the constant aim both of teaching people to develop practical alternative ways to deal with situations and of motivating them to use these techniques, as the course goes on. Part of each session is given over to a discussion of entries in participants' anger diaries and a discussion of the methods used to control their anger and the outcome. I have never yet run a group where not one participant had successfully tried out these techniques. This shows that the techniques are working for some participants, and helps to motivate the rest of the group. A follow-up session serves to examine participants' use of the techniques, again through the examination and discussion of diary entries, and to praise and reinforce this use. At this point, or in the final session, a quiz is often used to assess course members' knowledge and to identify any areas that need further work.

Post-course evaluation measures usually include some measure of how participants feel about the course; looking at its length, pace, relevance and their view of the tutors. Other popular measures include examining institutional behaviour, for example, through analysing participants' anger diaries. A variety of psychometric measures have also been used (Towl and Dexter, 1994). The strengths and weaknesses of these various measures and the results they have found are discussed below.

A major problem with a 'typical' anger-management programme was an absence of an emphasis on the experience of victims of violence and any debate about the immorality of temper loss and violent acts. My own disquiet about the absence of these factors, from the courses I ran in the mid-1990s, was fuelled by discussion in the media about reports from the USA. These suggested that violent men who were referred to anger-management programmes for assaulting intimate partners became less physically violent but more verbally and emotionally abusive. This echoed my own experiences whereby course members accepted the idea that violence was a maladaptive strategy for them, based purely on its consequences for themselves, but then found other ways to hurt people who upset them. This was encapsulated by a course member who said, 'I realize now that I can hurt more with my mouth than with my fists'. Discussing the effect of any sort of abusive behaviour on victims can help to move participants to a wider understanding of why any such behaviour is unacceptable. Arnold Goldstein, who has done a tremendous amount of work in this and related areas, in his talks and seminars, outlines and stresses the importance of exposing participants to moral arguments that are more sophisticated than those they currently use. This advances their moral development. He does this through the use of short debates. This technique can be readily added to anger-management programmes if done with great care. The emphasis must be on guiding the group to victim awareness and a moral perspective on their actions without trying to impose this.

Such anger-management programmes have been delivered by a range of staff, including psychologists, teachers, probation officers and prison officers. Indeed, using prison officers to deliver programmes has been a typical feature of the growth in offending-behaviour programmes within HM Prison Service. For example, Towl (1994) reports a pilot programme to train 50 prison officers from nine establishments to deliver anger-management group work.

These then, are the features of a 'typical' anger-management programme, as run in a variety of prison systems. As described above, a variety of methods have been used to evaluate the effectiveness of these programmes.

An immediate measure of the effectiveness of a programme is so-called 'happy sheets', in which participants rate how effective they think the particular course has been for them. If participants report that the programme was irrelevant or that they have no intention of using the techniques taught, such feedback has value. 'Happy sheets' which amount to 'consumer satisfaction' ratings allow judgements as to whether conditions are in place which are necessary, but not sufficient, to permit the conclusion that a programme has had the desired effect on participants' behaviour. Positive trends may be due less to a genuine recognition by respondents of the need to change their behaviour by using the techniques provided, than to a simple positive feeling about the course. This positive feeling is obviously desirable, but may arise because the course was a break from prison routine or because some of the exercises were quite fun, rather than anything more meaningful.

Another method, again often of more use when its results are negative, because it falls into the category of judging 'necessary but not sufficient' features, is an end-of-course quiz or test. The premise here is that it is necessary for course members to have understood and remembered the material, but this in itself is not sufficient for behaviour change to take place.

Anger diaries provide useful qualitative and quantative feedback, provided participants keep them and fill them in honestly.

Institutional measures are often looked at. For example, findings of guilt in adjudications after being placed 'on report' for breaking prison rules are an easily gathered and analysed measure. They have the strength that they are records of incidents investigated and then, at the adjudication, only proved after a hearing in which the prisoner can give evidence and the evidence from witnesses can be heard. However, the process of placing a prisoner on report for misbehaviour can often be a reflection of the attitudes and beliefs of staff as much as the behaviour of the prisoner.

Behavioural checklists filled in by members of staff in contact with the prisoner, can provide useful data. However, there are also obvious problems with determining the accuracy and 'inter-rater' reliability of these measures.

Psychometric measures can provide quantifiable information on a variety of aspects of cognition and behaviour. However, they do not prove behaviour change, even though they may be linked evidentially to behaviour change in previous research.

One problem with any participant measure is the pressure on participants to give positive results; whether in an anger diary or through their responses to psychometric measures. This may be because performance on the course, judged in whole or in part through these measures, may affect parole or other decisions. They may also have enjoyed the group, liked the facilitators and not want to let them down (as they would see it) by being honest, even if the truth is that they are still losing their temper. Similarly, staff filling in checklists may want to get a prisoner onto a course for very genuine reasons and so inflate their pre-course scores. After the course, they may feel the person is making a genuine effort to change and so give them some leeway, perhaps by being more optimistic when filling in a checklist or reluctant to place them on report.

Using a mixture of these methods, many attempts have been made to assess the effectiveness of anger-management groupwork with prisoners. Some of these are considered now.

Firstly, I will look at the results of some of the research using self-report inventories and assessment methods. One tool that has been used in a number of pieces of research in this area is the State Trait Anger Expression Inventory or STAXI (Spielberger, 1988). Towl and Dexter (1994) describe the STAXI as a self-report measure that looks at three components of anger expression: internally and externally directed anger and anger control. The anger experience is viewed as consisting of 'state anger': which is an individuals' variable subjective feelings of anger; and 'trait anger', which is a measure of the disposition of an individual to have those feelings in situations, with and without provocation.

Towl and Dexter (1994) report the results of an evaluation of nine anger-management courses run in prisons in England and Wales between 1991 and 1993. They used the STAXI administered prior to, and seven to 14 days after completing the course. In total 50 prisoners completed the course and the STAXI. Overall, they reported a significant reduction in the self-reported intensity of participants' angry feelings (state anger) after the course. However, for the sample as a whole, this decrease was largely caused by major changes in six participants. The majority of participants showed no significant decrease in their scores. The data showed a significant reduction for trait anger and a similarly positive result was reported for 'anger in' scores (internally directed anger). However, although 'anger out' (externally directed anger) scores did not decrease significantly for the group as a whole, they did for those scoring very highly on the STAXI scales. As would be hoped, a significant increase in overall anger control scores was reported which Towl and Dexter (1994) viewed as, 'indicating prisoners were investing more energy into monitoring and preventing their experience and expression of anger'. Although Towl and Dexter (1994) themselves stress the limitation of this research, overall its results are encouraging.

Law (1997) cites research using the Situations-Reactions Hostility Inventory and the STAXI as having consistently shown positive results across various populations, in that offenders believe they have more control of their anger and aggressive behaviour. Law (1997) goes on to report the

STAXI as showing one significant result in her evaluation of four anger-management courses, in indicating that participants were trying to control their anger more after the course. She also reported other non-significant but positive trends.

Hunter (1993) evaluated an anger-management programme in American federal prisons looking at a sample of 28 offenders who had completed the programme. The results showed a 'lower score on all measures of aggression, hostility and anger after treatment'. These results must be viewed with some caution as, contrary to most research in this area which has used an untreated control group, Hunter (1993) also found positive, although smaller, changes amongst them.

Hughes (1993) in another American study, faced a host of difficulties in evaluating an anger-management course; but, using a battery of assessment measures, found broadly positive results.

Ireland (2000), looking at a sample of 50 male young offenders who had completed an anger-management course, found a significant difference in self-reported angry behaviours after offenders had completed the course.

Overall, the results from self-report measures seem broadly positive, as do those for measures of disciplinary reports. McDougall et al. (1987) found evidence of a reduced rate of reports, overall, in young offenders after attendance on an anger management course. Law (1997) found a small reduction after a course in the already low number of disciplinary reports in her study. In Hunter's (1993) American study, a reduction in institutional infractions for verbal assaults of staff was reported for offenders who had completed an anger-management course.

When behavioural checklists have been used as an evaluatory method, Law (1997) reports some positive findings by other researchers and small positive changes in her own study. Ireland (2000), in her research with young offenders, reports a significant decrease in the number of angry behaviours in the institution's residential units which prison officers reported after the course.

Hughes (1993) looked at rates of reoffending after completion of an anger management programme in an institution. This study found that attendance made little difference to reoffending rates in general; although he reports more positive effects on the rate of reconviction for violent crime only.

Looking at this research, with the exception of the reoffending data, which has its own difficulties, many of the studies used quite short follow-up periods, often due to prisoners being transferred quite quickly out of the establishment. This makes conclusions drawn from even the positive findings tentative.

With the introduction of 'accredited' programmes, an alternative to anger-management programmes could be seen as the 'accredited' Reasoning and Rehabilitation (R & R) programme or the Enhanced Thinking Skills (ETS) course. Both of these are cognitive-skills courses. Research in a variety of penal systems has reported positive results for such courses. For example, Robinson (1995) found significant reductions in reoffending with, amongst others, violent offenders, after attendance on the R&R course. This would suggest that these courses, as they aim to, include components to address anger-management issues successfully. 'Accredited' programmes aimed specifically at addressing violent behaviour are being introduced to the Prison Service. These are the Cognitive Self Change Programme (CSCP) and the Controlling Anger and Learning to Manage It (CALM) Programme. These courses are both much longer, and therefore provide more sessions, than the anger-management programmes previously run. As part of the 'accreditation' process it is much more likely that these courses will be run the same way, with large numbers of offenders, and the results, both in the short and the long term, rigorously evaluated. These features reduce programme drift – the tendency for programmes when delivered to reflect the content of their manuals less and less (Hollin, 1995) contains a useful description of this problem with treatment programmes generally). Anger-management programmes are obviously vulnerable to this process.

SUMMARY

In this chapter I have looked at the factors that led to the introduction, growth and continuance of anger-management groupwork. I then described a 'typical' anger-management programme and the strengths and weaknesses of the various types of measures that have been used to evaluate these programmes. Looking at some of the research into the effectiveness of these programmes reveals that measures using self-report are often positive, and examples of positive results from other measures are described. The benefits of the 'accreditation' process for programmes using the body of knowledge commonly referred to as the 'What Works' principles, are that such courses contain features that research has shown to be important in reducing reoffending, coupled with mechanisms to ensure that the programmes fulfil their aims wherever and whenever they are run.

Chapter Eleven

Working with Lifers

Phil Willmot

Overview of the Lifer System

Following the abolition of capital punishment, a life sentence became the mandatory penalty for individuals convicted of murder. A discretionary life sentence can also be passed for other serious offences (including manslaughter, rape, attempted murder, armed robbery, arson and some drugs offences). The Crime (Sentences) Act, 1997, introduced a third category, whereby judges are obliged to impose a life sentence following a second or subsequent conviction for a serious sexual or violent offence (known as a Section 2 automatic life sentence), unless the judge considers that exceptional circumstances exist for not doing so.

No child under the age of 10 may be convicted of a criminal offence. Children and young persons under the age of 18 who are convicted of murder are sentenced to be detained at Her Majesty's Pleasure, and those convicted of other offences of exceptional gravity are sentenced to detention for life. For young people between the ages of 18 and 21 on conviction for murder or other serious offences, the sentence is one of 'custody for life'. Although there is no distinction in name, in practice this latter sentence when imposed for murder is administered as a mandatory life sentence and, for other offences, as a discretionary life sentence.

The minimum period to be served in custody by anyone convicted of murder, i.e. 'the tariff' which marks the gravity of the offence, is recommended by the trial judge and the Lord Chief Justice to the Home Secretary who makes the decision. Following the 'Doody judgement' (Smart, Pegg, Doody, Pierson. House of Lords judgement; 24 June 1993), the views of the judge and Lord Chief Justice are now disclosed to the lifer who is allowed to make representations before the tariff is determined.

Mandatory lifers are referred to the Parole Board three and a half years before their tariff expires to consider, where good progress has been made, suitability for transfer to open conditions, and to recommend a future date, generally between one and two years, to assess suitability for release. In formulating its recommendations the chief concern of the Parole Board is the risk that the lifer presents to the public. Final decisions concerning transfer to open conditions are made by the Secretary of State and release by the Home Secretary, both of whom must decide whether to accept the recommendations of the Parole Board.

Unlike those who receive mandatory sentences, prisoners serving discretionary sentences are informed in open court of the minimum period of time they must serve, the 'relevant part' of the sentence, and can appeal against the decision. These cases are managed and reviewed by the Parole Board before tariff expiry, in the same way as those of mandatory prisoners, including recommendations for a move to open conditions which are subject to ministerial approval. However, once the 'relevant part' has expired, for those remaining in custody the Parole Board sits as a Discretionary Lifer Panel (DLP) to assess suitability for release. The lifer may attend and be legally represented.

Following a judgement in the European Court (the Secretary of State *ex parte* Hussain, 1997), young people sentenced to life detention at Her Majesty's Pleasure are now dealt with as discretionary lifers and release is decided at oral hearings by the Parole Board (HMP panels). However the tariff continues to be set by the Home Secretary. Prison service staff now consider annual progress reports on all lifers subject to detention during Her Majesty's Pleasure whose tariff has not yet expired and bring to the attention of ministers exceptional progress which might justify a reduction. In addition, halfway through the tariff ministers personally examine progress reports on each case to consider whether the original tariff remains appropriate. These lifers are able to submit their own representations as part of this process. A prisoner may ask for a review of their unexpired tariff at any time.

The lifer population has shown a high growth rate over the past 40 years, with the number in 2001 exceeding 4000. Roughly 2.5 times as many lifers are received into prison each year as are released. Among those released, the average time they had served has increased from 9.1 years in 1979 to 12 years in 1989 and 14 years in 1997. This figure does not of course take into account those lifers who are not released. According to the joint thematic review of lifers (HM Inspectorate of Prisons for England and Wales 1999), if current trends continue, the lifer population will rise to almost 6,000 by the year 2007 (para 3.13).

Over 90 per cent of new lifers are adult men, while 5 per cent are young males and 5 per cent are female. The fastest-growing group of lifers are young men. According to research carried out in the joint thematic review, of those lifers in custody, 85 per cent were white, 9 per cent black, 4 per cent South Asian and 2 per cent from other ethnic groups. Among lifers on supervision in the community, 88 per cent were white, 9 per cent black, 2 per cent south Asian and 1 per cent from other ethnic groups.

According to prison statistics for England and Wales (1997), the average length of time served by those lifers released in 1997 had increased to 14 years for mandatory lifers and 13 years for discretionary, with 296 prisoners still in custody having served more than 20 years (18 per cent of all lifers sentenced between 1965 and 1977). Such calculations are conservative, since they do not consider those lifers who are still in prison.

Unlike determinate-sentence prisoners, life-sentence prisoners go through a set series of stages in their sentence. The length of time at each stage will vary according to the length of sentence and the degree of progress.

As a result of the increasing size of the lifer population, a 'revised strategy' for managing them was introduced by the Prison Service in 1989. The principles of this strategy are given by Mitchell (1990) and outlined below:

> Lifers should be treated as a seperate group because of the particular practical and psychological problems associated with the indeterminate sentence. However they should be integrated with other prisoners
> Lifers should progress from conditions of high security to more open conditions in order to give them a sense of purpose and direction
> Testing and assessment for release should take place in open conditions
> Pre-release preparation should be as thorough and varied as possible
> Lifers should have a career plan, involving goal setting, revision and progression.

Local prison stage

Although little attention is paid to lifers in local prisons, this can be a significant part of the life sentence. Though newly sentenced lifers should be allocated to a main centre after sentence, the joint thematic review found that

> . . . staff in local prisons have not received either appropriate guidance or resources, because the intention has always been that lifers should not remain there for lengthy periods but be moved to main centres as quickly as possible. However, the number of lifers spending in excess of a year in local prisons after sentence without any structured input before being moved to a main centre was a matter for serious concern. There is also an absence of adequate information to inform both risk assessment/management and sentence planning at the beginning of sentence.
> (HM Inspectorate of Prisons for England & Wales, 1999)

The joint thematic review found that, where psychologists were in post in local prisons, their main work was with groupwork interventions aimed at reducing their offending, and they did not work with newly sentenced lifers (para 5.21). Given the high risk of self-harm reported by Dooley (1990) at this stage, there is arguably a greater need for psychologists to be involved with lifers at this stage.

Main centre or first stage

According to the *Lifer Manual* (HM Prison Service, 1999a), the period in a main centre:

1   '... is usually three years, but this may be reduced for some prisoners (for example those with tariffs of less than 10 years and who are making exceptionally good progress)' (para 3.4);
2   '... the initial assessment must be completed . . . within three months of receipt of the offence-related documentation (the summary dossier)' (para 8.4);
3   '... Life Sentence Plan must be prepared for all lifers' (para 8.3);
4   '... the first F75 reports will be called for by Lifer Unit (after approximately 2½ years)' (para 3.4).

The joint thematic review criticized the variable quality of initial risk assessments in life-sentence plans, but commented that where psychologists were involved in preparing the risk assessments, the quality of risk assessments improved significantly (para 6.13). Work on addressing the issues identified from this assessment may also begin at the main centre.

Second stage prison

The *Lifer Manual* states that:

The lifer will be held in a category B training or dispersal prison until such time as he is considered suitable by Lifer Allocation Unit. . . for transfer to a category C prison. The time spent in a category B will form an important part of the sentence, during which:
a . . . much of the work necessary to address offending behaviour, as identified by the Life Sentence Plan will be carried out
b . . . the lifer will be expected to show significant progress before transfer to a category C prison' (HM Prison Service 1999a: para 3.5).

For category C prisons, the *Manual* states that (para 3.6) :

1 '. . . once considered suitable for conditions of lower security the lifer will
   be transferred to a category C prison. This transfer . . . will not normally
   be more than three years before the first Parole Board review. During the
   period spent in a category C establishment:'
2 '. . . offence related work continues, but the focus changes towards preparation for release on licence';
3 '. . . local town familiarisation visits may be allowed subject to the conditions set out elsewhere in the manual'.

For women, progress mid-sentence is marked by a transfer from a main centre
to a further closed prison and the *Lifer Manual* states that: 'at a second stage
establishment the ethos of the sentence changes noticeably . . . everything is
geared towards the first Parole Board review' (HM Prison Service, 1999a: para
9.6).

During the second stage of the sentence, the main focus will be on addressing
offending-behaviour issues and psychologists will be primarily involved in delivering offending-behaviour work in group-based or individual interventions
with lifers. In category 'C' conditions the focus changes towards preparation
for release on licence.

Open prison

The *Lifer Manual* states that a period in an open environment (category D) 'usually following satisfactory progression through category B and C closed conditions, is a prerequisite to release on life licence'.

The purpose of category D is to: 'test lifers in more challenging conditions
before being considered for transfer to a pre-release employment scheme (PRES)
or resettlement prison prior to release; and provide facilities for supervised outside activities and temporary release in preparation for release on licence' (HM
Prison Service, 1999a: para 3.7). The *Lifer Manual* notes that transfer to category D enables exploration of: 'areas of concern in conditions which are nearer
to those in the community than can be found in closed prisons . . . and require(s)
them to take more responsibility for their actions' (para 6.1).

As the joint thematic review points out, the move to open conditions is a significant change for lifers in terms of the physical environment, with little or no
physical security, freedom of movement and relatively few staff.

In open conditions lifers are gradually reintroduced to life in the community,
starting with escorted town visits and working up to obtaining full-time work
in the community and spending extended periods of home leave at their proposed release address. The work of psychologists in open conditions comprises

mainly risk assessment and management. The work may also involve equipping lifers with the necessary skills for life in the community. In theory, offence-related work should have been completed before a lifer arrives in open conditions, though in practice new issues sometimes emerge at this stage. Mitchell (1990) found that almost 10 per cent of his sample of lifers had been removed from open conditions, emphasizing the need for ongoing reviews of risk.

Life licence

On release from open conditions, lifers are subject to supervision by the National Probation Service on life licence, potentially for the rest of their lives. Life licence is similar to other types of licence supervision for determinate-sentence prisoners. Under the terms of the Victims' Charter (Home Office, 1990) the victims or their surviving relatives are consulted about the conditions of the licence and many life licences contain a condition preventing offenders from going to particular areas or approaching the victims or their families. Provided that the lifer abides by the conditions of his or her licence and does not give other cause for concern, the conditions of the licence are usually gradually relaxed, and the supervision element of the licence may be cancelled by the Lifer Unit after a minimum of four years. However, the licence remains in force and supervision can be reimposed or the lifer recalled to prison at any time if their circumstances or behaviour gives cause for concern.

Recall

If recalled to prison, a lifer will usually be returned to closed conditions and the process of risk assessment and preparation for release begins again. Depending on the circumstances of the recall it may not be necessary for the lifer to work through open conditions again and the lifer can be re-released within a period of months. However, in other circumstances, recall can result in many more years in prison, if serious concerns are raised.

Current Policy and Practice of Forensic Psyclogists Working with Lifers

The joint thematic review points out that the only role specified in the *Lifer Manual* for psychologists is that they should prepare F75 reports 'wherever possible' (HM Prison Service, 1999a: paras 6.6.7 and 7.1), and that 'the report should include any other information, such as specialist advice, that may assist in the review. The psychologist for example, must comment if necessary on matters relevant to the Sex Offender Treatment Programme' (para 7.3.8). However, the joint thematic review found that in practice psychologists contributed routinely to F75 reviews in only 54 per cent of cases. They concluded that 'given the fundamental importance of risk assessment and public protection, it (is) unacceptable that psychologists' input with lifers should be so variable. (para 7.7). The review went on to recommend a more coordinated and multi-disciplinary framework for dealing with lifers in which 'psychologists should have a lead role in assessing and reviewing criminogenic need, with probation staff progressing offence focused work in individual cases. The latter should have the key task of ensuring that every lifer is assisted in giving an 'active account' of the offence which does not minimize the extent of their involvement. Psychologists should be called upon for advice and specialist work in problematic cases (para 7.27).

There are a number of aspects of the life sentence which set them apart from other prisoners and create a unique set of issues which forensic psychologists in prison are called upon to work with.

Because the decisions about the progress and release of lifers are decided by the Lifer Unit and the Parole Board on the basis of reports by prison staff, the quality and content of those reports is extremely important to individual lifers.

The nature of the life sentence creates a unique set of psychological problems. Not only do lifers have to adapt to a very long period in prison, they also have to deal with the uncertainty of not knowing exactly how long they will spend there. While there is intensive preparation for release, the final decision to release a lifer may only occur a few days beforehand. Even after release, the process of adjusting to life in the community can be very arduous; it is not uncommon for lifers to be released after 20 years or even longer in prison.

The nature of the life sentence has led to various legal challenges. The indeterminate nature of their sentences and the unique influence that politicians have over them creates numerous questions about their human rights, and in the past lifers have successfully challenged various aspects of their sentences under the European Convention on Human Rights. Mitchell (1990) observed that lifers generally do not present problems of control or security. The fact that disruptive behaviour can have a detrimental effect on a lifer's move through the system or their release means that they are more likely to resort to litigation to resolve problems than to more direct and confrontational forms of protest. Also, Parole Board hearings for certain groups of lifers, at which they have the right to legal representation, have given lawyers greater access to the lifer system and the Parole Board.

The work of forensic psychologists with lifers falls under four broad headings:

mental health
risk assessment
offending-behaviour focus
preparation for release and resettlement.

Mental health

Research into the mental health of lifers has indicated that levels of disturbance are higher for lifers than for other groups of prisoners. Swinton et al. (1994) found that lifers were more psychiatrically disturbed than other prisoners in terms of both personality disorder and psychosis. Life-sentence prisoners have to adapt to serving a very long sentence and the added uncertainty of never knowing when, or even if, they will ever be released. In the case of offenders who have killed a partner or family member, there are the issues of dealing with bereavement, together with the guilt of knowing that they are the person responsible for that bereavement. Also, lifers are at a greater risk of completing suicide when compared to determinate-sentenced prisoners (Crighton, 2000).

Bereavement work is not a specific skill in which many forensic psychologists are trained, and practitioners should, wherever possible, refer the lifer to a more appropriate agency for this work. As well as the danger of working beyond the bounds of their competencies, there is a danger of role conflict between bereavement work and other, core, tasks such as risk assessment or offence-focused work.

Managing uncertainty Uncertainty is a constant source of stress for lifers, from first remand until the point of release, and beyond. Because key decisions about life-sentence prisoners have to be referred to the Lifer Unit, and sometimes to ministers, there is often a delay of several months for decisions about transfers or the ratifying of sentence-plan targets. The joint thematic review found that target periods for completing Parole Board reviews varied from six and a half months where no change was recommended and no consultation with ministers or the judiciary was needed, up to nine months where the review resulted in a recommendation for release (para 10.19). In practice however, delays can be even longer. Staff working with lifers therefore need to structure their expectations about the likely delays, and be familiar with the processes involved in decision-making so that they can provide some explanation. It is not uncommon for lifers exposed to such uncertainty to revert to previous dysfunctional strategies such as substance abuse or avoidance. The psychologist may therefore have role in preparing them for this and in training or rehearsing positive adaptation strategies.

Adapting to long-term imprisonment Flanagan (1992) argued that, although widely assumed, there was little empirical evidence for physical and mental deterioration during long-term imprisonment caused by extended exposure to highly regimented, unisexual prison life with limited stimuli. Instead, his review of the research suggested that no systematic or predictable effect of long-term imprisonment exists. Indeed, as Toch (1975) observed, 'paradoxically, some men flourish in this context. Weaklings become substantial and influential, shiftless men strive and produce; pathetic souls sprout unsuspected resources.'

However, Flanagan also argues that generalization about the damaging effects of long-term imprisonment is dangerous. On some measures of prisoner adjustment long-term prisoners, as a group, may be better adjusted to the demands of the prison environment than are other prisoners. However, the group average masks substantial differences in individual responses to confinement.

Zamble and Porporino (1992) found that, in general, although prisoners behave in a more introverted way whilst in prison, their previous social skills are not lost, but stored for future use and remain available for release. The joint thematic review suggested that, although long-term imprisonment may not in itself be damaging to robust personalities, its effects on dysfunctional personalities has not been established. For those coming into prison as young people, female prisoners and lifers who are known to have personality disorders, the effect of long-term containment without remedial help may well be result in further deterioration (para 3.29).

Intentional self-injury (ISI) and suicide Swinton et al. (1994) found that more than a quarter of lifers had a history of self-harm compared with 16 per cent of non-lifers. Dooley (1990) found that murderers made up 16 per cent of prison suicides, although they comprised just 4 per cent of the total prisoner population. Towl and Crighton (2000) also found that life-sentence prisoners have an appreciably higher risk of suicide than determinate-sentence prisoners. Likely critical points where there is a raised risk fall into a number of categories:

1 **Offence-related anniversaries**, not just of offences, arrest and imprisonment, but also of birthdays and other anniversaries of the victim or of family members.
2 **Prison-related life events**: e.g. being informed about tariff dates, transfers, reviews, adjudications.
3 **Perceived set-backs**: e.g. 'knockbacks' on reviews as well as otherwise relatively minor incidents which take on added significance. For example a life-sentence prisoner in open conditions who gets into a fight with another prisoner shortly before a Parole Board hearing might feel that this incident could jeopardize his chances of release, resulting in several more years in prison.

Risk assessment

Given that the overwhelming factor in determining a lifer's suitability for release is the risk of further serious offending, risk assessment is central to the life-sentence plan. A risk assessment using the 'Wakefield model' (Clark et al., 1993) is a central part of the life-sentence plan and should be carried out at the main centre. This involves an analysis of the index offence and the dynamic risk factors which contributed to the offence. It also feeds into the sentence-planning process by making predictions about the sorts of behaviours which individuals with these risk factors might display in the prison environment. Towl and Crighton (1995) have identified a number of areas requiring further work in this system, not least of which is the variable quality of initial risk assessments mentioned above.

Risk assessment of lifers is an ongoing and dynamic process which continues throughout the sentence. The initial formulation of the offending behaviour produced at the first stage may change as the lifer carries out offence-related work and develops more insight into his behaviour or as he discloses more information. Other risk factors may be included which are not relevant to the index offence if other previous offending or institutional behaviour are taken into account. This occurs most commonly in cases where a lifer has a previous conviction for a sexual offence. Because of the importance of reducing the risk of further serious offences, psychologists may find themselves called upon to assess the lifer's need and suitability for a sex-offender treatment intervention.

Because of the subjective and non-quantitative nature of the life-sentence-plan risk assessment, psychologists working with lifers should be familiar with more widely used clinical risk-assessment tools such as the HCR-20 (Webster et al., 1997) for prediction of violent behaviour, or the SRA-2000 (Thornton, 2002) for assessing risk of sexual offending. They also need to be aware of other established assessment tools for dynamic risk factors such as the Level of Service Inventory – Revised (LSI–R; Andrews and Bonta, 1995) and the Psychopathy Checklist – Revised (PCL–R; Hare, 1991) both of which are sometimes used in a range of forensic settings.

Because of their expertise in risk assessment, psychologists sometimes find themselves coming to very different conclusions from their colleagues about the risk presented by individual offenders. Webster et al. (1997) have highlighted the risks of unstructured clinical judgements about risk, where, for example, staff working without an effective model of risk assessment tend to give more weight to overt behaviours rather than underlying risk factors or longer-term patterns of behaviour.

For discretionary and HMP cases, once the tariff has expired, the prisoner is entitled to a hearing before a tribunal of Parole Board members in order for their case for release to be heard. The prisoner is entitled to legal representation at such a board and can call and cross-examine witnesses, including report writers. Because of the importance of these panels and the added pressure of being cross-examined by a lawyer, DLP and HMP panel reports should ideally only be completed by a chartered forensic psychologist with experience of writing lifer reports.

Offending-behaviour work

For risk to be effectively assessed and managed, a lifer will need to carry out an assessment of his offending behaviour. A number of frameworks have been used for this type of work, including the functional analysis model (Owens and Ashcroft, 1982) and the behavioural diagnosis model of Kanfer and Saslow

Table 11.1 Behavioural diagnosis (Kanfer and Saslow, 1969)

Stage	Issues to be covered
Initial analysis of the offending behaviour	Description of the offending behaviour
Clarification of problem situation	Conditions of the offence; when, where and how it occurred, the immediate precursors and consequences.
Motivational analysis	Internal and external factors which motivated offending behaviour, reinforcers of behaviour
Developmental analysis	Family, social and interpersonal history, key life events, patterns and changes relevant to offending behaviour
Analysis of self-control	Level and pattern of control that the offender has over offending behaviour, thoughts and emotions.
Analysis of social relationships	Significant relationships, support, peer environment
Analysis of social-cultural-physical environment	Social norms and attitudes in the offender's normal environment, interaction with offending behaviour

Source: Kanfer, F. H. and Saslow, G. (1969). Behavioural Diagnosis. In C. Franks (ed.) *Behaviour Therapy: Appraisal and Status*. New York: McGraw-Hill. Reproduced with permission of the McGraw-Hill Companies.

(1969). This provides a seven-stage framework for interviewing as shown in table 11.1.

The advantages of such a model are that it provides a clear structure and focus for what is an important process, it allows both interviewer and offender to progress systematically through the various aspects of the relevant behaviours; and it is a cognitive-behavioural model which can be applied to any set of offending behaviour.

Cullen and Newell (1999) stress the need to understand the offender's point of view and his reasons for offending, and a number of practitioners have used personal-construct theory (Kelly, 1955; Needs, 1988) as one approach of exploring how the offender views himself, other people and the world.

When the Parole Board assesses a lifer for release, the members consider the risk of that lifer committing *any* further serious offence. It may therefore be the case that offence-focused work will look at a broader range of issues than those surrounding the index offence. Again, this is most common among lifers with a previous conviction for a sexual offence, though other past serious offending patterns may also be significant.

In recent years the focus for offending-behaviour work has been groupwork programmes with a prescribed format. However, with lifers there is still great demand for individual interventions to address offence-specific risk factors which are not catered for by groupwork programmes, though such needs are not always met.

Psychologists also have a role in providing follow-up work or refresher training to lifers who have completed groupwork-based interventions aimed at reducing their risk of reoffending. For example a lifer may get to open conditions and have identified a need for training in problem-solving, even though he has completed a cognitive-skills group several years beforehand. In the absence of a refresher course, it may fall to the psychologist to provide this work.

Preparation for release and resettlement

Proper preparation for release is particularly important for lifers for a number of reasons:

1 Lifers will generally have spent longer in prison than determinate-sentence prisoners and may therefore have more problems adjusting to life in the community. For many, simple life skills such as handling money, budgeting, living independently or socializing with people outside the prison setting are skills which may need to be re-learnt.

2 Because of the serious nature of their offences, male lifers will have re-

stricted opportunities in terms of social support in the community. They may have to move to a different area if their case was particularly notorious or if the victims ask for them to move, they may also find themselves shunned by family and friends.

3   Lifers will also find restricted opportunities for employment, housing and leisure activities because of the nature of their offences.

4   Nearly all lifers will spend time in open conditions prior to release. While in open conditions they will spend progressively more time in the community in town visits, voluntary work, paid work and periods of home leave lasting several days when they will have the opportunity to stay at their release address. At this stage, risk assessment and management again becomes important as the lifer is exposed to different environments and potentially destabilizing influences such as alcohol and drugs. At this stage lifers may find they need to develop specific skills to deal with living in the community. For example, a lifer whose index offence was related to his heavy drinking may have developed a set of adaptive strategies in prison to avoid future problem drinking, but have gone through his sentence never having had to put those strategies into practice because alcohol was not widely available, or the predisposing factors which triggered his drinking were not present. Suddenly on home leaves he may find himself exposed to these stresses and in an environment where alcohol is once again freely available. In such circumstances he is likely to need 'remedial' work with a psychologist to strengthen his relapse-prevention strategies.

Work on life licence

Forensic psychologists are now increasingly being employed by the National Probation Service to carry out, amongst other things, risk assessments and interventions with particular high-risk offenders in the community. Where concerns are raised about a lifer on licence in the community, even though these are not serious enough to warrant recall to prison, forensic psychologists are likely to find themselves asked to work with the supervising probation officer in the risk assessment and management of lifers in the community.

SUMMARY AND CONCLUSIONS

'Working with life-sentence prisoners' is a heading which encompasses a broad range of the skills that forensic psychologists have to offer, both in prisons and in the community. Risk assessment and management, conducting individual case formulations and interventions, working with offenders at risk of self-harm, and with mentally disordered offenders, are all important skills which forensic psychologists bring to this group. In particular, the issues of risk assessment and risk management are central to working with lifers and should underpin all the work that is carried out with them. Because of this, forensic psychologists are uniquely placed to play a key role in the management of life-sentence prisoners.

NOTE

Extracts from *The Lifer Manual*, 1999, are reproduced by permission of HM Prison Service.

| Chapter | Twelve |

Working with Young Offenders and Juveniles

Martha Blom-Cooper

Introduction

Recent legislation and government initiatives have led to significant changes in the management of young people in the prison system. These include the provision of separate and distinct regimes for young (18–21 year old) and juvenile (12–17 year old) offenders. Young and juvenile offenders have, in recent years, had a higher profile in the minds of the public and government, encouraged by media reports of the most serious, albeit rare offences committed by the very young. The Crime and Disorder Act 1998 introduced a new range of sentences for juvenile offenders, replacing the Detention in Young Offender Institutions and Secure Training Orders with a Detention and Training Order. This added to the options already available to the courts under the Children and Young Persons Act 1933 (now the Powers of Criminal Courts (Sentencing) Act, 2001). The number of young people who are placed in the custody of the Prison Service has since increased and now stands at approximately 13,600, of whom approximately 3,100 are female (Home Office, 2001 (April)).

The Youth Justice Board was set up in 2000, its remit being to oversee the provision for juveniles, including setting standards for the treatment of this population (HM Prison Service, 2000c). This marked a growing realization that this ever-increasing population could not and should not be treated as 'miniature adults'. Senior Prison Service managers also recognized the different demands placed on those responsible for such young people in custody. These include the higher rate of 'acting out' behaviour and assaults and emotional problems. Given the relatively small numbers of prisoners accommodated in the female estate, young women between 15 and 21 are generally placed in units alongside adult prisoners. One notable exception was the Young Offender Unit at Holloway prison (Cain, 1999).

This chapter provides a brief overview of the research regarding the development of offending behaviour in juvenile and young offenders taking into account the emotional, physical and cognitive development of adolescents in particular. This outline of the key areas of work with juvenile and young offenders in the prison system will highlight current strategies for working with this age group and will propose future developments.

The Development of Offending Behaviour in Juveniles and Young People

Criminological research has clearly established that young people have a disproportionately greater involvement in crime. Rates of offending appear to peak between the ages of 15 and 18 years of age (Home Office, 1989a). Whilst the proportion of those engaged in property offences remained consistent with age, 14–15 year olds appeared more likely to engage in violence or criminal damage (Campbell and Harrington, 2000). Research suggests that juvenile offenders are generalist rather than specialist offenders as compared with adults. Although most outgrow youthful offending, evidence of numerous and varied early anti-social behaviours are a strong predictor of later offending (Loeber, 1982, Robins, 1978).

Many factors appear to contribute to the development of anti-social or offending behaviour. These include environmental factors such as poverty, resulting in poorer education, housing and childcare arrangements; and healthcare and social factors, for example peer groups and the presence of anti-social or absence of pro-social role models. Many young people convicted of serious offences have experienced childhood abuse (Boswell, 1995) or erratic and harsh discipline from parents. Recent research suggests that the use of drugs was a strong predictor of serious or persistent offending (Campbell and Harrington, 2000).

Thus, juvenile and young offenders are likely to have experienced one, and sometimes several problems such as childhood abuse, neglect, disrupted or chaotic care and educational and health problems. In response to this evidence, the Prison Service now places much greater emphasis on multi-disciplinary teams working to address the whole range of problems that a young person is likely to present. Research informing the development of interventions for young and juvenile offenders has resulted in a focus on cognitive-behavioural approaches aimed at developing pro-social behaviour using active, concrete teaching styles in high-intensity interventions which encourage the involvement of families where possible (Maguire, 1995 and Vennard et al., 1997). In addition, it is recognized that, particularly among the juvenile estate it is important to involve prisoners' families in decisions about the management and care of the young person.

Although the law clearly distinguishes between young and juvenile offenders in terms of chronological age, it is more difficult to draw clear distinctions between individuals in developmental terms. A wide range of physical, emotional and cognitive changes mark the period of adolescence. Individuals develop at different rates and with differing outcomes. Adolescents often struggle to balance their need for independence and self-esteem with a lack of confidence in taking on the challenges of personal responsibility in society. Some also experience difficulty considering the needs of others where these conflict with their own. Developmental processes, which may influence the likelihood of a young person engaging in delinquent behaviour, include management of emotions and aggressive behaviour, social class, moral reasoning (Kohlberg, 1969) and cognitive skills (Ross and Fabiano,1985).

However, practitioners have in the past tended to assume that adolescents possess the same personality or emotional constructs as adults and that they can be treated as 'miniature adults'. To some extent this view was encouraged by the dearth of research focusing on the experiences and needs of young people. Some notable exceptions, for example, Farrington (1989) subsequently led to researchers taking a greater interest in young people's delinquent behaviour. Researchers have addressed the delinquent behaviour of young men to a greater extent than that of young women. The lack of relevant research remains a significant problem for the management and treatment of female offenders, old or young. Evidence remains of uniform treatment of adult, young and juvenile female offenders. Until very recently, the Prison Service did not offer 'accredited' offending-behaviour programmes adapted to the needs of young or female prisoners. Programmes had been validated for adult populations from other countries only. The Prison Service is now piloting a number of programmes targeting the needs of more specific populations including young people and in doing so, is recognizing the differences between the populations. These issues will be expanded upon in the following sections.

Working with Young and Juvenile Offenders: Current Policy and Practice in HM Prison Service

This section summarizes the range of work in which psychologists working in young-offender institutions and juvenile units are currently engaged. Broadly, this work involves the assessment of risk of reoffending or suicide and self-injury; provision of individual interventions and groupwork programmes addressing cognitive and behavioural factors associated with an increased risk of offending; providing support for those at risk of suicide and self-injury and those staff responsible for their care; researching and advising on the development of regimes and the development and implementation of organizational strategies, for example those aimed at reducing the incidence of bullying in an establishment.

Assessment

Psychologists are frequently engaged in assessing the likelihood that offenders will reoffend for the purposes of making decisions regarding suitability for parole, and in order to make appropriate referrals for intervention. A number of well-recognized risk- and needs-assessment tools include versions for young- and juvenile-offender populations. These include the Level of Service Inventory (Andrews and Bonta, 1995) and the Adolescent Problems Inventory (Freedman et al., 1978). These are useful for a vast majority of offender groups. However, in the case of low base-rate behaviours such as homicide, assessments rely more heavily on clinical judgement. In this context, it is essential that psychologists are aware of the limited relevant evidence base when assessing such cases. Approaches to risk assessment such as functional analysis (Owens and Ashcroft, 1982) may prove to be helpful with such offenders.

When assessing young and juvenile offenders it is important to consider at what stage of development she or he may be. Many may not yet have developed fully in some aspect of personality or some emotional, cognitive or moral respect. Thus, assessments of these aspects of a young person's character should not be regarded as static but rather 'working assessments' that are expected to change over time. This is particularly important when working with a client group whose 'dynamic' risk factors are likely to be more evident. The need to avoid labelling individuals is particularly vital when assessing those whose personality is emerging. Whilst it is important to avoid labelling young people, it remains the responsibility of those involved in assessment to ensure access to appropriate resources.

Offending-behaviour programmes

The Prison Service provides a range of offending-behaviour programmes including the Enhanced Thinking Skills, Reasoning and Rehabilitation and Sex Offender Treatment Programmes. These programmes aim to challenge offenders' attitudes and to equip them with more constructive thinking and behavioural skills to help them avoid offending in future. They are based on the so-called 'What Works' literature which stipulates that, in order to be effective, interventions should, among other requirements, have a sound theoretical base; target factors demonstrated to be associated with offending; adopt cognitive-behavioural methods; and take into account the target group's learning styles. The literature (McGuire, 1995) emphasizes the need to consider 'responsivity' when designing effective treatment interventions. This involves the appropriate selection of intervention and matching the techniques employed in interventions to the learning styles of the target population. Programmes currently accredited by the Joint Prison and Probation Accreditation Panel are not tailored to the needs of young people in this way, although such programmes are currently being piloted.

Evaluations of how effective such programmes are when applied to young people have revealed a number of broad guidelines that should inform the future development of effective programmes. For example, behavioural approaches have been found to be more effective when compared with psychodynamic approaches. Regimes that incorporate physical activities, and offending-behaviour and educational components (Farrington et al., 2000) such as the High Intensity Treatment programme (Beck, 1997) reported a 10 per cent drop in reconviction rates. It appeared that this latter result was likely to be related to the offending-behaviour and educational components as opposed to the physical activities, thereby dispelling the myth that the military style discipline and high level of physical activity of 'boot camp' regimes could 'straighten out' young offenders.

The Reasoning and Rehabilitation Programme (Fabiano and Porporino, 1997) has recently been adapted for juvenile offenders (and renamed the Reasoning and Re-Acting Programme) and is currently being piloted. The adaptations include the development of materials using scenarios more within the life experience of young people and increasing the number, but shortening the length, of each session. This allows for more frequent reinforcement of ideas and practice of skills whilst taking into account the shorter attention spans of young people. The Prison Service has also recognized the need to focus on motivating young people to address their problem behaviour particularly those who will spend relatively short periods of their sentence in custody – some can remain in custody for as little as two months. Some broad-based interventions such as the 'Motivate Offenders to Re-Think Everything' aim to prepare young people to address their offending behaviour through completion of interventions that can be offered in the community following the custodial part of the sentence. New programmes currently being explored include a programme designed to increase the level of socio-moral reasoning at which an individual operates without confronting the individual and thereby encouraging defensiveness (Lunness, 2000).

Despite the obvious investment in developing interventions tailored to the specific needs of young and juvenile offenders, it is essential to evaluate the effectiveness of these approaches and to refine the teaching styles adopted to take into account the different levels of educational attainment and concentration of young people.

Organizational issues

It is widely recognized that young and juvenile offenders can present particularly challenging behavioural problems and that these impact on staff (Lyon and Coleman, 1994). The high level of assaults occurring in male young- and juvenile-offender establishments may be explained by the tendency of young men to 'act out' their feelings rather than express them constructively. Developmentally, it is expected that younger age groups will more often use physical aggression, particularly as a means by which to resolve conflict or obtain a goal. Managing behavioural problems on a daily basis can be challenging for all staff. Behavioural monitoring and incentive schemes can help staff to motivate offenders to behave in a more socially responsible manner. These schemes are most effective when behaviour is immediately followed by reinforcement, be it positive or negative, and when the incentives are meaningful to that individual and not simply based upon adult assumptions about what will act as an incentive.

Numerous studies have assessed the extent of bullying behaviour amongst young and juvenile offenders in establishments (Homberger and Farmer, 1998; Ireland, 2001a) and examined options for limiting opportunities to engage in such behaviour, for example by increasing levels of staff supervision. Only recently have researchers begun to focus on what motivates bullies (Ireland, 2001b). This issue is dealt with in more detail in chapter 15.

The research on the effects of long-term imprisonment is extremely limited and virtually non-existent in the case of young people (although see Ireland, 2000). We can only hypothesize how young people are affected by their removal from the home environment with the social support that it offers (even if it is sometimes anti-social in influence). Further research in this area might usefully add to our knowledge and management of young people, particularly those at an increased risk of suicide and self-injury. For example, a recent study explored young and juvenile offenders' experience of homesickness and the possible link between 'coping styles' and general health (Ireland, 2000). This study found that this population experienced more homesickness as compared with a control group.

The Prison Service has adapted the initial training programme for new officers, providing modules on the demands likely to be placed on staff in young- and juvenile-offender establishments. Prison staff have to balance their 'order and control' role with their 'caring' role as significant adults in the lives of impressionable young people. Psychologists can offer staff support in terms of helping them to understand the behaviour displayed by this offender group and help them to develop skills that they can use to manage their behaviour effectively (Cosgrave and Langdon, 2001). Additional training for staff is also being developed by psychologists for those already working with disturbed or disruptive young people, learning from the experiences of staffing Local Authority Secure Units.

'Holistic' regimes   Some establishments have developed a holistic approach to working with particular groups of offenders. Aylesbury Young Offenders Institution has created a therapeutic community in which young people are encouraged to take greater responsibility for the running of the unit and to support one another in resolving problems. Additional special units for young people serving long-term sentences including life sentences have recently been established. The emphasis has been on multi-disciplinary working and engaging the offender's family in the sentence-planning process that should much more closely reflect the very specific needs of the individual.

Support for vulnerable prisoners   Research suggests that young men under 25 years old, on remand or early in their sentence may present an increased risk of suicide or self-injury (Towl, 1997). Features of prison regimes may further increase this risk, for example limited time out of cell and isolation from social support networks. Of particular concern are those on remand or arriving at an establishment directly from sentencing in court, and particularly those sentenced to long-term or life sentences. The prevention of suicide and self-injury and the management of those at risk of attempting such actions is a high priority for the Prison Service (Towl et al., 2000). Whilst psychologists may initially be involved in the assessment of such individuals, they may also provide a key role in contributing to the care plan on which they will have advised. Intervention may focus on developing constructive 'coping' strategies. Strong emphasis is placed on the role of 'significant adults' for the young person involved whether this be family members, or members of prison staff identified as having personal responsibility for the welfare of that young person.

Professional and ethical issues

Working with young and juvenile offenders in custody confronts staff with a range of ethical and professional issues. The question of labelling young people as a result of the use of diagnostic assessment tools is one example. Setting and maintaining the limits of confidentiality can also present problems, particularly where young people are not aware of the consequences of disclosing new information (Plant, 2001). Those working with young people should be aware of the professional guidelines and legal requirements, for example the presence of 'appropriate adults (Police and Criminal Evidence Act, 1984). Quality work is frequently conducted with young people in custody. There is a professional imperative that the benefit of this is not lost when a young person returns to the community, where the real test will come. It is therefore important to ensure effective communication with outside agencies to ensure that young people do not fall into the gaps between services. This is particularly relevant to young and juvenile offenders who present with multiple social and personal problems, not effectively addressed in isolation (Leheup, 1998). The new partnership between the Prison and Probation Services will provide a structure for closer joint working.

Summary

Young and juvenile offenders present prison staff with many challenges. They often exhibit a wide range of social problems and emotional and cognitive deficits, some of which may be associated with their individual development. They may be disruptive, demanding and vulnerable.

The Prison Service has begun to acknowledge that the needs of young and juvenile offenders in custody are different and that these are only just beginning to emerge from the recent research in the area. In preparing to meet the needs of young and juvenile offenders in the future, Prison Service regimes and interventions need to be adapted as our knowledge about this population increases. Research on the efficacy of new interventions and regimes is essential. More importantly, research needs to focus on how young people adapt to prison life, its impact upon them and, indirectly, on treatment effectiveness, for example.

Forensic psychologists in the Prison Service are ideally placed to develop evidence-based practice and to contribute, through research, to the knowledge base regarding the needs of young and juvenile offenders and the most effective and ethical approaches to meeting these needs.

Chapter Thirteen

Working with Women Prisoners

Lorraine Mosson

Background

Women in prison

The increase in the number of women prisoners held by HM Prison Service in England and Wales is well documented (HMCIP, 1998: Wedderburn, 2000). In 1970, there were less than 1,000 women prisoners in England and Wales. In March 2002, the female prison population was 4, 210, within the context of a total prison population of 69, 780 (HM Prison Service *Weekly Operations Report* for that date). Both the baseline figure and the number of women in prison as a proportion of the total population have increased.

The reasons for this dramatic and continuing increase remain unclear and are the subject of considerable debate. Reasons put forward include: a significant change in the behaviour of women; changing attitudes amongst sentencers; an increased number of people coming before the courts; women in economic need (itself acting as a precursor to offending behaviour); an assumption amongst sentencers that imprisonment can stop drug abuse (e.g. Carlen, 2000; Wedderburn, 2000; HMCIP, 1998; Warner, 2000). There is perhaps no single cause; with a change in the number of women appearing in court and a change in sentencing patterns likely to be the primary factors (Player, 2000).

As the number of women in prison has increased there have been two significant changes in how they are managed within the prison system:

Women's Policy Group   WPG was established in 1998 to provide the Prison Service with a more strategic overview of the women's estate and to give direction to the provision of regimes for women. It was also tasked with ensuring that the policies and practices of the Prison Service are more effectively reflected the needs of women prisoners (Stewart, 2000).

Operational management of women's prisons   In his thematic review of women's prisons, the Chief Inspector noted the absence of co-ordinated operational planning and day-to-day management within the women's estate (HMCIP, 1998). An Operational Manager for Women's Prisons has since been established, and women's prisons taken out of the existing area structure for the management of prisons and constituted within one single 'area'. The Operational Manager for Women's Prisons now employs a Principal Psychologist with responsibility for the delivery of forensic psychology services within women's prisons.

Amalgamation of WPG and Operational Management Team   In 2002 the Women's Policy Group and the Operational Management Team were amalgamated to form the Women's Policy Estate Unit, to ensure greater consistency between strategy, policy and operations.

These have been significant developments in the women's prison estate, and these have provided an opportunity for concerted change, which has impacted on the work of forensic psychologists in women's prisons.

Psychologists in women's prisons

In his thematic review of women's prisons the Chief Inspector noted that only three women's prisons had at least one full-time psychologist (1998). In the four years that have elapsed since the publication of that review there has been an increased presence of forensic psychologists in women's prisons. By June 2002 forensic psychologists were employed by the Prison Service in 12 establishments in which women prisoners were located, with staffing ranging from a singleton psychologist to established departments with a range of staff at different levels.

Forensic psychologists working in women's prisons are involved in a wide range of activities and tasks, and operate at different levels within their establishments – from practitioner to senior manager. These reflect in broad terms the areas in which forensic psychologists are employed within male establishments. The key areas in which forensic psychologists contribute are offending-behaviour programmes and risk assessment, most notably with life-sentence prisoners. Forensic psychologists also contribute to training of prison staff, research (HM Prison Service, 1998), the development of regimes, and the development of strategy and policy at a local and national level (Towl and McDougall, 1999). The breadth of work undertaken by forensic psychologists in prisons is reflected in other chapters of this book; and in most cases these also apply to the work undertaken by forensic psychologists in women's prisons.

There are three key themes which underlie the work of forensic psychologists in women's prisons: marginalization of women in much of the literature and research that concerns forensic psychology; balancing priorities of risk and need; and finding the balance between perceptions of similarity and difference.

Marginalisation of women in research and forensic psychological literature
The generic area of forensic psychology is expanding rapidly with many exciting developments, particularly in the area of evidence–based practice (McGuire, 1995; Hodgkins, 2000; Towl and Crighton, 1996). Forensic psychologists working with women in prison frequently find that the emphasis in developments, literature and research continues to be on male offenders. This may in part be explained by the relative size of male and female offender populations: although the number of women in prison is increasing dramatically the number of women imprisoned in comparison with men remains relatively small (Warner, 2000).

Texts dealing with issues in forensic psychology frequently omit reference to women; or deal with them in a way that suggests that women are a homogeneous group not reflecting the diversity of women in prison (see Kelland and McAvoy, 1999 for a description of the diversity of the women's estate). Hodgkins and Muller-Isberner (2000), for instance, highlight that an important aspect of the treatment of mentally disordered offenders that has been neglected is the special needs of women and notes that 'mentally disordered women who offend are less numerous than males, but no less in need of treatment'.

Knowledge of the 'dynamic' and 'static' risk factors for male offenders has developed significantly but research into factors contributing to women's offending is relatively recent and is not well developed. Clark and Howden–Windell (2000) note that the dynamic risk factors for female offenders have not been fully investigated. McAvoy (1998) also noted the established body of research into the development and correlates of male offending, and commented that 'research into female offending is more scarce and less systematic'.

Clearly absence of literature specifically related to women offenders and factors influencing their offending has an impact on the practice of forensic psychologists working in women's prisons.

Finding the balance between risk and need   The emphasis in much of the literature on women prisoners relates to the needs of women prisoners rather than risk assessment and intervention to reduce reoffending. There is a greater emphasis upon risk assessment and intervention to reduce reoffending in research about male offenders. Texts referring to women in prison have almost exclusively focused on need in relation to health and lifestyle rather than exploring factors perhaps that relate more directly to offending (for example: Horn and Warner, 2000).

How are women's needs perceived? In his thematic review of women's prisons (1998) the Chief Inspector of Prisons commented 'women have different physical, psychological, dietary, social, vocational and health needs and they should be managed accordingly'. In their introduction to 'Positive Directions for women in secure environments' Horn and Warner (2000) comment that 'women in secure environments differ in significant ways from men: not simply in terms of the type of offences they tend to commit, but also in terms of their specific and varying needs'.

The needs of women in prison are identified as significant, and different from or greater than the needs of male prisoners in the following areas:

Women in prison as parents   Caddle and Crisp (1997) describe how 61 per cent of women prisoners surveyed were mothers of children under 18 years; and most were the primary carer before their imprisonment.

Experience of abuse and victimization   Morris et al. (1995) indicated that nearly one third of the women in their sample reported having been sexually abused before imprisonment. Nicholls (1998) found that 36 per cent of women in one establishment reported problems with sexual abuse in the past. McAvoy (1998) reported 20 per cent of her sample describing an abusive current relationship.

Self–harm   Nearly one quarter of the women in Morris et al.'s (1995) sample reported harming themselves prior to imprisonment. Singleton et al. (1998) reported that both sentenced and remand women prisoners reported more suicidal thoughts and suicide attempts than male sentenced and remand prisoners. Of sentenced women prisoners in their sample, 37 per cent, compared with 20 per cent of male prisoners, reported a suicide attempt in their lifetime. A recent Home Office study (Sattar, 2001) reported no statistically significant difference between genders regarding prisoners' type of death (natural and unnatural).

Drug use   One quarter of the sample of women in prison in Morris et al.'s study (1995) were classified as high drug-users and slightly more than one fifth as medium drug-users. Singleton et al. (1998) reported 40 per cent of women on remand with a dependence on heroin and 23 per cent of sentenced women in comparison with 25 percent of men on remand and 18 per cent of sentenced men.

Mental health   Singleton et al. (1998) report that 14 per cent of women in their sample had experienced functional psychosis in the past year in comparison with 7 per cent sentenced men and 10 per cent of men on remand. They also indicated that women prisoners were more likely to report neurotic symptoms than male prisoners; and that this was particularly marked amongst sentenced prisoners. In Maden et al.'s study (1994), psychiatric contact prior to the sentence was reported by 45 per cent of women compared with 36 per cent of men. They write, 'our study cannot explain the observed gender differences in psychiatric disorder. They must arise from an interaction of rates of mental disorder among offenders and the operation of procedures at various stages of the criminal justice system which are intended to divert mentally disordered offenders away from the prison system.'

Personality disorder: Maden et al. (1994) reported 18 per cent of women in prison in their sample with a personality disorder, compared with 10 per cent of men, but noted concerns about the validity of the finding. Bolger (1998) reports research carried out in Holloway in 1992 in which the PDQ–R (Personality Diagnostic Questionnaire – Revised) was used. Responses to the self-report questionnaire suggested that only 8 per cent of women completing the questionnaire did not have a personality disorder. The validity of the finding however is reduced as the methodology did not include a structured clinical interview; as Bolger herself acknowledges.

It is clear that women in prison have specific and in some cases different needs from men in prison. However, the Home Office is clear in its statement of the role of the Prison Service in public protection. Sometimes, staff who work with women prisoners are caught between responding to expressed or perceived need in relation to mental or physical health and lifestyle, and carrying out assessments and interventions to reduce risk of reoffending and ultimately promote public protection. This applies to forensic psychologists when prioritizing use of limited resources. Perhaps the challenge for forensic psychologists working with women in prisons is to resist responding to a dichotomy or choice; and instead to find a balance in which both the individual's and the public's needs are met.

Similarity and difference　　Forensic psychologists working with women in prison face a second apparent dichotomy which at one extreme presents women in prison as exactly the same as men in prison; and at the other presents women as entirely different. Opting for either of these two approaches in isolation may have a profound impact on the practice of a forensic psychologist.

The remainder of this chapter will draw on these three themes and focus on policy and practice relating to the areas that currently dominate the work of forensic psychologists working with women in prison:

1   assessment: risk assessment;
2   psychological intervention: groupwork programmes.

Risk Assessment

What is risk assessment?

Risk assessment is a key task for forensic psychologists working within the Prison Service (Clark, 1999).

Towl and Crighton (1996) define risk assessment as 'a combination of an estimate of the probability of a target behaviour occurring with a consideration of the consequences of such occurrences'. Within the forensic setting 'target behaviour' may be any behavioural category, including violence or sexual offending, suicide and self–harm. Towl and Crighton describe a five-stage process: specification of the target behaviour; examination of the knowledge base about that behaviour using actuarial data where possible and exploration of the individual case; identification of factors that might increase or decrease risk of target-behaviour occurrences; estimation of the probability of target-behaviour occurrence and assessment of the consequence of target-behaviour occurrence; assessment of the acceptability of that risk; and specification of appropriate monitoring arrangements.

In order to undertake a reliable and valid risk assessment related to an individual and his or her future reoffending, it is important to have available baseline data about that offence type and offender type; and to have an understanding of the dynamic factors that increase and decrease risk. The information should be specific to the target behaviour and to the offender type.

Clark (1999) describes how forensic psychologists are slowly progressing from 'professional judgement' to processes based on objective criteria and consistent methods; and describes a range of methods including clinical inference and actuarial prediction, as well as techniques involved in consideration of dynamic social factors, personality factors and behavioural monitoring.

Risk assessment with women in prison

The accuracy of risk assessment with women in prison is limited by the availability of relevant actuarial data and knowledge of those dynamic factors which relate to women's offending. McAvoy (1998) noted that research into female offending is more scarce and less systematic than for male offending. Clark and Howden–Windell (2000) comment that dynamic factors contributing to wom-

en's offending 'have not been fully investigated'. Dynamic risk factors contributing to women offending have rarely been correlated with reconviction.

Literature on risk assessment often does not refer in sufficient detail to women
(for example, Towl and Crighton, 1996; HM Prison Service 2000a); and literature about women in prison often does not refer to risk assessment (for example, Horn and Warner, 2000).

Previous research relevant to risk assessment with women in prison   Morris et
al. (1995) conducted research into the needs of women in prison. Almost a quarter of the women in that study reoffended within two to six months of their release. There appeared to be common experience among those reconvicted:
unsatisfactory accommodation, difficulties in managing financially, drug use,
alcohol use, and employment difficulties. Graham and Bowling (1995) published
a study into young people and crime. They suggested that there was a difference
between young men and young women in their ability to desist from crime. They
described how young men are less likely than young women to leave home, enter
into stable relationships with the opposite sex, form new families and become 'eco-
nomically independent, socially responsible and self-reliant individuals'. The study
indicated that these were important predictors of avoidance of offending for young
women. McAvoy (1998) compared first-time and repeat women offenders with
the aim of increasing insight into the characteristics of repeat offenders. The main
findings of this study were that repeat offenders have more developed criminal
careers, have greater cognitive deficits and were more likely to have been victimized as an adult; and that self-efficacy, proximity of criminal others and victimization by a partner are relevant to the levels of female offending.

Current research relevant to risk assessment with women in prison   The
studies above provide useful information and develop our understanding of
factors contributing to women's offending, in terms of what initiates offending, what maintains it, and what encourages avoidance. However, there has
been an absence of a systematic study into women's offending. In response to
this, Women's Policy Group within the Prison Service commissioned research
into the factors contributing to offending in the female prison population. The
research focuses on individual characteristics and the situational circumstances of an offender which when altered leads to a change in the probability
of reconviction (Andrews and Bonta, 1994a, cited in Clark and Howden-
Windell, 2000).

The resulting survey of the female prisoner population (Howden–Windell,
1998) comprises retrospective and prospective studies. The retrospective component of the survey is intended to assess the prevalence of factors that have
been identified in previous studies and to identify other crime-related factors

that may be prevalent, using a representative sample of 215 women prisoners discharged in 1995. The prospective study will include 200 offenders who will be interviewed within three to four months of release to assess the prevalence of factors, and then followed up through the Offenders Index post-release to establish levels of reconviction.

In the unpublished findings from the retrospective study, the following were found to be predictive of recidivism for women prisoners in this sample:

Criminal history: (e.g.) Age at first conviction, a previous custodial sentence.

Education and employment Women without formal educational qualifications and women who been previously been in unskilled employment were more likely to be reconvicted.

Drug abuse Alcohol abuse was not related to reconviction.

Lack of continuity of care Lack of care before the age of 18 years.

Attitude / behaviour in prison History of absconding, previous breach of bail conditions etc were found to be predictive of recidivism.

The authors of the study conclude that

the best predictors of recidivism in the female prison population are those predictive in the male prison population. This would suggest that approaches which have been developed to tackle these factors in male offenders should work with female offenders. This does not of course rule out the importance of making offending programmes responsive to female offenders in the way they are delivered.

Certain factors often referred to in literature about women and offending were found not to be predictive of recidivism in this sample – including mental health and victimization/abuse histories. The authors concluded from their own study that 'having mental health problems does not predict reconviction'.

The second stage of this research is under way. It is hoped that this study will demonstrate whether the factors identified in the retrospective study are indeed predictive for women offenders. Preliminary findings from the OASys (a joint HM Prison Service and National Probation Service project) suggest that the most common factors causing women prisoners to reoffend were related to drug misuse and thinking skills, followed by relationships and attitudes.

The Psychopathy Checklist – Revised (Hare, 1991) is being increasingly used in some male prisons on the basis that scores obtained are correlated with violent recidivism. Such psychometric tests are sometimes used by forensic psychologists in prisons to contribute to estimates of the risk of reoffending and to inform decisions about interventions and treatment to reduce risk (Clark, 1999). As evidence is collected regarding the validity of using the PCL–R with women in the UK, its use by forensic psychologists in women's prisons may or may not increase with both lifers and determinate-sentence prisoners. McAvoy (1998) suggested that the Level of Service Inventory – Revised may also be a robust measure when used with women offenders and that it may have a key role to play in the development of treatment interventions and risk assessment with women.

Application of risk assessment with women in prison: Life-sentence prisoners

Perhaps the most common application of risk assessment procedures with women in prison is with life-sentence prisoners. There are currently (June 2002) 160 women serving life sentences in prisons in England and Wales. They are held in 12 prisons, Bullwood Hall and Durham being the prisons in which they are held following conviction and sentencing in court. Eleven of the women life-sentence prisoners are young offenders (aged 21 or under). There are 4,900 men serving life sentences in England and Wales of whom 150 are young offenders. Between 1987 and 1997, there was an 85 per cent increase in the female life-sentence population, compared with a 58 per cent increase in the male life-sentence population. The increase in the female lifer population was primarily accounted for by adults (increased from 66 in 1987 to 128 in 1997) rather than young offenders (eight in 1987; and nine in 1997: HM Inspectorate of Prisons and Probation, 1999).

The thematic review of lifers published in 1999 noted the remarkable finding that of 52 female lifers released since 1981, no reconvictions for a standard list offence had been recorded against them; compared with the 46 per cent two-year reconviction rate for female determinate-sentence prisoners discharged in 1994 (HM Inspectorate of Prisons and Probation, 1999).

Forensic psychologists working with women lifers are involved sometimes in preparing the life-sentence plan, which follows the prisoner through her sentence and includes a risk assessment (Clark, 1999). More significantly, they are involved in the review processes that take place regularly throughout a life sentence and contribute to the decisions that are made about a female lifer's suitability to move from main centre to a second-stage prison; from second-stage prison to open conditions; and then from open conditions to release into the community. Risk assessment forms a key part of this process. Forensic psychologists are also involved in undertaking psychological interventions with prisoners to assist in reducing their risk of reconviction.

The thematic review of lifers noted that initial and subsequent risk assessment with male and female life-sentence prisoners is often not based sufficiently on factors that are known to be directly linked with offending. Input by psychologists was recognized as improving the quality of risk assessments.

The absence of research and actuarial data about female offenders and more specifically about lifers has limited forensic psychologists in their ability to undertake full and valid risk assessments with female lifers. Review Boards to discuss individual lifers and their progress in detail are held regularly. In the absence of clear information about factors relating directly to offending, Review Boards for women lifers have sometimes developed plans and targets on the basis of perceived need rather than on reduction of risk of reoffending. The retrospective and prospective crime-related needs research currently being undertaken by the Prison Service potentially may improve the quality of risk assessments undertaken by forensic psychologists working with life-sentence prisoners; and improve the quality of target-setting and planning for women lifers.

Psychological Interventions with Prisoners: Groupwork Programmes

A key way in which forensic psychologists intervene with prisoners is through groupwork; and forensic psychologists in the Prison Service have long been involved in the development, implementation and delivery of groupwork programmes (Towl, 1995b; Blud, 1999). Groupwork with women in prison has been an important part of the work of forensic psychologists.

In the mid- to late 1990s there was a significant change in the way in which groupwork programmes were delivered in the Prison Service. On the basis of a body of research sometimes referred to as the 'What Works' literature, the Prison Service established a set of criteria against which groupwork interventions aimed at reducing the risk of reoffending were to be assessed and accredited. In 1996 an accreditation panel was established 'to ensure that programmes run in prison are quality programmes which meet the requirement of appropriateness by laying down guidelines for effective design, management and delivery' (Blud, 1999), and to ensure that they meet criteria to improve their effectiveness in reducing offending. Essentially the Prison Service has developed a policy relating to groupwork programmes that gives priority to 'accredited' offending-behaviour programmes. They are enshrined in the Home Office Business Plan (2001) and have become a key performance target for the Prison Service. The government allocated significant funds to their development as part of the comprehensive spending review. This has had an impact on the work of forensic psychologists in women's prisons.

Offending-behaviour groupwork in women's prisons

Offending-behaviour groupwork-based interventions already accredited to date by the Joint Accreditation Panel include: Enhanced Thinking Skills (ETS), Reasoning and Rehabilitation (R&R), Controlling Anger and Learning to Manage It (CALM), and Cognitive Self-Change Programme (CSCP) for violent offenders; and a range of sex-offender treatment programmes for men (HM Prison Service 2002). These are manualized approaches to working with offenders in groupwork programmes.

Cognitive-skills programmes   To date, two offending-behaviour programmes have been delivered within the female estate: ETS and R&R; both of which are cognitive-skills manualized groupwork programmes. ETS and R&R were based on research suggesting that offenders differ significantly from non-offenders in the number and range of thinking skills deficits they exhibit – including self-control, cognitive style, interpersonal problem-solving, values and critical reasoning (Blud, 1999).

ETS and R&R were both based on literature and research conducted primarily with male offenders and there was considerable initial concern that the programmes would not therefore be suitable for use with women prisoners. The issue of similarity and difference was central to the debate that led to the introduction of these programmes into the female estate. Initially it was assumed that men and women were sufficiently different to warrant major revisions or different programmes. Many practitioners argued persuasively, however, that the programmes should at least be piloted with women.

Forensic psychologists have taken a significant role in implementing these interventions in women's prisons. Forensic psychologists often take responsibility for quality control, supervision of tutors and ensuring the clinical integrity of the programme (Blud, 1999). In the case of cognitive-skills groupwork with women this has meant contributing to the revision of materials and exercises to ensure they are appropriate for use with women; and working with the concept of responsivity. Essentially, responsivity refers to the way a programme is matched with the learning style of its participants. In supervision of groupwork facilitators, the forensic psychologist is able to raise questions about the specific needs of the women in the group; how the programme might meet those needs; how the facilitatory style is matching with the women's learning needs; and then encourage facilitators to consider the dynamics arising from the gender of the group and the tutors.

Cognitive-skills groupwork programmes are now delivered in the majority of women's prisons. Forensic psychologists in this area now express few concerns about the materials and generally report a positive response to the groupwork in terms of level of participation and 'customer feedback'.

Initial reconviction data from the 'accredited' cognitive-skills programmes have been published by the Prison Service which suggests that they may well be having some impact on reconviction rates (Blud, 1999). The data, however, does not yet distinguish between men and women prisoners. Initial and unpublished data from psychometric testing completed at pre-, post- and follow-up stages by participants in cognitive-skills programmes suggest that (1) women prisoners are more 'needy' than male prisoners in terms of thinking skill deficits and (2) that women prisoners show greater positive changes on all measures than their male counterparts.

What next in terms of 'accredited' offending-behaviour groupwork for women?   At present the range of offending-behaviour groupwork available in male prisons is significantly wider than in women's prisons. Currently for instance there is not a structured sex-offender groupwork for women.

Women's Policy Group and the Operational Management team for women's prisons has been active in trying to expand the range of offending-behaviour programmes available for women. Unfortunately, new programmes such as CALM (Controlling Anger and Learning to Manage it); and the Cognitive Self Change Programme for violent offenders are not being piloted in the female estate. Such omission at this stage in programme development reinforces the argument that women are frequently marginalized within developments in forensic psychology in prisons.

It also appears that CALM may not be introduced in the foreseeable future because its authors claim that women require a separate programme – reinforcing the view that sometimes women are perceived as too different from men in prison. Assuming a significant gender difference can build in a delay in piloting new initiatives with women.

Other groupwork with women

Groupwork with women in prison is developed with three purposes which are sometimes overlapping and sometimes discrete:

1   to reduce risk of reoffending;
2   to address and change institutional behaviour;
3   to address mental health needs.

A programme for female and juvenile young offenders was developed at HMP and YOI New Hall (Mosson, 1998) based on the findings of Morris et al. (1995) and Graham and Bowling (1995). King and Brosnan (1998) outline the range of psychological group work programmes delivered at HMP and YOI Holloway: assertion training, anger management, fighting depression, domestic violence, self-help workshop, self-harm workshop and relaxation training. Moynihan (1998) describes groupwork developed for young offenders located on the psychiatric unit at Holloway. A female life-sentence prisoner essentially has access to only one 'accredited' prison service programme, a male life-sentence prisoner has access to a broad range of programmes targeted at a range of their needs.

One significant area of development in the female estate is Dialectical Behaviour Therapy (DBT). DBT has been developed by a psychologist, Marsha Linehan, and is aimed primarily at helping women who meet the criteria for Borderline Personality Disorder (King and Moynihan, 1998a). Its likely impact on reoffending is unclear, particularly given that the initial findings of the crime-related needs survey of women prisoners (2000) that mental health and experience of victimization are not predictive of recidivism in women prisoners.

Borderline Personality Disorder is controversial in itself. Reported prevalence varies between studies. Bolger (1998) reported a prevalence amongst women prisoners of 60 per cent. Singleton et al (1998) who used a more rigorous methodology (a structured clinical interview rather than a self–report questionnaire) reported a prevalence of 20 per cent amongst female prisoners, 14 per cent amongst male sentenced prisoners and 23 per cent amongst male remand prisoners. Borderline Personality Disorder is viewed by some practitioners as too common to be a useful diagnosis; and some consider that it is an acquired syndrome rather than intrinsically part of personality disorder.

DBT is nevertheless an important development since it responds to the needs of women outlined above in the absence of other interventions. It raises the question again of how we balance need and risk. It is interesting that DBT is only recently being piloted with male prisoners when prevalence of Borderline Personality Disorder may be at similar levels in both estates. This highlights the disparity between the female estate, where there is support for responding to needs not directly linked with offending, and the male estate where the emphasis is more notably on need related to offending rather than needs associated with mental and psychological health.

Conclusion

Forensic psychologists working with women in prison are involved in broadly similar areas of work to their colleagues in the male estate. The emphasis of their work, however, is often different. That difference in emphasis sometimes reflects policy at a national level, decisions about resources at a local level, the marginalization of women in research and literature, and sometimes the individual practitioner's own priorities.

Essentially, forensic psychologists working with women in prison have to balance dilemmas that are brought into sharper focus for them than for their colleagues working with men in prison. Is work prioritized in response to need or risk? Is practice, be it in risk assessment or in psychological intervention, based on the assumption that women are the same as men or different? Moving away from the marginalization of women in research and literature, and achieving a different balance in their application with women and men, may allow those dilemmas to be more readily resolved and effectively managed.

Chapter Fourteen

Working with Suicidal Prisoners

David Crighton

Background

From the 1970s to the 1990s HM Prison Service adopted a system of suicide prevention based primarily on medical assessment and management of suicide and self-injury. The main thrust of the management of such behaviours was intended to be a combination of regular observations combined with attempts to physically prevent suicides, generally by locating prisoners in 'unfurnished' cells.

This approach replaced largely *ad hoc* arrangements in place within individual Prison Service establishments. Several revisions were made to this basic approach over subsequent years, the last taking place in 1989. Between 1971 and 1989 the rate of suicide in prisons had continued to increase, in line with previous trends (Crighton and Towl, 1997; Towl and Crighton, 1998).

The procedures for managing those felt to be at a significantly increased risk of suicide were contained in a Prison Service Circular Instruction CI 20/1989 (Home Office, 1989a; HMCIP 1990). This required that prisoners should be subject to screening interviews by health care staff on reception into prison. These would later be followed up by an initial assessment by a primary-care medical practitioner. Health-care staff conducting such assessments were required to refer those felt to be at high risk of suicide for urgent medical assessment. In addition the police or court escorts, by means of exceptional risk forms, could identify 'high risk' prisoners. These were to be forwarded to the prison as part of the prisoner's record.

It was made explicit that all members of staff had a duty to identify prisoners thought to be at increased risk of suicide and, by using standardized documentation, refer them for an assessment by health-care staff. Such assessments were to be concerned with the level of risk of suicide and, in line with the results reported by Topp (1979); emphasis was placed on the presence of psychiatric illness (especially 'clinical' depression).

Current Policy and Practice

The current approach to the management of suicide and self-injury in prisons in England and Wales was introduced in the form of an Instruction to Governors in 1994 (HM Prison Service 1994a) and additional detailed guidance (1994b). This instruction and supporting guidance introduced a new approach to suicide with three key elements:

1   a policy statement;
2   specification of management responsibilities;
3   specification of key standards and procedures.

The policy appears to have been heavily influenced by research into suicide and self-injury in prisons, and especially the work of Liebling (1991). It was also strongly influenced by the 1990 report of HM Inspector of Prisons (HMCIP, 1990; Crighton, 2000). Both suggested the need for several fundamental changes of approach to suicide in prisons.

Firstly, the new policy covered suicide and 'self-harm'. This represented a significant change in that it treated these as related behaviours. Previous practice had been to draw a clear distinction between suicide and self-injury.

The new policy also markedly reduced the emphasis on assessments by healthcare and medical staff. The aim of the new policy was to put in place a multidisciplinary approach that focused on residential prison staff and residential managers.

The new approach divided the management of high-risk prisoners into 'primary' and 'special' care. Primary care included a wide range of factors thought to be involved in creating a safe environment for prisoners. The development of positive staff-prisoner relationships, the creation of positive environments and regimes and the maintenance of ties with the outside community were particularly stressed as ways of improving a prisoner's ability to cope with custody.

'Special care' referred to those prisoners identified as being in crisis and likely to intentionally injure or kill themselves. The new policy shifted clearly away from stressing the role of 'mental illness' in suicide and intentional self-injury.

Management

Overall responsibility for suicide and self-injury moved from medical staff to prison managers, who were to be accountable for implementing the new approach. Each establishment was required to set up a multi-disciplinary

'Suicide Awareness Team' (SAT). The role of these teams was to implement and monitor the new approach to managing suicide and self-injury at establishment level.

As noted above it was a central tenet of the new approach that improving conditions in prisons would help to reduce levels of suicide deaths and intentional self-injury. In turn this would allow a move away from attempts to physically prevent self-destructive behaviours, by means of, for example, 'unfurnished' cells.[1] Positive regimes and staff–prisoner relationships were seen as a keystone of the approach.

Primary-care procedures

The primary-care procedures in the new policy were specified in considerable detail.

> Prisoners were to be assessed on reception into custody, with the risk of suicide or 'self-harm' being assessed as part of a broader health care screening process. Health care staff were to complete a report (called an F2169) on all prisoners on the day of first reception and, where necessary, subsequently.
>
> On first reception, and on reception following conviction, sentence or transfer, prisoners had to be examined by a medical practitioner within 24 hours. As part of this there was a formal requirement that information received from other agencies about possible risk of 'self-harm' should also be used as part of this assessment. Audit systems and 'key standards' were also established as part of the new policy.
>
> Two radical developments in the new policy were to be the formal involvement of prisoners in the prevention of suicide and self-injury, and also the involvement of voluntary agencies (primarily the Samaritans) across all establishments. Both were to be involved in developing awareness, in a befriending role and in providing input to SATs. This aspect of the policy drew heavily on early pioneering work, where prisoners had been involved in such work. It also drew on international experience where prisoners had worked in this area to good effect (Towl et al., 2000; Snow, 2000).
>
> Analogous to community approaches allowance was also made for the admission of prisoners to the prison's health care centre or to NHS hospitals. As in the community though this was now seen as a last, rather than a first, resort.

The effectiveness of current practice

In 1999 HM Inspectorate of Prisons undertook a thematic review, which addressed the issue of the efficacy of current practice, within its broader remit of reviewing suicide in prisons (HM Inspectorate of Prisons for England and Wales, 1999a).

The authors began by acknowledging the role of the 1990 Chief Inspector of Prisons Report in producing the new policy outlined above. In August 1992 the Prison Service responded to this report with the publication of a paper 'The Way Forward', which in turn gave rise to the detailed policy of 1994 (HM Prison Service 1994a; 1994b). The Prison Service's Suicide Awareness Support Unit was given a key role in the implementation of this policy at establishment level.

Policies The review found that virtually all establishments had a Suicide Awareness Team (SAT) and local policies and training programmes in suicide awareness. Most SATs were reported to meet quarterly, although some met on a monthly basis. Only 5 per cent met less often than quarterly. Overall the authors felt that this was appropriate and reflected operational need, with some prisons having very few incidents of suicide or self-injury (e.g. Open Prisons). The review did, though, note inconsistencies in the effectiveness of different teams, ranging from the innovative and excellent through to the weak and ineffectual.

A need for different strategies The report's authors were very critical of the idea that a single policy was appropriate for all groups within the prison system, for example, recommending that different strategies were required for juvenile prisoners, where they suggested a need for a specific response to the rising rate of intentional self-injury and falling suicide rates. They also suggested that a different approach was required for women prisoners, apparently on a similar basis to juveniles.

Local prisons were also felt to be in need of a modified approach. A number of key aspects of the suicide-prevention strategy, the report suggested, were not functioning in local prisons. The notion of 'personal officer schemes'[2] for example had never worked well in local prisons: indeed it could be argued that such schemes were never workable in prisons with a constantly changing population.

Training Levels of training were reported as being very variable and a survey of 593 staff found that 68 per cent reported having received no training in relation to suicide or self-injury. In addition they noted an emphasis within training sessions on the correct completion of the paperwork, rather than on its function.

Perhaps not unrelated to this, they suggest a reticence on the part of staff to approach prisoners they believe may be at increased risk of suicide. Concerns that discussing suicide may serve to precipitate it persisted amongst a number of staff.

Prisoner support schemes   Such schemes were to be introduced as part of the new strategy from 1994 onwards. These were to increase levels of peer support for those assessed at high risk of suicide and self-injury. The survey of Board of Visitor (BOV) Chairs found that by 1999 most establishments had involved prisoners in this manner.

The involvement of the Samaritans had developed well, with 93 per cent of BOV Chairs reporting regular visits by this voluntary group to their establishment. In other respects progress had been less impressive, with only 40 per cent of establishments having a dedicated telephone line to the Samaritans. Dedicated 'crisis suites', for those felt to be at acute risk of suicide or self-injury, had been set up in only 32 per cent of local and 40 per cent of training prisons.

Personal Officer schemes   Personal officer schemes pre-dated the 1994 policy changes, and indeed were in place in many prisons before the 1990 report (HM CIP, 1990). As such they were to be a key building block of the new policy.

The survey of BOVs here highlighted that 87 per cent of establishments had such schemes, although very wide variations in terms of effectiveness were noted. The reports from training prisons again tended to be more positive than those from local and remand prisons where such schemes were often token.

Completion of F2052SH forms   Serious concerns were also evident from the completion of the F2052SH forms. Completion of these appeared to have become an end in itself, rather than as a basis for effective care-planning and risk management as intended. The quality of support offered was noted to be often very poor.

Significant differences between local and training prisons were also suggested. In local prisons forms were more likely to be raised by health care staff (38 per cent) than prison officers (27 per cent). In training prisons this was reversed to 24 per cent and 40 per cent respectively. Following on from this it was noted that 46 per cent of 'at-risk' prisoners were located in the health-care centre in local prisons, compared to 19 per cent in training prisons.

Prisoners were more likely to be managed on 'normal location' in training prisons than in local prisons (54 per cent vs. 33 per cent). Case conferences to close F2052SHs (a requirement of the system) were also more likely to take place in training prisons than local prisons (62 per cent vs. 53 per cent), and were reported to be more frequent for men than women.

The report authors went on to make a number of specific recommendations for changes to the system. These included the following:

1   Senior managers should sample F2052SH forms for quality and compliance with the policy.
2   Support plans (which were absent in 36 per cent of cases) should be present.
3   Managers should address the quality of support plans.
4   Multi-disciplinary case conferences should take place before closing all cases.

Regimes   Improving prison regimes had been seen as central to reducing suicide and self-injury. However, the growth in the prison population served to slow down such improvements. Regimes in local prisons also seemed to suffer disproportionately. The routine was disrupted more often in local prisons (38 per cent) than in training prisons (11 per cent). The environment was estimated as free from bullying in 27 per cent of local prisons but 50 per cent of training prisons. Induction was thought to equip prisoners to seek assistance with problems in 56 per cent of local prisons and 80 per cent of training prisons. Most seriously staff-prisoner relations were judged to be of a quality where prisoners could approach staff to discuss their problems in only 69 per cent of local prisons compared to 81 per cent of training prisons.

The overall conclusion of the authors was that local prisons were operating regimes that were likely to engender feelings of frustration and anger. Directly linked to this, such regimes also appeared poorly suited to managing those at risk of suicide and self-injury.

The inspectorate report went on to make a series of suggestions for the development of healthy prisons. In fact these seemed to be generally non-controversial in terms of their general desirability (Towl et al., 2000). Such views did however serve to shift the emphasis of suicide management away from the individual 'pathology' of prisoners, in favour of a focus on a range of environmental factors in prisons.

The review by the Prisons Inspectorate also identified a clear lack of compliance with the Prison Service policy on suicide and self-injury. In direct contravention of the policy, they noted a continued dependence on fixed interval checks as a way to manage suicide risk.

Another area on which they commented was the continued use of isolation and 'unfurnished' accommodation, rather than, as recommended by the new policy, hospital ward-type accommodation or purpose-built 'crisis suites'. From a survey of four health-care centres in 1997/8 the report's authors noted that 36 patients were secluded, with an average episode of seclusion lasting 50 hours.

Criticism was levelled at the continuing use of seclusion in the Prison Service, arguing that the use of such seclusion is 'anti-therapeutic' in the context of self-injury (Crighton, 1997; Crighton and Towl, 2000; Towl and Forbes, 2000).

Contemporary Developments

The Prison Service is in the process of implementing new screening procedures for prisoners on reception. Until recently the approach has been based on a screening tool (F2169) which aims to cover a very broad range of health and personal difficulties. The relevance of much of this material immediately on arrival in prison has been questioned, leading to a revised screening tool. This has been designed to focus on areas of immediate health and welfare concern. It has also been suggested that it will allow staff more time to assess difficulties in a detailed manner (McHugh, 2000).

The current system of communicating concerns between the Prison Service and private escort contractors and the police has also come under review. In the past a form (POL1) would be completed only on prisoners who had caused concern. This form included concerns over suicide and self-injury, as well as concerns about violence towards others. This approach had the theoretical advantage of only drawing attention to prisoners who had caused concern. However, the absence of such a form, for whatever reason, was generally taken to imply that there were no identified concerns. From January 1999 this form was replaced by the Prisoner Escort Record (PER), which detailed information on all prisoners.

From the mid-1990s the Prison Service has conducted small-scale research in prison cell design (McHugh, 2000). These have generally involved designs that, amongst other attributes, have fewer ligature fixing points. The cost of such approaches to the whole prison service is however considerable. It is also unlikely, given the relative infrequency of suicide, that small-scale research will yield significant effects in reducing suicides in prison, at least for the immediate future.

Staff training in suicide awareness has also received attention. The current training programme dates from 1993. This was replaced by an updated programme from April 2000. The new programme has been described as aiming to increase staff confidence in approaching and supporting suicidal individuals, via the teaching of practical skills (McHugh, 2000). This is to be complemented by a new training programme for senior managers who take responsibility for establishing Suicide Prevention Teams (SPTs).

From 2000 onwards there have been a number of changes in relation to the implementation of policy, although the basic tenets of the Prison Service approach remain unchanged. These changes have been primarily aimed at driving forward the implementation of current policy more effectively and giving a more explicit emphasis on 'prevention' rather than simply 'awareness' (Towl, 2000).

A key part of this has been an increased emphasis on the need to care for prisoners whilst in custody. As part of this, suicide prevention has received greater support nationally. The Suicide Awareness Support Unit has been renamed the Suicide Prevention Group, and has expanded in terms of its remit and staffing to include broader research and establishment support roles.

Part of this new remit has been renewed attempts to develop the physical prevention of suicides, drawing on the experience of prison and healthcare services nationally and internationally. This is clearly distinct from historical approaches of isolating prisoners, in that the aim is to address and eliminate areas of risk in the physical environment. The approach therefore involves the development of safer cells, which provide fewer opportunities for suicide.

Likewise an increasing number of prisons now have 'crisis suites'. These are primarily located in local and/or remand prisons, which tend to have the greatest numbers of suicide deaths. Such suites, in combination with hospital ward-type accommodation in prison health-care centres, have replaced the use of 'unfurnished' or 'strip' cells.

Organizational changes have also been implemented in the field. Establishment SATs have been renamed Suicide Prevention Teams, with a view to increasing the stress on the prevention role. Less superficially, such groups are now required to report to area suicide prevention co-ordinators via area meetings. Co-ordinators are often area psychologists and act as the chair of area suicide-prevention meetings. These are intended to address the wide variations in practice between establishments. Although in their infancy, Prison Service areas which piloted such groups suggest positive effects in improving practice (Towl, 2000).

The resources allocated to suicide prevention have also been improved, with establishment SPTs increasingly having active involvement from specialist staff (e.g. forensic psychologists and forensic nurses). A number of 'high risk' prisons are also to have full-time suicide prevention co-ordinators whose remit is to ensure compliance with key standards.

SUMMARY

In this chapter the area of suicide and self-injury prevention in the Prison Service has been reviewed. From around 1971 to 1994 the policy of the Prison

Service was based on the medical assessment and management of those felt to be at increased risk of suicide, with self-injury being seen as a largely distinct problem.

From 1994 this policy shifted radically. Based on then-current research and the findings of HM Inspectorate of Prisons (HMCIP, 1990) the policy changed in a number of key respects. Firstly, the new policy sought to treat self-injury and suicide as part of a continuum of similar behaviour. Secondly, the policy moved the responsibility for prisoners at increased risk away from medical staff and to Prison Service managers. Thirdly, the policy aimed to introduce a multi-disciplinary model of assessment and care, based on the residential wings, and involving all Prison Service staff. Finally, the new policy introduced the notion of formally involving outside agencies and also prisoners themselves as a fundamental part of suicide prevention.

In line with this the new policy sought to move away from attempts to physically prevent suicides and to replace this with attempts at primary prevention and specialist care. Primary prevention stressed the need to create safe environments and positive staff-prisoner relationships. Specialist care was to be focused on those in acute crisis.

With the benefit of hindsight it could be argued that the changes introduced in 1994 were over-ambitious, particularly in view of the resources available and the growth of the prison population. The policies also lacked a clear focus on individualized accountability. The role of specialist staff tended to become marginalized in this area (e.g. the effective removal of input from psychologists).

The move to a single policy for all Prison Service establishments also appears somewhat misguided. It seems clear that different types of prisons have often quite distinct needs. It can also be suggested, with hindsight, that moving so decisively away from attempts at physical prevention was perhaps a mistake.

In current practice a number of these difficulties have begun to be addressed. Recent developments have included the research into 'safer cells' to reduce the ease with which prisoners can find means to kill or injure themselves. An increased focus of resources on 'high risk' prisons (predominantly those with the highest turnover of prisoners) is also developing.

There has also been a slow but discernible growth in some Prison Service areas of the level of specialist input to suicide prevention, predominantly in the form of forensic psychologists and nurses. It can convincingly be argued that there is a pressing need to develop levels of specialist input and support in relation to suicide and intentional self-injury in prisons. The experience of the Prison Service suggests that non-specialist staff are often not sufficiently equipped to assess and manage prisoners at inflated risk of suicide. There is also a growing body of international research suggesting that specialist input can have very marked positive effects in relation to the quality and efficacy of risk assessment and risk management of suicide and self-injury in the community and in custody (Hawton, 1994; Snow, 2000). This is an area where psychologists have had only limited involvement, but have much to offer.

NOTES

1   This term refers to cells where the majority of furnishing has been removed, along with other materials that might be used to complete suicide.
2   Personal officer schemes involve the allocation of an officer or small team of officers as keyworker(s) for prisoners.

| Chapter | Fifteen |

Working with Bullies and their Victims

Jane Ireland

Bullying is an important issue in prisons and has been found to occur among all types of prisoners – adults, young offenders, juveniles, men and women. Estimates of the extent of bullying are reported to be high: in a review of studies that asked prisoners directly if they had bullied others or had been bullied, Ireland (in press) reported estimates of up to 67 per cent for prisoners reporting to have bullied others and 57 per cent for prisoners reporting to being bullied. However, when interpreting estimates of the extent of bullying it is important to consider the environment in which it is taking place and the characteristics of the prisoner population that it houses.

Ireland (in press) proposes a model of bullying in which aspects of the prison environment, largely outside the control of prison authorities, are seen to interact with the individual characteristics that a prisoner brings with them to this environment. The environmental characteristics include aspects of the physical environment such as limited staff supervision, high population density, and aspects of the social environment such as the existence of an inmate subculture that supports aggression. Individual characteristics include the intrinsic characteristics that bullies are perceived to possess, such as positive beliefs about the use of aggression and the physical/social ability required to successfully bully their peers. Indeed as stated by Ireland (in press): 'Bullying is very much a product of the interaction between the prison environment and those housed within it. The environment acts to influence and reinforce the behaviour of prisoners who are predisposed towards bullying others'.

Hence the combination of environmental and individual characteristics can increase the likelihood that bullying will occur. Since much of this is outside the control of prison authorities, eradicating bullying completely from prisons should be considered an unobtainable goal. Indeed, tackling bullying effectively is a difficult task and this should be acknowledged in any intervention strategy. Instead, the focus of intervention strategies should be on *reducing* bullying by attempting to impact on the environmental and individual characteristics that promote it. The present chapter focuses on one element of such strategies, namely how to deal with those prisoners identified as either bullies and/or victims following an incident of bullying.

HM Prison Service published its first anti–bullying strategy in 1993 (HM Prison Service, 1993). This was updated in 1999 when a mandatory anti-bullying strategy was produced (HM Prison Service, 1999b). The 1999 strategy represented a comprehensive update of the 1993 strategy and included detailed methods of preventing bullying and a clearer supporting rationale for the interventions suggested. In terms of how bullies and victims should be dealt with the emphasis was on challenging bullies and supporting victims.

Regarding bullies, the focus was on challenging their behaviour constructively based on principles of negative reinforcement where the incentives to bully, in the form of intrinsic rewards, were removed. Incorporating strategies and targets into sentence plans, reviewing their position on the incentive scheme, moving them to another unit in the prison, changing their labour allocation (if they had been bullying others whilst at work) and developing interventions that aimed to increase victim empathy and encourage prosocial behaviour were also promoted. It was also suggested that where resources allowed, the bully could be moved to a dedicated unit to address their behaviour. Such units have been referred to as 'anti-bullying units', although the strategy suggests that a neutral name may be more appropriate. Placing bullies on report, in segregation or transferring them to another establishment were also suggested although it was recognized that these options should be dependent on the seriousness of the incident. Finally, the strategy emphasized the use of 'stage systems' to manage bullying behaviour where a set of procedures would be put in place each time a prisoner bullied others (HM Prison Service, 1999b). These 'stage systems' relate to the creation of action plans where a series of graded targets is set for the bully. The specific targets set are determined by the type of bullying behaviour presented and the 'attitude' of the bully.

Regarding victims, the strategy focuses on encouraging them to report bullying to staff by assuring them that the information received will be treated in the strictest confidence. It is recommended that victims are involved in planning a strategy to deal with their 'specific problems' and that they are kept informed of developments relating to their own case. The strategy also proposes examples of good practice such as using personal officers as sources of support, offering victims counselling, allowing them to receive support from their peer group, either from listeners or through the development of 'buddy' schemes. The development of programmes designed to help victims adapt effectively to the prison environment in order to reduce their vulnerability to bullying was also proposed (HM Prison Service, 1999b).

Whilst there is much to comment on the positive elements of this strategy such as increasing the involvement of victims (particularly by keeping them informed of progress on their case) and emphasizing the use of already-existing systems to tackle bullying (i.e. sentence planning systems and incentive schemes), there are also some limitations that are worthy of further discussion. For example, the creation of dedicated units to address the behaviour of bullies (i.e. 'anti-bullying units') is problematic for a number of reasons. These units are based on the notion that a prisoner bullies solely because there is something intrinsically wrong with him or her. By removing them from their peers, 'treating' them and then putting them back with their peers it is expected that their behaviour will have been improved in some way. However, this fails to acknowledge the importance of the environment in promoting and maintaining bullying. This is reflected by Mellor (1998) who argues that we should move away from viewing bullies as intrinsically and 'irrevocably bad' and removed from the environment in which they act, instead viewing bullying as: 'a result of the social situation they find themselves in . . . there's nothing intrinsically wrong with them. In a different environment, they might not bully at all' (p. 32).

If the behaviour of a bully is to be managed effectively it needs to be done within the environment in which the bullying takes place (see Ireland, in press, and O'Donnell and Edgar, 1996, for a further discussion of the problems associated with dedicated units). The same can be said about the suggestion that victims need to plan a strategy for dealing with their 'specific problems'. Again, this suggests that victims have somehow contributed to their victimization and that there is something intrinsically 'wrong' with them. This fails to take into account the impact of the environment on their status as a victim. Outside of a prison setting they may not present as victims at all.

The suggestion of offering support through the use of a 'buddy' scheme also presents problems. Such schemes have also been suggested by researchers (often termed 'chaperone' schemes: Brookes et al., 1994; Willmot, 1997) and involve 'trustworthy and mature' prisoners being encouraged to look after victims of bullying. However, staff need to ensure that these 'trustworthy and mature' prisoners are not in fact bullies. In view of the lack of research addressing the *actual* characteristics of the different groups involved in bullying it can be very difficult to identify with any certainty who the bullies are, particularly the 'pure bullies' (Ireland, in press). In choosing 'chaperones' or 'buddies' staff need to be careful that they have not placed the victim at risk. The victim in this instance may find it difficult to report to staff that they are being bullied – who would believe the victim who tells staff that they are being bullied by a prisoner whom the staff have specifically chosen to protect them? Furthermore, if similar schemes were developed solely by prisoners they could in some instances, where the original principles of the scheme became subverted, be described as 'protection rackets', condoned by the prison authorities and construed both as a form of bullying and a potential threat to the management of the prison regime. Authorities need to be careful that they are not seen to be legitimizing such 'protection' schemes. In view of these issues 'buddy/chaperone' schemes should not be recommended (Ireland, in press).

In addition, the Prison Service strategy does not give many concrete suggestions about the sorts of 'support' that should be provided for victims, nor does it distinguish between the ways in which 'pure bullies' and 'bully/victims' should be dealt with. This latter consideration is particularly important. Research into bullying has identified four distinct groups:

1   **'Pure bullies'** – those who solely report bullying others;
2   **'Pure victims'** – those who solely report being a victim of bullying;
3   **'Bully/victims'** – those who report both bullying others and being victimized themselves; and finally
4   **The 'not involved' group** – those who report no bullying or victimization.

The prevalence of prisoners belonging to each group tends to be fairly consistent across studies, with bully/victims (3) and those not involved (4) tending to be the most frequently reported groups, followed by pure victims (2) and pure bullies (1). Intervention strategies that operate on the principle that there are just two groups involved in bullying – bullies and victims – fail to recognize the existence of bully/victims, and are unlikely to be effective.

However, although there are some limitations in the current strategy it is worth recognizing how advanced the Prison Service is in developing anti–bullying strategies in comparison with services outside of the UK, with a number of these services using the UK strategy to develop their own. In addition, it should be acknowledged that no anti-bullying strategy will be perfect and that limitations are likely to occur in any strategy attempting to deal with a behaviour as difficult to manage as bullying. The fact that a strategy is in place which is emphasized by the Prison Service and is now mandatory for all establishments demonstrates the most important element of any strategy – a commitment to dealing with bullying. Thus, the following section aims to develop this anti-bullying strategy further by proposing suggestions for dealing with the different groups involved.

What Should Be Done?

The following suggestions are presented in three sections headed: Investigation, Dealing with the Different Groups and Bullying as a Continuum. Each will be discussed in turn. It should be noted that they represent only *some* of the possible strategies/interventions and that they are presented in summary form. Readers are referred to Ireland (in press) for a more detailed discussion of their possible applications.

Investigation

Investigation is a crucial part of intervention that is required *before* any action is taken. The focus of investigation should be on checking:

1   whether or not an incident of bullying has occurred;
2   what actually happened during the incident;
3   whether the incident is a one-off event or related to other incidents;
4   whether the individual is a pure bully, a bully/victim or a pure victim;
5   the motivation of the bully and the specific role that he or she took during the incident, i.e. as a leader, assistant or follower; and
6   the effect on the victim(s).

Dealing with the different groups

When it is established which prisoners were involved in the incident and what specific role(s) they played, the next task is to decide how best to manage their behaviour. Correctly identifying bullies and/or victims is important since this will impact on the specific interventions to be used. Whatever the case, the emphasis should be on addressing the behaviour in the environment in which bullying occurred. Isolating bullies and/or victims from their peers and 'treating' them is unlikely to be effective. What follows therefore are suggestions on how best to respond to pure bullies, pure victims and bully/victims.

Pure bullies   the emphasis should be on setting targets with them for appropriate behaviour. This is perhaps similar to the 'stage systems' proposed in the 1999 Prison Service strategy (HM Prison Service, 1999b). Essentially such systems should involve an individual behavioural contract for each bully. These contracts need to be monitored over time and include options for rewarding good behaviour. These 'rewards' should principally relate to positive feedback i.e. acknowledging when they have followed the rules (Ireland, 1999a). Ideally this should be communicated to them in a multi-disciplinary format such as during a sentence-planning board. It is important to tell bullies when they *have* followed the rules as well as when they have not. Equally important is exploring the motivation behind bullying, i.e. what were they achieving from it? The aim should be on teaching them more appropriate and pro-social ways of achieving their goals. Alternative approaches that include encouraging bullies to empathize with their victims are unlikely to prove useful. Research findings have suggested that bullies have a limited capacity for empathy, namely showing concern for others and perspective-taking (Ireland, 1999b). In view of this intervention strategies are better focused on addressing the costs and benefits of their behaviour. However, it should be recognized that pure bullies may be particularly skilled at bullying and may be able to avoid detection for long periods of time. This undoubtedly impacts on any analysis of the costs and benefits of bullying for them, with the benefits outweighing the costs (at least initially) in these cases and thus any intervention of the 'costs and benefits' of bullying should take this into account.

The skills that such bullies may possess in avoiding detection make it difficult to assess how much impact interventions will have on them. Following intervention they may well reduce their use of the specific behaviours that they know are being monitored. Instead they may bully others using other more subtle forms that they know will be harder to detect and are not being monitored. This re-emphasizes the importance of investigation into when, where and how they are likely to bully others. This should be an ongoing process which is reviewed over time so that a full picture of their behaviour can be obtained. Essentially staff should aim to complete a full risk assessment of the bully's behaviour. This should follow accepted frameworks for conducting risk assessments (e.g. Towl and Crighton, 1996) that includes assessing:

> what factors may help to increase the risk of the target behaviour occurring (in this case bullying);
> what may decrease the risk of its occurrence;
> how likely it is to occur; and
> the consequences of the behaviour.

If staff are able to assess the risk that the bully poses to others and predict the circumstances in which this is increased or decreased, it should be possible to put preventative strategies in place to reduce the likelihood of further bullying. In some circumstances this may include increasing staff supervision of the bully's behaviour. However, there needs to be a careful balance between observing bullies more closely and carrying this out to such an extent that staff can be accused of harassment or victimization. The extra supervision should be subtle but not intrusive. For example, increasing the visibility of staff may be just as important as increasing the actual 'physical' supervision and may help to improve levels of perceived supervision. Other suggestions include making the supervision less predictable – bullies may be very good at predicting when they will have an opportunity to bully others, namely when supervision is less likely. It becomes harder for them to bully if it becomes more difficult for them to predict when there will be a 'gap' in supervision (Ireland, in press). Indeed, it has long been realized by researchers that predictable supervision patterns in prisons are one factor that may help to increase the likelihood of violence taking place (Toch, 1978). This is recognized in the current Prison Service strategy which emphasizes the importance of varying the times when prison officers patrol prisoner living areas (HM Prison Service, 1999b).

Bully/victims   Intervention with such prisoners can also include elements of the above. However, there should be an increased emphasis on *support* and they should be viewed primarily as a victim group. Researchers have suggested that bully/victims represent aggressors whose bullying has become a strategy that they have adopted to prevent future victimization. Their aggression may be a way in which they are communicating to the rest of their peer group that they are not an 'easy' target. Teaching bully/victims more appropriate ways of dealing with conflict may therefore be of use. For example, deterring them from using retaliatory aggression as a possible response to being bullied and providing them with an opportunity to be placed on a course that promotes appropriate responses to conflict situations, e.g. using assertiveness as opposed to being aggressive, may be useful (Ireland, 1999a). However, there should be an assessment of where the skill deficits are expected to lie and it should be acknowledged that an individual may not necessarily show the same degree of assertiveness in all situations. For example, Ireland (2001b) reported a trend for bully/victims to be *under-*assertive in some situations (specifically, general social interactions) but *over-*assertive in others (those involving actual, potential or perceived conflict). Any intervention would need to recognize that bully/victims may have *specific* deficits in displaying assertive behaviour. In addition, bully/victims do not appear to have the same reduced capacity for empathy as pure bullies (Ireland, 1999b). Thus, interventions with this group could also consider victim awareness issues, such as the impact of their aggressive actions on others.

Recognizing how bully/victims may present themselves to staff is also important. It is likely that this group have already come to the attention of staff but not because of their status as a victim. Bully/victims tend to display a range of behaviours that could bring them into conflict with staff. For example, Ireland (2001b) reports how they are more likely than the other groups to display negative behaviour towards staff and the prison regime, such as being placed on adjudication or being abusive to officers. They are also more likely to report drug-related behaviours such as selling and/or using drugs. One possible consequence of these behaviours is that they become viewed more as 'troublemakers' than potential victims because they simply do not fit the stereotype of a victim (Ireland, in press). Thus, one of the most crucial areas to consider when working with bully/victims is the importance of exploring the function that these 'other' behaviours serve for them and trying to assess how they may relate to their status as a bully/victim. Thus, those that work with bully/victims should be trying to answer questions such as:

> What other sorts of behaviours have they displayed that have brought them to the attention of staff?
> What function do these other behaviours serve for them and how do they relate to their status as a bully/victim?

One of the consequences of the aggressive/delinquent behaviour shown by a bully/victim is that they become easier to identify than the pure victim who causes no concern to staff. Recognizing the distinction between bully/victims and pure victims is important if 'treatment' is to be tailored to each group. Recognizing the existence of bully/victims is particularly important in view of research that has found them to be the most frequently reported group in comparison to pure bullies and pure victims (e.g. Bolt, 1999, reported that 25 per cent of all prisoners were classified as bully/victims compared to 15 per cent classified as pure bullies and 16 per cent as pure victims). The implication of this is that bully/victims may be responsible for a sizeable proportion of victims. Trying to manage their behaviour through a combination of identifying the behaviours that they are likely to display and the specific skills that they lack, and offering them support (details of which are listed in the following section) is likely to be the most effective approach.

Pure victims   With this group staff need to be much more attentive to the subtle behaviours that could indicate that they are being bullied. Whereas the bully/victim may 'act out' (by being aggressive/delinquent), possibly in the hope that staff will recognize their distress, pure victims may not be as obvious (Ireland, in press). Nevertheless, there are similarities between the interventions that can be used with pure victims and those proposed for bully/victims. However, whereas the emphasis with bully/victims should be on both managing their aggressive behaviour in a similar way to pure bullies *and* on providing support, the focus with pure victims should primarily be that of support. Some of the most suitable ways of supporting victims involve:

1   **Identifying victims through the symptoms that they show**
    Victims are unlikely to inform staff when they are being bullied for a range of reasons. These include not wanting to violate the informal but powerful inmate code that states that prisoners should not inform on others, or not wanting to admit to being a victim for fear of this being perceived as an indication of weakness.

2   **Limiting the opportunities that other prisoners have to bully them,** either by dealing appropriately with the behaviours of bullies, or by helping the victim to generate strategies by which they can deal with conflict. These can include educating victims on subtle ways of avoiding situations/times in which they may be targeted; for example, if they get bullied during movement asking them to ensure that they are one of the last prisoners to join movement so that they have to walk at the back near the officers. It can also include helping them to develop skills in certain areas, such as assertiveness. Indeed, pure victims appear to be more *under*-assertive than bully/victims (Ireland, 2001a). However, such interventions need to acknowledge that being passive during a conflict situation can be adaptive in some circumstances, particularly if the victim has assessed the risk for potential injury for themselves to be high (Ireland, 2001a). This recognizes the importance of assertiveness skills being applied in appropriate contexts; victims should not be encouraged to be assertive in a situation where they consider themselves to be at risk of injury and where 'being assertive' is likely to increase this risk of injury. Indeed, Ireland (in press) argues that intervention strategies should perhaps focus on how victims respond *following* an incident of bullying as well and encourage them to use assertiveness skills in reporting incidents of bullying to staff and requesting action.

3   **Including them more fully during investigations,** an area that was touched upon in the 1999 Prison Service strategy (HM Prison Service, 1999b). This involvement should include obtaining their perspective on the bullying incident and acknowledging how they want the matter dealt with. However, their involvement in the final decision regarding the action against the bully needs to be carefully managed and overall responsibility should clearly remain with staff. The overall aim of involving the victim is to try and empower the individual as much as possible in decisions made about their care. In consideration of the effect that bullying

may have had on them, e.g. increased feelings of powerlessness, empowering them as part of the investigation process therefore becomes potentially very helpful.

4 **Being seen to take a collaborative approach to the problem** It should be made clear to the victim that they do not have to deal with the bullying on their own. The emphasis should be on joint working, with both the victim and staff taking responsibility for developing strategies to deal with the bullying. One of the best forums for this may be through the use of multi-disciplinary case conferences where the victim can attend and play a significant and key role in decisions made. Such an approach will also communicate to the victim how serious the authorities are about dealing with the bullying.

5 **Not placing pressure on victims to name the bullies** Although borne out of good intentions and a wish to support the victim by protecting them from the bully, it can be detrimental in the long run if staff engage in such behaviour. This can recreate the original feelings of powerlessness that the victim may have experienced during the bullying incident itself. It may also discourage the victim from telling staff if they are victimized in the future (Ireland, 1999a). Should the victim disclose the name of the bully this should be purely a voluntary admission.

Bullying as a continuum

Finally, it is important to recognize that prisoners who bully and prisoners who are bullied are not polar opposites: bullying others and being bullied may be construed as varying along a continuum of behaviour (Ireland, 1999c), with 'being bullied' at one end and 'bullying others' at the other (see figure 15.1 below).

Prisoners can present at any point along this continuum. Although it is uncertain how 'stable' the classifications of pure bully, bully/victim and pure victim are, it could reasonably be anticipated that a prisoner's classification into these groups may change over time. This may be particularly true for

Bullying Others   Being Bullied

Figure 15.1

bully/victims who are perceived as actively trying to change their classification by resisting the label of 'pure victim' and possibly aspiring to the role of 'pure bully'. If they are successful their classification could change (although this process would be expected to occur over a relatively long period of time) and it is important that any intervention recognizes this possibility as it should be important in informing how the prisoner's behaviour is managed subsequently. Indeed, interventions with bullies and/or victims should focus on their *recent* behaviour and deciding from this how best it should be managed.

SUMMARY

Creating and implementing effective interventions for bullies and/or victims is difficult in view of the lack of research addressing this area. However this chapter has attempted to present broad guidelines on how to deal with the behaviours of bullies and/or victims and has highlighted specific interventions that may or may not be appropriate (e.g. anti-bullying units and 'buddy' schemes).

It is important that intervention strategies recognize the limits in which they operate. Bullies are a difficult group to manage, particularly since their behaviour is a product of both environmental *and* individual factors. In view of this the focus of intervention is perhaps better placed on monitoring their behaviour and limiting the opportunities for bullying. With regards to victims, the emphasis should be on offering them support and opportunities where they may be empowered, primarily by increasing their involvement following the incident of bullying.

However, what has been presented here is a summary of the interventions that can potentially be applied to deal with bullying. They are by no means comprehensive and should be employed in the context of a wider anti-bullying strategy that includes both reactive and preventative components. Similarly, although the interventions presented here have concentrated on bullies and/or victims, the importance of the wider peer group should not be ignored; bullying is not a behaviour that occurs between a small number of individuals, it is a product of the peer group as a whole and if it was not supported to some extent by the peer group it would be unlikely to occur. Including all of the peer group, namely those prisoners who are 'not-involved' in bullying and staff (who also form part of the peer group) becomes important. Bullies and/or victims cannot be managed and/or supported in isolation. This has to be achieved within the context of a wider social group.

ACKNOWLEDGEMENTS

Thanks to Dr Sandy McEwan for earlier comments on this chapter.

Chapter Sixteen

Managing Disruptive Prisoners

Sarah Selvey

Introduction

The problem of managing persistently disruptive prisoners is one faced by all prison systems: Coyle (1987) estimated that although representing a small minority – between just 0.2 per cent and 5 per cent of the UK prison population – their behaviour causes significant difficulty.

It is surprising then that it was only in the mid-1980s that HM Prison Service developed a detailed management strategy to deal with the problem. Prior to this most disruptive prisoners were managed by the Continuous Assessment Scheme (CAS), a process involving regular transfer between prison segregation units. Although this strategy shared the problem of disruptiveness amongst high security prisons, the scheme involved little structured assessment and a Home Office report in 1984 (Home Office, 1984) acknowledged that the prison system lacked adequate facilities for dealing with persistently difficult and intransigent prisoners.

As a result a detailed strategy to address the management of disruptive prisoners by the establishment of small special units was outlined in a Home Office report in 1987 (Home Office, 1987). The aim of these was to identify triggers to disruptiveness, to encourage behavioural change and, where feasible, reintegrate prisoners into the normal prison system. This strategy had strengths over the CAS system, including the provision of varied regimes and a significant reduction in assaults. However, the units were largely unsuccessful in reintegrating prisoners into mainstream prisons. In fact the special units were seen as rewarding by the majority of prisoners. Most had been placed there, in an open environment with well-supported regimes and high levels of interaction with staff, after months of segregation on CAS, and understandably they were frequently unwilling to leave. Additionally the system did not allow for the removal of subversive prisoners, who orchestrated problems but did not openly participate in disorder.

Future strategy development was influenced by significant security lapses, the political climate at the time and consideration of penal policy towards the management of disruptive prisoners in other countries. Following high-profile escapes from Whitemoor in 1994 and Parkhurst Prison in 1995, the Learmont Inquiry (Home Office, 1995) recommended a prison to accommodate the most disruptive prisoners. A project team was duly established to consider the feasibility of a 'supermax' prison. This concept, a complete institution run on a super maximum security basis, has proliferated in the United States whilst in Europe penal policy has tended towards highly secure units within existing prisons (Vagg, 1994). The US approach has not been without its critics and McConville (1995:4) has argued that it has been characterized by a 'lack of moral involvement with and responsibility for the prisoners . . . [and] . . . a reduction of staff discretion and a reliance on procedure rather than relationship in the handling of prisoners'. The project team rejected the idea of implementing supermax facilities in favour of adapting the existing special units into a system of Close Supervision Centres, or CSCs (HM Prison Service: the Spurr Report, 1996). These centres would emphasize engagement with staff, provide greater structure than the special units and be based on a staged progression system, with access to successive levels earned by co-operative behaviour.

The newly established CSCs were opened in February 1998 operating as part of a national management strategy aimed at securing the return of problematic or disruptive prisoners to a settled and acceptable pattern of institutional behaviour.

The initial functions were:

> to remove the most seriously disruptive prisoners from mainstream dispersal or training prisons;
> to contain highly dangerous or disruptive individuals in small highly supervised units with safety for staff and prisoners;
> to provide the opportunity for individuals to address their anti-social disruptive behaviour in a controlled environment;
> to stabilize behaviour and prepare for a return to the mainstream with minimum disruption.

Fourteen months later, in April 1999, an additional function was added which acknowledged that progression was not a realistic option for some prisoners and involved 'the long-term containment of those who continue to pose a serious threat to the safety of staff and prisoners'. However, the dual purpose created by this addition proved difficult to achieve, with those prisoners who wanted to progress requiring very different management from those needing control and close supervision. This created role-conflict issues for officers which may make them more susceptible to demonstrating hostile orientation towards prisoners (Wilson, 2000).

During the first two years of its operation the CSC system has experienced close scrutiny through independent research commissioned by the Prison Service (Clare and Bottomley, 2001). Whilst a few prisoners did progress there were a small group of prisoners who were persistently non-compliant and others for whom it was judged too risky to staff or other prisoners for them to be located in less controlled environments. The researchers argued that the underlying principle of prisoner 'progression', through a variety of incentives and earned privileges, was flawed and did little to encourage co-operation or progression. This approach assumes a 'rational choice' model of human behaviour, an instrumental reasoning which places material rewards and punishments at the centre of motivation and fails to consider less 'rational' factors which may motivate behaviour, and the influence on prisoners from pressures arising within prison culture. Liebling (in Clare and Bottomley, 2001:159) argues that this model is not appropriate for emotionally unstable and often brutalized prisoners, who bring with them a legacy of distrust and antagonism, considerable experience of material deprivation, and who have little control over their own behaviour.

The researchers further argued that the dual assessment of compliance and risk reduction caused confusion amongst both prisoners and staff, with improved behaviour and suitability to progress being poorly defined and often subjective. Regime compliance was frequently the main criterion by which prisoners were judged, despite this conformity offering no guarantees that the underlying causes of disruptive behaviour had been addressed nor that ability to function on returning to the main prison system had increased. Undoubtedly future strategy needed clear definitions of what constituted progress for each individual prisoner. Many of the research recommendations have already been adopted and others will be incorporated into Phase II development of the CSC system (Luchford, 2000), which It is anticipated will be fully operational in 2002.

The disruptive prisoner

Prisoners described as dangerous or disruptive have been found to differ significantly from the normal long-term prisoner population, including number of transfers and higher levels of violence. Clare and Bottomley (2001) suggest that such prisoners cannot be safely contained within a therapeutic setting as they exhibit volatile, violent and aggressive behaviour for which they express low levels of responsibility. Many have histories of local authority care and special schooling, often reporting physical or sexual abuse in childhood. Over half of the CSC prisoner population have reported past contact with psychiatric services and over a third have previously been in special hospitals. More than half have deliberately and repeatedly self-harmed (Clare and Bottomley, 2001).

Whilst all prisoners located in special units exhibit control problems of a serious nature prior to admission, wide variation in the different forms and motivations behind these behaviours has been found (Coid, 1998). A proportion of the prisoners feel persecuted by others, spend periods in highly suspicious states of mind, and are likely to employ or threaten violence in order to avoid confrontation, whereas others derive extreme pleasure and excitement from violent behaviour, with some reporting compulsive urges to kill within prison. Coid (1998) found other prisoners profoundly anti-authoritarian and unwilling to accept any rules or restrictions on their behaviour. For some, violence appeared their only solution to resolving difficulties and grievances with others, a strategy employed within conflicts throughout their lives.

Further research (Home Office, 2000a) suggests there may be two broad categories of disruptive prisoner: the over-controlled who are able to regulate their behaviour appropriately but who tend to be solitary, isolated and withdrawn; and the under-controlled who exhibit severe mood swings, are more extrovert, impulsive and generally under-socialized. The latter demonstrate more psychopathic traits (characteristics such as callousness, lack of empathy and anti-social lifestyle) and have greater criminal histories with more convictions for violence and serious acquisitive crime. In contrast the offending of the over-controlled is more likely to take the form of less frequent but serious violence resulting from inter-personal problems.

The most recently reported research (Clare and Bottomley, 2001) indicates that the CSC population has high levels of personality disorder with nearly two thirds of the prisoners at the time meeting the criterion for diagnosis on DSM-IV[1] (American Psychiatric Association, 1994). Most common were borderline, anti-social, narcissistic and paranoid disorders. Whilst it is highly likely that severity of personality disorder in the CSC population is greater than amongst other prisoners the prevalence of mental illness is also high. It appears to be the co-occurrence of these two factors that distinguishes CSC prisoners from the rest of the sentenced prison population.

Assessment

The starting point for the management of disruptive prisoners within the centres involves extensive multi-disciplinary assessment and formulation of their individual needs into a care and management plan. A co-ordinated approach aims to produce a shared understanding of the prisoner's needs in terms of control and treatment, the balance between these two requirements varying with each individual. Staff contributing to the plan include unit managers, prison officers, probation officers, psychologists, psychiatric nurses, health-care officers and managers, security officers, teachers and members of chaplaincy.

A comprehensive understanding of the beliefs, emotional experience and behavioural patterns of each prisoner allows the identification of rewards that are meaningful to the individual and can be responsive to small incremental improvements in behaviour. The risk of harm to others is determined by analysing the antecedents to violent behaviour. The CSCs utilize a model (Douglas et al., 1999) which views risk assessment and management as a dynamic process rather than a static event. This model moves from viewing the 'difficult' prisoner as unidimensional to an interactive process (McConville, 1995) where it is important to assess triggering contingencies and institutional response. Towl and Crighton (1996) highlight the importance of examining the individual's personality, the situations in which the behaviour is more likely to be exhibited and, most significantly, the interaction between the individual's disposition and relevant situations. In later research, Ward and Eccleston (2000) discuss the importance of incorporating both situational and environmental information, arguing that because individuals will change in response to contextual factors monitoring is a crucial component of risk assessment and during the initial reception period a prisoner's risk may be managed by environmental and situational manipulation which Cooke (in Coid, 1998) argues is often 'more productive with difficult prisoners than direct interaction.'

A psychologist is allocated to each newly arrived prisoner. The psychological assessment aims to identify treatment needs, factors which contribute to or are supportive of offending ('criminogenic' factors), particularly those relating to offences committed in prison, and protective factors that minimize or negate the risk of disruptive behaviour, such as supportive interpersonal relationships (Andrews, 1995). A multi-modal functional analysis of the prisoner's disruptive, institutional behaviour is established, drawing on the 'case formulation' approach described by Howells et al. (1997). This approach involves extensive interviews with the prisoner, often using 'motivational interviewing' (Miller and Rollnick, 1991), and completion of psychometric questionnaires. Collateral evidence from file is also utilized in supporting evidence of behaviour and previous assessments. Psychometric measures vary according to the individual but in general a standard package is given to all prisoners which includes assessment of psychopathy (PCL–R: Hare, 1991), assessment of anti-social personality disorder (APQ: Blackburn and Fawcett, 1996), a measure of the experience and expression of anger (STAXI: Spielberger, 1988) and the assessment of maladaptive schema (Young et al., 1995).

There are key questions that the psychologist undertaking assessment needs to address:

> Why has the prisoner been disruptive/difficult?
>
> What have been the difficulties for him in the prison system?
>
> What are the over-developed and under-developed problematic behaviours?
>
> How are the problematic behaviours maintained and reinforced?
>
> What environmental, cognitive and affective factors were involved in the development and maintenance of the behaviour?
>
> What environmental factors may impede progress and change, and which may be protective to this process?
>
> What has been the prisoner's response to previous treatment interventions?
>
> What is the prisoner's attitude towards prison staff and specialists and how is he likely to respond to the environment?

Behaviours and general functioning at the time of the offence(s) are identified and relevant offence paralleling behaviours (Jones, 2001) then determined. Evidence for the presence of parallel behaviours is monitored on a daily checklist and contributes to risk-assessment and risk-reduction measures.

When assessment of the prisoner's needs has been completed the individual care plan is determined. The multi-disciplinary team meet to summarize agreed treatment needs, establishing which member of the team or group of individuals will be responsible for addressing those needs, the type of intervention planned and a time scale. The team review progress against targets on a monthly basis and once the prisoner has met those set out in his initial care plan there is an expectation that his behaviour should have stabilized and adapted to the stage where he can safely progress to the next regime level. At the final CSC stage (in general, after moving through three successive levels) the plan is focused towards reintegration and may include short trial periods on normal location in preparation.

Whilst all members of the multi-disciplinary team contribute to the care plan it is the prison officers, who spend most time in interaction with the prisoners, who play a crucial role. 'It is primarily they', Coid (1998) explains, 'who are the central agents in exerting a therapeutic or ameliorating influence on the prisoners' behaviour'. Each new prisoner is allocated a team of up to four personal officers to ensure continuity of contact and these are responsible for setting out compliance requirements with the regime. A high level of interaction is expected and the officers also meet formally with the individual on a weekly basis to discuss any current difficulties and, where appropriate and under supervision from a psychologist, undertake offending-behaviour work using 'motivational interviewing' skills (Miller and Rollnick, 1991) and pro-social modelling.

Despite the heterogeneous nature of the prisoners' presentation there are clear patterns in their treatment needs, with overwhelming deficits in cognitive skills and maladaptive deeper-level thoughts (*schema*). The prisoners appear to possess a range of cognitive schema about themselves, people in authority and potential victims of their violence (such as over-attribution of hostile intent and a sense of entitlement to revenge) which serve to sustain anti-social behaviour. Assessment also indicates that unwillingness to accept personal responsibility, poor emotional control (principally of anger), manipulative behaviours, impulsivity, vulnerability to negative peer influence and poor interpersonal skills are common areas of need.

The identification and modification of core beliefs and assumptions about self and others has therefore been highlighted as a key intervention target. However, these beliefs tend to be highly emotionally charged, may operate outside conscious awareness and are difficult to modify because they are laid down early in life with the associated emotions often negative and traumatic (Home Office, 2000). As Leibling observes (in Clare and Bottomley, 2001), 'prisoners' emotional volatility is inextricably linked to perceptions of fair or unfair treatment and to perceptions of respect . . .[which]. . . are mediated via personal encounters with staff'. Any punitive sentiment becomes counter-effective by reinforcing cognitive schema relating to authorities as cruel and unfair and their own position as wronged. A strategy to address maladaptive beliefs therefore needs to be part of the entire unit ethos.

The model of treatment and risk management operating within the CSC system is very demanding of staff and can only be undertaken by highly trained and skilled individuals who understand each prisoner's difficulties. Forensic psychologists have played a key role in the development of an appropriate training strategy. A comprehensive training needs analysis (Thorne, 2000) has identified suitable core sessions, essential for staff prior to working on the centres and locally delivered sessions providing relevant staff with detailed understanding of the behaviour patterns, core beliefs and general functioning of each individual prisoner in their units. The core modules include understanding the role of personality in disruptive behaviour, dealing with hostage incidents, motivational interviewing, behavioural target setting, providing constructive feedback and rewarding positive change. To derive maximum benefit local modules are delivered after staff have spent some months on the CSC, enabling them to use their own experience in exploring and gaining greater understanding of individual prisoner behaviour patterns.

Consideration is given to how disruptive prisoners may seek out re-enforcement of their anti-authoritarian belief systems, and strategies staff can use to counter these beliefs. In addition local training addresses the processes which affect staff working in this environment. McConville (1995) in his review of special units urged that 'staff must be prepared for the social dynamics' to counter against two possible 'maladaptive staff reactions'. The first of these McConville describes as 'moral disengagement' where he cautions that 'distancing from inmates . . . combined with intense staff solidarity, can lead to stereotyping, callousness and even brutality' (p. 75). The second reaction may arise in response to conditioning attempts by prisoners such as trying to split the staff group into factions and exploiting disorganized or vulnerable situations. The staff team risks becoming divided and demotivated.

The nature of the CSC prisoner population and the need to balance the dual role of risk management and treatment means that periods of stress are inevitable for staff; something that has been shown to impair individual and organizational decision-making (Daniels, 1999), which clearly needs to be minimized in this type of environment. Stress-management policy utilizes a multifaceted approach incorporating training, support and supervision, co-ordinated by a forensic psychologist. Regular training raises awareness of different 'coping styles' and teaches adaptive strategies. Frequent team-building sessions are held and training time is also provided to allow staff to explore their personal reactions and feelings provoked by the difficult nature of their work. The support service provides individual confidential sessions to staff, group psychological debrief following incidents and advice to unit managers to encourage empowerment and autonomy.

Intervention

An integrated approach, which aims to deliver robust risk management and individualized treatment, has to be sensitive and the unit intervention strategy utilizes a range of therapeutic approaches for both one-to-one and group work. Current practice has been shaped by, and needs to be continually responsive to, assessment-needs analysis, groupwork facilitator experience and the latest evidence-based practice in providing appropriate responses to individuals with personality disorders and co-existent clinical syndromes such as anxiety, alcohol/drug dependence and depression.

Providing interventions in any forensic milieu is a challenge in itself, presenting a range of organizational, operational and ethical difficulties. Delivering effective treatment to a population of anti-social, personality-disordered prisoners, some of whom are also experiencing anxiety and depression, creates additional dilemmas. Their interpersonal dynamics typically involve intimidation and aggression, and levels of distrust are such that establishing trust is very challenging. It is crucial then that a safe environment, where all staff support a therapeutic ethos, is established. Initial intervention work focuses on addressing needs such as anxiety, depression and self-harm along with other therapy-interfering behaviours, such as emotional regulation and distress-tolerance skills (Linehan, 1993) before groupwork can be undertaken. A collaborative case conceptualization model (Padesky and Greenberger, 1995) is adopted by psychologists to assist in the difficult, but essential, process of building therapeutic alliance.

Experiential evidence from psychologists who have undertaken groupwork has indicated that difficulties are faced in engaging the CSC prisoner population. Whilst not all of these problems are inherently unique to the CSCs, nevertheless many are of more extreme or more frequent occurrence than those found with groupwork in more typical prisoner groups. In particular, group cohesion, the maintenance of treatment motivation and support and supervision for facilitators have proved critical to the successful completion of CSC groupwork.

During such work inter-group dynamics may change frequently and have a greater effect than is usual in other prisoner populations. Friendships between group members form and break regularly. On the relatively rare occasions when group participants all work together they often attempt actively to sabotage therapeutic goals. Personality factors which can threaten groupwork delivery include attention span deficits, frequent boundary testing, 'disruption delight' – when prisoners appear to engage in planned strategies to cause most disruption to the group content – and poor behavioural controls. For example, CSC prisoners, more frequently than other prisoner groups, may want to withdraw from the group in protest at other external events. In addition frequent mood swings can make the pre-planning of likely responses to groupwork material extremely difficult (Morgan and Trinder, 1999).

Because of the difficulties experienced by this prisoner group in managing interpersonal relationships and coping with change, facilitator team continuity is important. Appropriate preparation, debrief and supervision time is paramount in ensuring facilitators gain a thorough understanding of the beliefs and behaviour patterns of participants from the psychologist so they are able to respond effectively to frequent group challenges. Supervisors need to allow time to explore how facilitators may feel, both personally and professionally.

The principles that are important for the effective treatment of offending behaviour (McGuire, 1995) have, wherever feasible, been incorporated into groupwork strategy, which has included the delivery of offending-behaviour groupwork using a cognitive-behavioural approach to target thinking and problem-solving skills as well as interpersonal and emotional difficulties.

However, for a significant number of CSC prisoners (certainly when they first arrive on the unit), cognitive-behavioural programmes will be inappropriate and for these individuals a combination of one-to-one skills-training interventions and pro-social modelling, provided on an ongoing basis by unit staff, is utilized as part of their initial intervention care plan. At a later stage, shorter, less structured groupwork may prove crucial in preparing these offenders for successful completion of longer cognitive-behavioural interventions. The prisoner is able to gain familiarity with the group process, including fundamental elements such as session times, agreeing a group contract and expectations of both self and facilitators. Perhaps more importantly, shorter module groups enable assessment of suitability for further intervention of this type in terms of levels of understanding, ability to exercise behavioural control within a group setting and the potential for disruption, and therefore threats to progress, of other group members. It also allows for assessment of therapy-interfering factors and for more effective delivery of more complex programmes.

SUMMARY

National management strategy for disruptive prisoners has a relatively short but nevertheless eventful history which has seen a number of policy changes in response to accumulating expertise in handling this population. Most recently the development of a dual model of treatment and risk, managing a fine balance of control and mental health needs, has been implemented. It is hoped that the introduction of this model may prove contrary to Coid's (1998) assertion that 'safe containment and reduction of risk may be more realistic goals than routinely pursuing a treatment option'.

The nature of the disruptive population and the CSCs' duality of function make for an incredibly challenging milieu. The needs of each prisoner can only be adequately addressed by a multi-disciplinary, highly skilled staff team who understand the prisoners' difficulties and are able to provide a safe and supportive environment, where some level of trust can be established and maintained and an appropriate individualized care plan developed which has meaning for the prisoner. Psychologists have played and will continue to play a key role in four main areas of unit strategy; prisoner assessment and intervention, staff training and supervision, staff support and the provision of research and consultancy advice to unit managers.

Phase II of the CSCs will see refinement of the system with clarity of purpose furthered by the expansion in terms of geographical location to accommodate sub-types of 'disruptive' prisoner and focus on their distinct needs. There will also be full implementation of an individualized care-plan approach, which ensures comprehensive mental health needs are addressed as well as factors relating to offending and troublesome prison behaviour. Within this structured environment where staff will have a clearly defined role, a greater number of disruptive prisoners may achieve the stability in their behaviour to engender successful reintegration into mainstream prisons or other appropriate environments.

NOTES

1 DSM-IV is a multi-axial system that allows clinical assessment in five areas, one of which (Axis II) relates to personality disorders and mental retardation.

References

Abel, G.G., Blanchard, E.B. and Becker, J.V. (1978) An integrated treatment programme for rapists. In R. Rada (ed.) *Clinical Aspects of the Rapist*. New York: Grune and Stratton.

Adams, C. and Fay, J. (1981) *No More Secrets: Protecting Your Children from Sexual Assault*. San Luis Obispo, CA: Impact Press. Quoted in Marshall et al. (eds), 1990.

Adams, J. (1995) *Risk*. London: UCL Press.

Adams, R. and Campling, J. (1994) (eds) *Prison Riots in Britain and the USA* (2nd edition). London: Macmillan Press.

American Psychiatric Association (1994) *Diagnostic and Statistical Manual of Mental Disorders* (4th edition). Washington, DC: American Psychiatric Association.

Amir, M. (1971) *Patterns of Forcible Rape*. Chicago: Chicago University Press.

Analoui, F. (1993) *Training and Transfer of Learning*. Aldershot: Avebury.

Andrews, D.A. (1990) The role of the anti-social attitudes in the psychology of crime. Paper presented to the Canadian Psychological Association, Ottowa. Cited in Attrill, G. 1999.

Andrews, D.A. (1995) The Psychology of criminal conduct and effective treatment. In J. McGuire (ed.), *What Works, Reducing Re-offending* (Chichester: Wiley), 35–62.

Andrews, D.A. and Bonta, J.L. (1994) *The Psychology of Criminal Conduct*. Cincinnati, Ohio: Anderson.

Andrews, D.A. and Bonta, J. L. (1995) *Level of Service Inventory – Revised Manual*. Toronto: Multi Health Systems. Cited in Attrill, 1999 .

Andrews, D.A., Zinger, I. Hoge, R.D., Bonta, J., Gendreau, P. and Cullen, F.T. (1990) Does correctional treatment work? A clinically relevant and psychologically informed meta-analysis. *Criminology, 28*, 369–404.

Aos, S., Phipps, P. , Barnoski, R., and Lieb, R. (1999) *The comparative costs and benefits of programs to reduce crime: a review of national research findings with implications for Washington State*. Document number 09-05-1202, Washington State Institute for Public Policy.

Attrill, G. (1999) Violent Offender Programmes. In Towl and McDougall (eds), 1999.

Bailey, J. and Hudson D. (1997) An Introduction to Basic Counselling Skills Training Course. Internal document, HM Prison Service.

Bailey, J., McHugh, M., Chisnall, L. and Forbes, D. (2000). Training staff in suicide awareness. In Towl et al., 2000.

Bandura, A. (1973) *Aggression: A Social Learning Analysis*. Englewood Cliffs: Prentice Hall.

Bandura, A. (1977) Self efficacy: Towards a unifying theory of behavioural change. *Psychological Review*, 84, 191–215.

Beck, A.J. (1987) *Recidivism of Young Parolees*. Washington, DC: Bureau of Justice Statistical Special Report.

Beck, A.T. (1976) *Cognitive Therapy and the Emotional Disorders*. New York: International Universities Press.

Beck, G. (1997) The development of a new regime for young offenders. *Journal of Prison Service Psychology*, vol. 1.

Beech, A., Fisher, D. and Beckett, R. (1999) *STEP 3: An Evaluation of the Prison Service Sex Offender Treatment Programme*. London: Home Office.

Blackburn, R and Coid, J. (1998) Psychopathy and the dimensions of personality disorder in violent offenders. *Journal of Personality and Individual Differences*, 25, 129–45.

Blackburn, R and Fawcett D. J. (1996) Manual for the Antisocial Personality Questionnaire (APQ). Unpublished manuscript, University of Liverpool.

Blud, L. (1999) Cognitive Skills Programmes. In Towl and McDougall, 2000.

Bolger, L. (1998) The prevalence of personality disorder in a women's prison. *Research and Development Bulletin: Females in Custody*, vol. 6, 6–8. HM Prison Service.

Bolt, C. (1999). A questionnaire survey to establish the incidence and nature of bullying, at HMP Holme House. Unpublished report, Psychology Dept, HMP Holme House, UK.

Boswell, G. (1995) *Violent Victims: The Prevalence of Abuse and Loss in the Lives of Section 53 Offenders*. London: The Prince's Trust.

Bottoms, A.E. and Rex, S.A. (1998) Pro-Social Modelling and Legitimacy: Their Potential Contributions to Effective Probation Practice. In Rex, S. and Matravers, S. (eds) *Pro-Social modelling and Legitimacy*. The Clarke Hall Day Conference. Cambridge: Institute of Criminology.

Bowen, D.E, Ledford, G.E. Jr and Nathan, B.R. (1991) Hiring for the organisation not the job. *Academy of Management Executive*, 5 (4), 35–51.

Bower, G. H. and Hilgard, E. R. (1981) *Theories of Learning* (5th edition). Englewood Cliffs: Prentice-Hall.

Boytzis, R.E. (1982) *The Competent Manager: A Model for Effective Performance*. Chichester, Wiley.

Brand, S. and Price, R. (2000) *The Economic and Social Costs of Crime*. Home Office Research Study no. 217. London: Home Office.

Brecher, E.M. (1978) *Treatment Programmes for Sex Offenders*. Washington, DC: Government Printing Office.

British Psychological Society (BPS) (1997) *Ethical Guidelines in Forensic Psychology*. Leicester, UK: BPS.

BPS (2001) *Supervised Practice Guidelines*. Leicester, UK: BPS.

Brody, S. (1976) *The Effectiveness of Sentencing*. Home Office Research Study no. 35. London: HMSO.

Brookes, M., Cooper, R., Trivette, E. and Willmot, P. (1994). Bullying Survey at HMP Lincoln. Unpublished Psychology Research Report, East Midlands, 19.

Burke, R.J. and Deszca, E. (1982) Preferred organisational climates of Type-A individuals. *Journal of Vocational Behaviour*, 21, 50–9.

Bush, J. (1995) Teaching self-risk management to violent offenders. In McGuire (ed.), 1995.

Caddle, D. and Crisp, D. (1997) *Mothers in Prison*. Home Office Research Findings no 38. London: Home Office.

Cain, S. (1999) Summary of the Young Offender Population. Unpublished study.

Campbell and Harrington (2000) *Youth Crime: Findings from the 1998/99 Youth Lifestyles Survey*. Home Office Research Findings no.126, London: Home Office.

Carlen, P. (2000) Women's imprisonment – reform and risk. *Prison Service Journal*, 132, 7–11.

Carter, N., Klein, R. and Day, P. (1992) *How Organisations Measure Success*. London: Routledge.

Christensen, L. and Mendoza, J. L. (1986) A method of assessing change in a single subject: An alteration of the RC index. *Behaviour Therapy*, 17, 305–8.

Clare E and Bottomley K (2001), assisted by Grounds, A., Hammond, C., Liebling, A. and Taylor, C. *Evaluation of Close Supervision Centres*. Home Office Research Study no. 210, Centre for Criminology and Criminal Justice, University of Hull and Institute of Criminology, University of Cambridge.

Clark, D. (1999) Risk assessment in prisons and probation. In Towl and McDougall (eds), 1999, 15–18.

Clark, D. and Howden-Windell, J. (2000) A Retrospective study of criminogenic factors in the female prison population. Unpublished Prison Service study.

Clark, D.A. (1988) Wakefield Prison Anger Management Course Tutors Manual. Unpublished document, HMP Wakefield.

Clark, D.A. (2000) *Effective Regime Measures Research*. Unpublished paper. HM Prison Service, Research and Development Section

Clark, D.A., Fisher, M.J. and McDougall, C. (1993) A New Methodology For Assessing Risk in Incarcerated Offenders. *British Journal of Criminology*, 33, 436–48.

Coid, J.W. (1991) Psychiatric profiles of difficult/dangerous prisoners. In K. Bottomley and W. Hay (eds) *Special Units for Difficult Prisoners*. Hull, UK: Centre for Criminology and Criminal Justice, University of Hull.

Coid, J.W. (1998) The management of dangerous psychopaths in prison. In Millon, T., Simonsen, E., Birkett-Smith, M. and Davis, R.D. *Psychopathy, Antisocial, Criminal and Violent Behaviour*. New York: Guilford Press.

Coleman, J. and Hendry, L. (1990) *The Nature of Adolescence* (2nd edition). Routledge, London.

Colledge, M., Collier, P. and Brand, S. (1999) *Crime Reduction Programme and Constructive Regimes in Prison. Programmes for Offenders: Guidance for Evaluators*. Crime Reduction Programme Guidance Note 2. Research, Development and Statistics Directorate. London: Home Office.

Cooke D.J. (1991) Violence in prisons: The influence of regime factors. *Howard Journal*, 30, 95–109.

Cooke D.J, Baldwin, P. J. and Harrison, J. (1990) *Psychology in Prisons*. London: Routledge.

Cooke, D.J. and Michie, C. (1998) Predicting recidivism in a Scottish prison sample. *Psy-*

chology, Crime and Law, 4, 169–211.

Cosgrave, N. and Langdon, P. (in preparation) *Training Staff Who Work With Challenging Adolescents: An Evaluation of a Novel Programme.*

Coyle, A. (1987) The management of dangerous and difficult prisoners. *Howard Journal* vol. 26 no 2. May, 139–52.

Craig, R. L. (1987) *Training and Development Handbook: A Guide to Human Resource Development* (3rd edition). New York: McGraw-Hill Book Company.

Crighton, D.A. (1997) The Psychology of Suicide. In Towl (ed.), 1997.

Crighton, D.A. (1999) Risk assessment in forensic mental health, *British Journal of Forensic Practice,* 1, (1), February.

Crighton, D. A. (2000) Suicide in prisons: a critique of UK research. In Towl et al. (eds), 2000.

Crighton, D.A. and Towl, G. J. (1997) Self-inflicted deaths in England and Wales 1988–1990, and 1994–95, In Towl (ed.), 1997.

Crighton, D.A. and Towl G. J. (2000) International self-injury. In Towl et al., 2000.

Crime and Disorder Act 1998. London: HMSO.

Critchley, E. (1968) Reading Retardation, Dyslexia and Delinquency. *British Journal of Psychiatry,* 114, 1537–47.

Cullen, J.E., Jones, L. and Woodward, R. (eds) (1997) *Therapeutic Communities for offenders.* Chichester :Wiley .

Dalkin, A. and Skett, S. (2000) *Working with young offenders,* In Towl and McDougall, (eds),1999.

Daniels, K. (1999) Affect and strategic decision making. *Psychologist,* 12, 24–48.

Department of Health (1996) *Directorate of Psychological Services Report,* Series 2, no. 177, National Treatment Outcome Research Study. London: Department of Health, November.

Dolland, J. and Miller, N.E. (1950) *Personality and Psychotherapy: An Analysis in Terms of Learning, Thinking and Culture.* New York: McGraw Hill.

Dooley, E. (1990) Prison suicide in England and Wales, 1972–1987. *British Journal of Psychiatry,* 156, 40–5.

Douglas, K.S., Cox, D.N. and Webster C.D. (1999) Violence risk assessment: Science and practice, *Legal and Criminological Psychology,* 4, 149–84.

D'Zurilla, T.J. and Goldfried, M.R. (1971) Problem solving and behaviour modification. *Journal of Abnormal Psychology,* 78, 107–26.

Evans, J. and Henson, C. (1999) The role of psychologists in hostage and other serious incidents. In Towl and McDougall (eds), 1999.

Executive Office of the President, Office of National Drug Policy (1996) *Treatment Protocol Effectiveness Study.* Executive Office of the President, Office of National Drug Policy (on-line at www.ncjrs.org).

Eyre, E. C. and Pettinger, R. (1999) *Mastering Basic Management* (3rd edition). Basingstoke: Macmillan Press.

Fabiano, E., La Plante, J. and Loza, A. (1996) Employability: From research to practice. *Forum on Corrections Research,* 8 (on-line at www.csc.scc.gc.ca/text/pblct/forum).

Fabiano, E. and Porporino, F. (1997) *Reasoning and Re-Acting: A Handbook for Teaching Cognitive Skills.* Ottawa: T3 Associates.

Farrington, D., Hancock, A., Livingstone, M. Painter, K. and Towl, G.J. (2000) *Evaluation of Intensive Regimes for Young Offenders.* Home Office Research Findings no. 121, London: HMSO.

Farrington, D. (1983) Randomized experiments on crime and justice. In M. Tonry, and N. Morris (eds) *Crime and Justice: An Annual Review of Research*, 4 (Chicago: Chicago University Press), 257–307.

Farrington, D. P. (1989) Early predictors of adolescent aggression and adult violence. *Violence and Victims*, 4, 79–100.

Finkelhor, D. (1979) Psychological, cultural and family factors in incest and family sexual abuse. *Journal of Marriage and Family Counselling*, 4, 41–9.

Flanagan, T.J. (1992) Long-Term Incarceration: Issues of Science, Policy and Correctional Practice. *Forum on Corrections Research*, 4 (on-line at www.csc.scc.gc.ca/text/pblct/forum).

Freedman, B.J., Rosenthal, L., Donahoe, C.P., Schlundt, D.G. and McFall, R.M. (1978) A social-behavioural analysis of skill deficits in delinquent and non-delinquent adolescent boys. *Journal of Consulting and Clinical Psychology*, 46, 1448–62.

Friendship, C., Blud, L., Erikson, M., Travers, R. and Thornton, D. (in press) Cognitive behavioural treatment for imprisoned offenders: An evaluation of HM Prison Service's Cognitive Skills Programme. *Legal and Criminological Psychology.*

Friendship, C. and Thornton, D. (2001) Sexual reconviction for sexual offenders discharged from prison in England and Wales: Implications for evaluating treatment. *British Journal of Criminology*, 41, 285–92.

Friendship, C., Thornton, D., Erikson, M and Beech, A.R. (2001) Reconviction: A critique and comparison of two main data sources in England and Wales. *Legal and Criminological Psychology*, 6, 121–9.

Garston, G.D. (1972) Force versus restraint in prison riots. *Crime and Delinquency*, 18, 411–21.

Gates, M. Dowden, C. and Brown, S.L. (1998) Case need domain: 'Community functioning'. *Forum on Correction Research*, 1(on-line at www.csc.scc.gc.ca/text/pblct/forum).

Gendreau, P. (1996) The principles of effective intervention with offenders in A.T. Harland (ed.) *Choosing Conventional Options that Work: Defining the Demand and Evaluating the Supply.* Thousand Oaks, CA: Sage Publications.

Gendreau, P. and Andrews, D.A. (1991) Tertiary prevention: What the meta-analyses of the offender treatment literature tell us about 'what works'. *Canadian Journal of Criminology*, 32, 173–184.

Gendreau, P. and Ross, R.R. (1980) Effective correctional treatment: Bibliotherapy for cynics. In Ross, R.R. and Gendreau, P. , 1980.

Gendreau, P., Paparrozzi, M., Little, T. and Goddard, M. (1993) Does 'punishing smarter' work? An assessment of the new generation of alternative sanctions in probation. *Forum on Correction Research*, 5 (on-line at www.csc.scc.gc.ca/text/pblct/forum).

Goggin, C., Gendreau, P. and Gray, G. (1998) Case need domain: 'Associates and social interaction'. *Forum on Correction Research*, 10 (on-line at www.csc.scc.gc.ca/text/pblct/forum).

Goldstein, A. (1988) *The Prepare Curriculum.* Champaign: Research Press. Cited in Attrill, 1999.

Goldstein, I. L. (1980) Training in work organizations. *Annual Review of Psychology*, 31,229–72.

Goldstein, I. L. (1986) *Training in Organizations: Needs Assessment, Development and Evaluation.* Monterey CA: Brooks Cole.

Graham, J. and Bowling, B. (1995) *Young People and Crime.* Research Study no. 145. London: Home Office.

Gudjonsson, G. H. (2000) Psychometric assessment. In C.R. Hollin (ed.) *Handbook of Offender Assessment and Treatment* (Chichester: Wiley), 111–12.

Hare, R. D. (1991) *Manual for the Hare Psychopathy Checklist – Revised.* Toronto: Multi-Health Systems.

Hawton, K. (1994) Causes and opportunities for prevention. In Jenkins, R. Griffiths, S. and Wylie, I. (eds) *The prevention of suicide.* London: HMSO.

Helderman, C. and Sugg. D. (1996) *Does Treating Sex Offenders Reduce Reoffending?* Research Findings no.45. London: Home Office.

Hill, G. (1985) Predicting recidivism using institutional measures. In D.P. Farrington and R. Tarling (eds) *Prediction in Criminology.* New York: State University of New York Press.

HM Chief Inspector of Prisons for England and Wales (HMCIP) (1990) *Review of Suicide and Self-harm.* London: HMSO.

HMCIP (1998) *Women in Prison: A Thematic Review.* London: Home Office.

HM Inspectorate of Prisons for England and Wales (1999a) *Suicide is Everyone 's Concern: A Thematic Review.* London: HMSO.

HM Inspectorate of Prisons for England and Wales (1999b) *Inspection of Closed Supervision Centres.* London: Home Office.

HM Inspectorates of Prisons and Probation (1999) *Lifers: A Joint Thematic Review by HM Inspectorates of Prisons and Probation.* London: Home Office.

HM Prison Service (1990) Suicide prevention and follow-up to deaths in custody. Addendum to CI 20/89. London: HMSO.

HM Prison Service (1993) *Bullying in Prison: A Strategy to Beat It.* London: HMSO.

HM Prison Service (1994a) *Caring for the Suicidal in Custody.* Instruction to Governors 1/94.

HM Prison Service (1994b) *Caring for the Suicidal in Custody: Guide to Policy and Procedures.* HM Prison Service.

HM Prison Service (1996) Management of Disruptive Prisoners: CRC Review Project Final Report (the Spurr Report).Unpublished report, HM Prison Service.

HM Prison Service (1998) *Research and Development Bulletin: Females in Custody,* vol. 6, August.

HM Prison Service (1999a) *The Lifer Manual.* Prison Service Order no. 4700.

HM Prison Service (1999b). *Anti-Bullying Strategy.* Prison Service Order no.1702.

HM Prison Service (2000a) *Research and Development Bulletin: Risk Assessment.* vol 9, July.

HM Prison Service (2000b) Criminogenic Needs Survey. Unpublished document, Research and Planning Department. HM Prison Service.

HM Prison Service (2000c) *Eleven Criteria for Accredited Programmes.* London: HM Prison Service.

HM Prison Service (2000d) *Regimes for Prisoners Under 18 Years Old.* Prison Service Order no.4950.

HM Prison Service (2002), *What Works in Prison Strategy.* London: HM Prison Service.

Hodgkins, S. and Muller-Isberner, R. (eds) (2000) *Violence, Crime and Mentally Disordered Offenders.* Chichester: Wiley.

Hoghughi, M. (1988) *Treating Problem Children: Issues, Methods and Practice.* Thousand Oaks, CA: Sage Publications.

Holding, D.H. (1965) *Principles of Training.* Oxford: Pergamon.

Hollin, C. (1999) Offender Treatment. Where have we been? Where are we going? *Forensic Update,* 57, 3–6.

Hollin, C.R. (1995). The meaning and implications of 'programme integrity'. In McGuire, (ed.), 1995.

Hollin, C.R., Epps, K.J. and Kendrick, D.J. (1995) *Managing Behavioural Treatment: Policy and Practice with Delinquent Adolescents.* London: Routledge.

Homberger, M. and Farmer, S. (1998) Survey of the prevalence of bullying at HMYOI and RC Feltham. *Research and Development Bulletin,* vol. 5. HM Prison Service.

Home Office (1984) *Managing the Long Term Prison System: Report by the Control Review Committee.* London: HMSO.

Home Office (1985) *see* Police and Criminal Evidence Act 1984.

Home Office (1987) *Special Units for Long Term Prisoners: Regimes Management and Research. A Report by the Research and Advisory Group on the Long Term Prison System.* London: HMSO.

Home Office (1989a) *Criminal Statistics England and Wales 1988.* London: HMSO

Home Office (1989b) *Circular Instruction 20/89: Suicide Prevention.* London: HMSO.

Home Office (1990) *Victim's Charter: A Statement of the Rights of Victims of Crime.* London: HMSO.

Home Office (1995) *Review of Prison Service Security in England and Wales and the escape from Parkhurst Prison on Tuesday 3rd January, 1995* (the Learmont Inquiry). London: HMSO CM3020.

Home Office (1998a) *British Crime Survey.* London: HMSO.

Home Office (1998b) *see* Crime and Disorder Act 1998.

Home Office (1999) *Home Office Statistical Bulletin.* London: HMSO.

Home Office (2000a) *HMIP Inspection of Close Supervision Centres August-September 1999 A Thematic Inspection.* London: HMSO.

Home Office (2000b) *The Effectiveness of Prison Drug Treatment Services: A Review of the Literature.* Research, Development and Statistics Directorate. London: Home Office.

Home Office (2001a) *HM Prison Service Statistics.* London: HMSO.

Home Office (2001b) *Business Plan 2001 – 2002.* London: HMSO.

Home Office (2001c) *Home Office Annual Report.* London: HMSO.

Horn, R. (2000) Assessing criminogenic needs: The development of a process. *Research and Development Bulletin,* 9, 3–6. HM Prison Service.

Horn, R. and Warner, S. (2000) *Positive Directions for Women in Secure Environments.* Issues in Forensic Psychology 2. Leicester, UK: BPS.

Howden-Windell, J. (1998) Current research: Criminogenic needs survey of the female prisoner population. *Research and Development Bulletin,* 6, 3. HM Prison Service.

Howells, K., Watt, B., Hall, B. and Baldwin, S. (1997) Developing programmes for violent offenders. *Legal and Criminological Psychology*, 2, 117–28.

Hughes, G. V. (1993). Anger management program outcomes. *Research in Offender Programming Issues*, 5, 1, 5–9.

Hunter, D. (1993). Anger management in the prison: An evaluation. *Research on Offender Programming Issues*, 5, 1, 3–5.

Ireland, C. A. (2001) Homesickness and coping in a sample of male young offenders. Paper presented at the Division of Forensic Psychology Conference, University of Birmingham, April 2001.

Ireland, J.L. (1999a). A recent bullying survey: Results and recommendations for intervention. *Prison Service Journal*, 123, 27 – 30.

Ireland, J.L. (1999b). Provictim attitudes and empathy in relation to bullying behaviour among prisoners. *Legal and Criminological Psychology*, 4, 51–66.

Ireland, J.L. (1999c). Bullying in Prisons. In Towl and McDougall (eds),1999, 19–22.

Ireland, J.L. (2000) Do anger management courses work? *Forensic Update*, 63 (October).

Ireland, J.L. (2001a). How does assertiveness relate to bullying behaviour among prisoners? *Legal and Criminological Psychology* 7, 87–100.

Ireland, J.L. (2001b) Bullying behaviour among male and female adult prisoners: A study of perpetrator and victim characteristics. *Legal and Criminological Psychology* 6, 229–46.

Ireland, J.L. (2001c) The relationship between social problem-solving and bullying behaviour among male and female prisoners. Paper presented at the Division of Forensic Psychology Conference, University of Birmingham, April 2001.

Ireland, J.L. (forthcoming) A comparison of bullying behaviour among young and juvenile male offenders. *Journal of Adolescence*.

Ireland, J.L. (in press) *Bullying Among Prisoners: Evidence, Research and and Intervention Strategies*. London: Brunner Routledge.

Jacobson, N.S., Follette, W.C. and Revenstorf, D. (1984) Psychotherapy outcome research. Methods for reporting variability and evaluating clinical significance. *Behaviour Therapy*, 15, 336–52.

Jacobson, N.S., Follette, W.C. and Revenstorf, D. (1986) Toward a standard definition of clinically significant change. *Behaviour Therapy*, 17, 308–11.

Jacobson, N.S., Follette, W.C. and Revenstorf, D. (1988) Statistics for assessing the clinical significance of psychotherapy techniques: Issues, problems and new developments. *Behavioural Assessment*, 10, 133–45.

Jacobson, N.S., Roberts, L.J., Berns, S.B. and McGlinchey, J.B. (1999) Methods for defining and determining the clinical significance of treatment effects: Description, application and alternatives. *Journal of Consulting and Clinical Psychology*, 67, 300–7.

Jacobson, N.S. and Truax, P. (1991) Clinical significance: A statistical approach to defining meaningful change in psychotherapy research. *Journal of Consulting and Clinical Psychology*, 59, 12–19.

Jenkins, J.C. (1976) What is to be done: Movement or organisation? *Contemporary Sociology*, 8(2) 222–8.

Jones, L. (2001) Anticipating offence paralleling behaviour. Paper presented to Division of Forensic Psychology Tenth Annual Conference, University of Birmingham.

Kanfer, F. H. and Saslow, G. (1969) Behavioural Diagnosis. In C. Franks (ed.) *Behaviour Therapy: Appraisal and Status.* New York: McGraw-Hill.

Kelland, D. and McAvoy, P. (1999) Working with women prisoners. In Towl and McDougall (eds),1999.

Kelly, G.A. (1955) *The Psychology of Personal Constructs.* New York: Norton.

Kershaw, C., Goodman, J. and White, S. (1999) Reconvictions of offenders sentenced or discharged from prison in 1995, England and Wales. *Statistical Bulletin,* no. 19/99. London: Home Office.

King, R. and Brosnan, F. (1998) Psychological group programmes for female prisoners at HMP Holloway. In *Research and Development Bulletin: Females in Custody,* 6, 6–8. HM Prison Service.

King, R. and Moynihan, S. (1998) Dialectical Behaviour Therapy – DBT – A new programme for difficult to manage behaviour in Holloway. *Research and Development Bulletin: Females in Custody,* 6, 17–18. HM Prison Service.

King, R. and Moynihan, S. (1998) An evaluation of an eight week pilot of dialectical behaviour therapy for women with borderline personality disorder. *Research and Development Bulletin: Females in Custody,* 6, 18–20. HM Prison Service.

King, R.D. (1999) The rise and rise of supermax: An American solution in search of a problem. *Punishment and Society,* 1: 163–86.

Kohlberg, L. (1969) Stage and sequence: The cognitive development approach to socialisation. In D. Goslin (ed.) *Handbook of Socialisation Theory and Research.* New York: Rand McNally.

Kohlberg, L. (1969) *Stages in the Development of Moral Thought and Action.* Holt, Reinhart and Winston, New York.

Lanceley, F.J. (1981) The anti-social personality as a hostage taker. *Journal of Police Science and Administration,* 9(1) 28–34.

Law, K. (1997). Further evaluation of Anger Management courses at HMP Wakefield: An examination of behavioural change. *Inside Psychology: The Journal of Prison Service Psychology,* 3(1), 91–5.

Law, M. (1998) Case need domain: 'Attitude'. *Forum on Correction Research, 10* (on-line at www.csc.scc.gc.ca/text/pblct/forum).

Laws, D.R. (ed.,1989) *Relapse prevention with sex offenders.* New York: Guilford Press.

Lee, E.T. (1992) *Statistical Methods for Survival Data.* New York: Wiley.

Leheup, R. (1998) Rethinking Provision for Delinquents. *Young Minds,* no. 38.

Liebling, A. (1991) Suicide in Prisons. Unpublished PhD thesis, University of Cambridge.

Linehan M.M. (1993) *Skills Training Manual for Treating Borderline Personality Disorder.* New York: Guilford Press.

Lipsey, M.W. (1992) Juvenile delinquency treatment, a meta-analysis enquiry into the variability of effects. In Cook, T.D., Cooper, H., Cordray, D.S., Hartmann, H., Hedges, L.V., Light, R.J., Louis, T.A. and Mosteller, S. (eds) *Meta-Analysis for Explanation: A Casebook.* New York: Russell Sage Foundation Group.

Lipsey, M.W. and Wilson, D.B. (1998) Effective intervention for serious juvenile offenders: A synthesis of research. In Loeber, R. and Farrington, D.P. (eds), *Serious and Violent Juvenile Offenders: Risk Factors and Successful Interventions.* Thousand Oaks, CA, Sage Publications.

Lipton, D., Martinson, R. and Wilks, J. (1975) *The Effectiveness of Correctional Treatments.* New York: Praeger.

Lloyd, C., Mair, G. and Hough, M. (1994) *Explaining Reconviction Rates: A Critical Analysis.* Home Office Research Study, no. 136. London: Home Office.

Loeber, R. (1982) The stability of anti-social and delinquent child behaviour. A review. *Child Development,* 53, 1431–46.

Lösel, F. (1995) The efficacy of correctional treatment: A review and synthesis of meta-evaluations. In J McGuire (ed.), 1995.

Luchford, D. (2000) Future management of disruptive prisoners: Phase II of the CSC system. Internal policy review document. HM Prison Service?

Lunnen, K.M. and Ogles, B.M. (1998) A multiperspective, multivariable evaluation of reliable change. *Journal of Consulting and Clinical Psychology,* 66, 400–10.

Lunness, T. (2000) SMART Thinking: Social and Moral Reasoning with Young People – Stop to Think or Think to Stop? Presentation to Youth Justice Matters Conference, March 2000.

Lyon, J. and Coleman, J. (1994) *The Nature of Adolescence: Working with Young People in Custody – Training Pack.* HM Prison Service/Trust for the Study of Adolescence.

Lyon, J, Dennison, C. and Wilson, A (2000) *Tell Them So They Listen: Messages From Young People In Custody.* London: Home Office.

MacKenzie, D.L. and Souryal, C. (1994) *Multisite Evaluation of Shock Incarceration: Evaluation Report.* Washington DC: National Institute of Justice.

MacKenzie, I. K. (1978) Hostage-captor relationships: Some behavioural and environmental determinants. *Police Studies,* 7(4) 219–23.

Maden, A., Swinton, M. and Gunn, J. (1994) A criminological and psychiatric survey of women serving a prison sentence. *British Journal Of Criminology,* 34, 2.

Maguire, M. (1997) Crime Statistics, Patterns and Trends: Changing Perceptions and their Implications. In Maguire, M., Morgan, R. and Reiner, R. (eds) *The Oxford Handbook of Criminology.* Oxford: Clarendon Press.

Marshall, W.L., Anderson, D and Fernandiz, Y. (1999) *Cognitive Behavioural Treatment of Sex Offenders.* Chichester: Wiley.

Marshall, W.L. and Barbaree, H.E. (1990) Outcome of comprehensive cognitive-behavioural treatment programs. In W.L. Marshall et al., 1990.

Marshall, W.L., Laws, D.R. and Barbaree, H.E. (1990) *Handbook of Sexual Assault: Issues, Theories, and Treatment of the Offender.* New York: Plenum Press.

McAvoy, P. (1998) *Factors Linked to Female Recidivism: A Comparison of First Time and Repeat Offenders.* Unpublished MSc thesis, University of London, Birkbeck College.

McConville, S. (1995) Special Units for Disruptive and Difficult Prisoners: A Review of the Literature and Principal Issues. Unpublished Prison Service Paper.

McDougall, C., Barnett, R. M., Ashurst, B., and Willis, B. (1987) Cognitive control of anger. In McGurk et al. (eds), 1987.

McFall, R.M. (1990) The enhancement of social skills: An information processing analysis. In Marshall et al., 1990.

McFall, R.M. and Dodge, K.A. (1982) Self-management and interpersonal skills learning. In Karoly and Kanfer (eds) Self-management and behaviour change: From theory to practice.

McGuire, J. (ed.,1995) *What Works: Reducing Offending. Guidelines from Research and Practice.* Chichester: Wiley.

McGuire, J. and Priestley, P. (1995) Reviewing 'What Works': Past, present and future. In McGuire (ed.), 1995.

McGurk, B.J., Thornton, D.M., and Williams, M. (eds) (1987) *Applying Psychology To Imprisonment: Theory and Practice.* London: HMSO.

McHugh, M. J (2000) Suicide prevention in prisons: policy and practice. *British Journal of Forensic Practice,* 2, 1), 12–16.

Meichenbaum, D. (1977) *Cognitive-Behaviour Modification: An Integrative Approach.* New York: Plenum Press.

Mellor, A. (1998), cited by D. Birkett, In defence of the bully. *Guardian Weekend,* 25 April, 24–33.

Mezey, G.C. and King, M.B. (eds) (2000) *Male Victims of Sexual Assault.* Oxford: Oxford University Press.

Miller, W.R. and Rollnick, S. (1991) *Motivational Interviewing: Preparing People to Change Addictive Behaviour.* New York: Guilford Press.

Miron, M.S.T. and Goldstein A.P. (1978) *Hostage.* Michigan: Behaviordelia Inc.

Mitchell, B. (1990) *Murder and Penal Policy.* Basingstoke: Macmillan Press.

Monahan, J. and Steadman, H.J. (eds) (1994) *Violence and Mental Disorder: Developments in Risk Assessment.* Chicago: Chicago University Press.

Morgan, W. and Trinder, H. (1999) Experience of running enhanced thinking skills with disruptive prisoners: A discussion document. Internal review, HM Prison Service.

Morris, A., Wilkinson, C., Tisi, A., Woodrow, J. and Rockley, A. (1995) *Managing the Needs of Female Prisoners.* London: Home Office.

Mosson, L. (1998) Development of a young offender course at HMP and YOI New Hall: A preliminary report. In *Research and Development Bulletin: Females in Custody,* vol. 6, 12. HM Prison Service.

Motiuk, L. (1998) Using dynamic factors to better predict post-release outcome. *Forum on Correction Research,* 10 (on-line at www.csc.scc.gc.ca/text/pblct/forum).

Moynihan, S. (1998) Group work with young offenders located on the psychiatric unit. In *Research and Development Bulletin: Females in Custody,* vol. 6, 13–14. HM Prison Service.

Murphy, W.D. (1990) Assessment and modification of cognitive distortions in sex offenders. In Marshall et al. (eds), 1990.

Needs, A. (1988) Psychological investigation of offending behaviour. In F. Fransella and F. Thomas (eds) *Experimenting with Personal Construct Psychology.* London: Routledge.

Needs, A.P.C. (1995) Social skills training. In G.J. Towl (ed.), 1995b.

Needs, A. and Towl, G.J. (1997) Reflections on clinical risk assessments with lifers. *Prison Service Journal,* 113, 14–17.

Neisser, U. (1976) *Cognition and Reality.* San Francisco: W.H. Freeman.

Nicholls, C. (1998) Perception of needs survey of women prisoners at HMP/YOI Foston Hall. *Research and Development Bulletin: Females in Custody,* 6, 4–6. HM Prison Service.

Novaco, R.W. (1975). *Anger Control: The Development and Evaluation of an Experimental Treatment.* Lexington DC: Heath, Lexington Books.

O'Donnell, I. and Edgar, K. (1996). *Victimisation in Prisons*. Home Office Research Findings no. 37 (Research, Development and Statistics Directorate), 1–4.

Owens, G. and Ashcroft, J.B. (1982) Functional analysis in applied psychology. *British Journal of Clinical Psychology*, 21, 181–9.

Padesky, C.A. and Greenberger, D. (1995) *Clinician's Guide to Mind Over Mood*. New York: Guilford Press.

Palmer, E. and Hollin, C. (1995) Education and work programmes in prisons: Effect on recidivism. Unpublished Report for HM Prison Service Planning Group.

Paolucci, E.O., Violata, C. and Schofield, M.A. (1998) Case need domain: 'Marital and family'. *Forum on Correction Research*, 10 (on-line at www.csc.scc.gc.ca/text/pblct/forum).

Paternoster, R., Bachman, R., Brame, R. and Sherman, L.W. (1997) Do fair procedures matter? The effect of procedural justice on spouse assault. *Law and Society Review*, 31, 163–204.

Patrick, J. (1992) *Training: Research and Practice*. London; Academic Press.

Pavlov, I.P. (1927) *Conditioned Reflexes* (trans. G.V.Anrep). New York: Oxford University Press.

Piaget, J. (1932) *The Moral Judgement of the Child*. New York: Macmillan.

Pithers, W.D. (1990) Relapse prevention with sexual aggressors: A method for enhancing therapeutic gain and enhancing external supervision. In Marshall et al. (eds), 1990.

Plant, B. (2001) Disclosure of unused material, *Forensic Update*, 64.

Player, E. (2000) Justice for Women. *Prison Service Journal*, 132, 17–22.

Police and Criminal Evidence Act 1984. London: HMSO.

Porporino, F.J. and Robinson, D. (1991) Adult basic education: Can it help reduce recidivism? *Forum on Corrections Research*, 3 (on-line at www.csc.scc.gc.ca/text/pblct/forum).

Prins, H (2002) Risk assessment – Still a risky business. *British Journal of Forensic Practice*, 4 (1), 3–8.

Probation Studies Unit (1998) *Assessment Case Management and Evaluation System: A Practical Guide*. Oxford: Probation Studies Unit.

Quinsey, V., Harris, G., Rice, M. and Lahumière, M. (1993), Assessing treatment efficiency in outcome studies of sex offenders, *Journal of Interpersonal Violence*, 8, 512–23.

Raven, J., Raven, J.C. and Court, J.H. (1995) *Manual for Raven's progressive matrices and vocabulary scales*. Oxford: Oxford University Press.

Raynor, P. and Vanstone, M. (1994), *Straight Thinking on Probation: Third Interim Report*. Mid-Glamorgan Probation Service.

Redondo, S., Sanchez-Meca, J. and Gramido, V. (1999) The influence of treatment programmes on the recidivism of juvenile and adult offenders: A European meta-analytic review. *Psychology, Crime and Law*, 5, 251–78.

Rice, M. E. Quinsey, V.L., and Houghton, R. (1990). Predicting treatment outcome and recidivism among patients in a maximum security token economy. *Behavioural Sciences and the Law*, 8, 313–326.

Robins, L. (1978) Sturdy predictors of adult anti-social behaviour: Replications from longitudinal studies. *Psychological Medicine*, 8, 611–22.

Robinson, D. (1995). The impact of cognitive skills training on post-release recidivism among Canadian federal offenders. Internal research paper no. R41, Ottawa: Correctional Service of Canada.

Robinson, D., Porporino, F.J. and Beal, C.A. (1998) Case need domain: Personal and emotional orientation'. *Forum on Correction Research*, 10 (on-line at www.csc.scc.gc.ca/text/pblct/forum).

Ross, R. R. and Fabiano, E. A. (1985) *Time to Think: A Cognitive Model of Delinquency Prevention and Offender Rehabilitation*. Johnson City, TE: Institute of Science and Arts.

Ross, R.R. and Gendreau, P. (1980) *Effective Correctional Treatment*. Toronto: Butterworth.

Russell, M.N. (1990). *Clinical Social Work*. Newbury Park: Sage Publications.

Rutter, M., Giller, H. and Hagel, A. (1998) *Anti-Social Behaviour by Young People*. Cambridge: Cambridge University Press.

Sampson, R.J. and Laub J.H. (1993) *Crime in the Making: Pathways and Turning Points Through Life*. Cambridge, MA: Harvard University Press.

Satar, G. (2001) *Rates and Causes of Death Among Prisoners and Offenders under Community Supervision*. Home Office Research Study no. 231. Research, Development and Statistics Directorate. London: Home Office.

Saylor, W.G. and Gaes, G.G. (1996) The effect of prison employment and vocational training/apprenticeship training on long-term recidivism. *Forum on Corrections Research*, 8 (on-line at www.csc.scc.gc.ca/text/pblct/forum).

Schacter, S. and Singer, J.E. (1962) Cognitive, social and physiological determinants of emotional states. *Psychological Review*, 69, 379–99.

Schneider, B. (1987) The people make the place. *Personnel Psychology*, 40, 437–53.

Schneider, B., Kristoff-Brown, A., Goldstein, A., and Brent Smith, D. (1997) What is this thing called fit? In Andreson, N., and Herriott, P. (eds) *International Handbook of Selection and Assessment*. Chichester: Wiley.

Singleton, N., Meltzer, H., and Gatward, R. (1998) *Psychiatric morbidity among prisoners in England and Wales*. London: HMSO.

Skinner, B.F. (1971) *Beyond Freedom and Dignity*. New York: Knopf.

Snow, L. (2000) Suicide prevention within New York City Department of Corrections facilities. *British Journal of Forensic Practice*, 2(1), 36–41.

Spielberger, C.D. (1988) *State-Trait Anger Expression Inventory Revised Research edition (STAXI Professional Manual)*, Florida: Psychological Assessment Resources, Inc.

Spielberger, C.D., Reheiser, E.C. and Sydeman, S.J. (1995) Measuring the experience, expression and control of anger. In Kassinove, H. (ed.) *Anger Disorders: Definition, Diagnoses and Treatment*. Washington, DC: Taylor and Francis.

Spivak, G., Platt, J.J. and Shure, M.B. (1976), *The Problem-Solving Approach to Adjustment*. San Francisco, CA: Jossey-Bass.

Stewart, C. (2000) Responding to the needs of women in prison. *Prison Service Journal*, 132, 41–3.

Strentz, T. (1979) Law enforcement policy and ego defences of the hostage. *FBI Law Enforcement Bulletin*, April, 2–12.

Strentz, T. (1980) The Stockholm Syndrome: Law enforcement policy and ego defences of the hostage. In F. Wright, C. Bahn, and R.W. Riever (eds) *Forensic Psychology and Psychiatry: Annals of the New York Academy of Science* (New York: New York Academy of Sciences), 347.

Sturmey, P (1996) *Functional Analysis in Clinical Psychology*. Chichester: Wiley.

Swinton, M., Maden, A. and Gunn, J. (1994) Psychiatric disorder in life sentence prisoners. *Criminal Behaviour and Mental Health*, 4, 10–20.

Taylor, G. (1998) Offender needs: Providing the focus for our correctional interventions. *Forum on Corrections Research*, 10 (on-line at www.csc.scc.gc.ca/text/pblct/forum).

Taylor, R. (1999) *Predicting Reconvictions for Sexual and Violent Offences Using the Revised Offender Group Reconviction Scale*. Home Office Research Finding no. 104. Research, Development and Statistics Directorate. London: Home Office.

Thorne, K (2000) CSC Training Needs Analysis. Internal communication, HM Prison Service.

Thornton, D. (1987) Moral development theory. In McGurk et al. (eds), 1987.

Thornton, D. (2002) *Constructing and Testing a Framework for Dynamic Risk Assessment*. Unpublished paper: HM Prison Service, London.

Tingey, R.C., Lambert, M.J., Burlingame, G.M. and Hansen, N.B. (1996) Assessing clinical significance: Proposed extensions to method. *Psychotherapy Research*, 6, 109–23.

Toch, H. (1975) *Men in Crisis: Human Breakdowns in Prison*. Chicago: Aldine Publishing Co.

Toch, H. (1978) Social climate and prison violence, *Federal Probation*, 42, 21–5.

Topp, D.O.(1979) Suicide in prison. *British Journal of Psychiatry*, 134, 24–7.

Towl, G.J. (1994). Anger control groupwork in practice. In E. Stanko (ed.) *Perspectives on Violence*. London: Howard League Handbooks, Quartet Books Ltd.

Towl, G.J. (1995a) Anger management groupwork. In Towl, G.J. (ed.), 1995b.

Towl, G.J. (1995b) Groupwork in prisons. A national survey. *Prison Service Journal*, 97, 5–9.

Towl, G.J. (ed), (1997) *Suicide and Self-injury in Prisons*. Leicester, UK: BPS.

Towl, G.J. (1999) Suicide in prisons in England and Wales, 1988–1996. In G.J. Towl, M.J. McHugh and D. Jones (eds), *Suicide in Prisons: Research, Policy and Practice*. Brighton: Pavilion Publishing.

Towl, G.J. (2000) Reflections upon suicide in prisons. *British Journal of Forensic Practice*, 2 (1), 17–22.

Towl, G.J. (2002) Working with offenders: The ins and outs. *Psychologist*, vol.15, no.5, 236–9. Leicester, UK: BPS.

Towl, G.J. and Crighton, D. (1995) Risk assessment in prisons: A psychological critique. *Forensic Update*, 40 (Leicester: Division of Criminological and Legal Psychology).

Towl, G.J., and Crighton, D.A. (1996) *The Handbook of Psychology for Forensic Practitioners*. London: Routledge.

Towl, G.J., and Crighton, D.A. (1997) Risk assessment with offenders. *International Review of Psychiatry*, 9, 187–93.

Towl, G.J. and Crighton, D.A. (1998) Suicide in prisons in England and Wales from 1988 to 1995. *Criminal Behaviour and Mental Health*, 8, 184–92.

Towl G.J. and Crighton, D.A. (2000) Risk assessment and management. In Towl et al. (eds), 2000.

Towl, G.J. and Dexter, P. (1994). Anger management groupwork in prisons: An empirical evaluation. In *Groupwork*, vol. 7(3) (London: Whiting & Birch), 256–69.

Towl, G.J. and Forbes, D.I. (2000) *Working with suicidal prisoners*. In Towl et al. (eds), 2000.

Towl, G.J. and Hudson, D. (1997) An Introduction to Groupwork Facilitation Training Course. Unpublished document, HM Prison Service.

Towl, G.J. and Jennings, M. (1990). *An Anger-Control Course at HMP Highpoint*. Directorate of Psychological Services Report, Series 2, no.177, November.

Towl, G.J. and McDougall C. (1999) *What Do Forensic Psychologists Do? New Directions in Prison and Probation Services*. Issues in Forensic Psychology 1. Leicester, UK: BPS.

Towl, G.J., McHugh, M.J. and Jones, D. (eds) (1999), *Suicide in Prisons: Research, Policy and Practice*. Brighton: Pavilion Publishing.

Towl, G.J., McHugh, M. and Snow, L. (2000) *Suicide in Prisons*. Leicester, UK: BPS.

Trotter, C. (1993) *The Supervision of Offenders: What Works*. Sydney: Victorian Office of Corrections.

Trotter, C. (1996) The impact of different supervision practices in community corrections: Cause for optimism. *Australian and New Zealand Journal of Criminology*, 29, 29–46.

Tullor, W.L., Mullins, T.W. and Caldwell, S.A. (1979). Effects of interview length and applicant quality on interview decision time. *Journal of Applied Psychology*, 64 (6), 669–74.

Vagg, J. (1994) *Prison Systems*. New York: Oxford University Press.

Wanous, J.P (1992) *Organisational Entry: Recruitment, Selection and Socialisation of Newcomers* (2nd edition.). Reading, MA: Addison-Wesley.

Ward, D. (1987) *The Validity of the Reconviction Prediction Score*. Home Office Research Study, no. 94. London: HMSO.

Ward, T. and Eccleston, L. (2000) The Assessment of Dangerous Behaviour: Research and Clinical Issues. *Behaviour Change*, vol. 17. no. 2, 53–68.

Wardlaw, G.(1983) Psychology and the resolution of terrorist incidents. *Australian Psychologist*, 18(2) 179–90.

Warner, S. (2000) Women and child sexual abuse: Childhood prisons and current custodial practices. In Horn and Warner, 2000.

Watson, J.B. and Rayner, R. (1920) Psychology as the behaviourist views it. *Psychological Review*, 20, 158–77.

Webster, C.D., Douglas, K.S., Eaves, D. and Hart, S.D. (1997) *HCR-20 Assessing Risk For Violence* (2nd edition). Burnaby: Mental Health, Law and Policy Institute, Simon Fraser University.

Wedderburn, D. (2000) Justice for women: The need to reform. *Prison Service Journal*, 132, 2–4.

Whiddet, S. and Hollyforde, S. (1999), *The Competencies Handbook*. London: Chartered Institute of Personnel and Development.

Wilde, J. (1996) Treating anger, anxiety and depression in children and adolescents. *Accelerated Development*.

Willmot, P. (1997) The development of an anti-bullying strategy at HMP Lincoln. *Journal of Prison Service Psychology*, 3, 81–6.

Willmot, P. (2000). *What else works?* Internal publication, Psychology Group HM Prison and National Probation Service.

Wilson, P. (2000) Experiences of staff working in close supervision centres. Unpublished MST thesis in Applied Criminology and Management (Prison Studies), Institute of Criminology, University of Cambridge.

Wong, S. and Gordon, A. (1999) *Violence Risk Scale* (2nd edition). Canada: Regional Psychiatric Centre (Prairies) and University of Saskatchewan.

Woolf, Lord (1991) *Prison disturbances, April 1990.* Cm 1456, London: HMSO.

Young, J.E., Schmidt, N.B., Joiner, T.E. and Telch, M.J. (1995) The schema questionnaire: Investigation of psychometric properties and the hierarchical structure of a measure of maladaptive schemas, *Cognitive Therapy and Research,* vol. 19 (3), 1995, 295–321.

Zamble, E. and Porporino, F. (1992) Coping, imprisonment and rehabilitation. *Criminal Justice and Behaviour* 17 (1), 53–70.

Appendix: Revolving Doors Agency

Revolving Doors Agency is an independent charity set up in 1993 to demonstrate new ways of working with people with mental health and multiple needs in contact with the criminal justice system. It runs experimental link worker schemes, which go into police stations, prisons and courts to support those people who fall through the net of mainstream services.

Link workers aim to help this vulnerable and sometimes chaotic group achieve a greater degree of stability in the community by improving their access to crucial services such as GPs, housing and social care. They make use of assertive outreach techniques and provide casework support as a whole team to those with the most complex needs. Joint working with mainstream agencies is key to the approach and includes being based with a local team. Staff backgrounds include social work, nursing, occupational therapy and supported housing, making a range of skills available to clients who need to navigate complex social, health and benefits systems.

Prison provides an opportunity to engage vulnerable people when they most need it, with the aim of establishing a supportive relationship prior to release. Referrals are taken of people returning to the local community after short sentence or remand. Those identified at police stations are also supported throughout their time in prison and afterwards. The key is to bridge the gap between community and criminal justice services, for example link workers provide training for prison officers to increase their awareness of mental health needs and of ways to gain access to services in the community.

The agency uses the learning from the schemes to assist other organizations seeking to set up or develop similar projects at the interface of mental health and criminal justice.

More information on: www.revolving-doors.co.uk
E: admin@revolving-doors.co.uk
T: 020 7242 9222

Index

Full details of works given here in the
form of the author name(s) and date may
be found in the References.